THE
NATURE
AND
POWER
OF
PRAYER

**30 Bible Lessons to Effective Prayer
That Will Change Your Life!**

PASTOR GREG SCALZO

www.xulonpress.com

To my beautiful wife Patty. Your love and encouragement, your sacrifice and dedication, and the courage and discernment with which God has blessed you, have made these years of ministry together possible. I am so thankful to the Lord for you and our children.

INTRODUCTION

———————∝———————

Prayer is an essential part of being a Christian and permeates every aspect of our lives as believers in Jesus. And because it is so primary and integral to our walk, a study on prayer will necessarily reveal the basic truths of the faith in many foundational areas. *The Nature and Power of Prayer* then is an excellent book for new Christians desiring to understand the essential teachings of the Scriptures. And I believe it will help answer questions even for those who have not yet made their decision but are honestly considering the claims of Christ. However, I have tried not to sacrifice depth of study in making the material understandable, and I believe the lessons will give fresh revelation even to mature believers while setting forth a clear review of first principles. It is my hope that the book will also prove a useful tool for them to use in sharing the joy of our faith with others.

Our nation today often seems chaotic. Things are changing rapidly, and usually not for the better. The culture seems unrecognizable to many older Americans, and our nation's social ills abound. Moreover, new threats and dangers have come to the forefront that seemed unthinkable only a couple of decades back. Increasingly, Americans are sensing that something is terribly wrong as uncertainty has replaced the stability that allowed our nation to prosper under the protection of Almighty God. The Bible makes clear that prayer is one of the key components for national restoration and healing (2 Chronicles 7:14). If ever there was a need for a populace that can pray in the will and power of God, it is now.

On a personal level, life can seem very daunting. Saved back in 1981, a prayer relationship with the Lord has been intertwined in every area of my life since. I cannot imagine handling the difficulties of this world without the continual privilege of bringing each situation before the Creator. And over the years I have been blessed to see many, many mighty and wondrous answers to prayer. I want the readers of this book to experience the same. I know that modern existence can be hectic and available time always seems at a minimum. So I have developed the format of this Bible workshop on prayer with daily lessons that contain vital information but are short enough to be read over the morning's cup of coffee or at a break time. Each lesson could also be used in a time of meditating over the Scriptures before going to God in prayer. Psalm 5 verses 1 to 3 says:

Psalm 5:1-3
> 1 Give ear to my words, O LORD,
>   Consider my meditation.
> 2 Give heed to the voice of my cry,
>   My King and my God,
>   For to You I will pray.
> 3 My voice You shall hear in the morning, O LORD;
>   In the morning I will direct it to You,
>   And I will look up. (NKJV)

In these lessons, we will consider many Bible verses. This is important. It makes no difference what I say or any other minister says if it is not supported by the Scriptures. If the analysis and conclusions are correct, then clear, solid and plentiful Scriptural evidence should be there to reinforce the accuracy of the teaching.

The Lord Jesus viewed prayer as a high and holy thing, not to be corrupted. It was so valued by Him that the greatest account we have of the Lord demonstrating His zeal and anger was when He overturned the tables and drove out the money changers from the Temple in Jerusalem. Jesus referred to Scriptures in Isaiah and Jeremiah when He taught:

Mark 11:17
> 17 …"Is it not written: 'My house will be called a house of prayer
>   for all nations'? But you have made it 'a den of robbers.'" (NIV)

The focus of the Temple should have been sincere prayer, and this extended to the Levitical sacrificial system. But humans corrupted the specialness of both the offerings and the location for selfish benefit. Jesus knew this and displayed a powerful anointing to restore His Father's house as a house of prayer for all nations. My hope is that this workshop will help to bring a time of refreshing into your life and that your home may also be called a house of prayer.

Pastor Greg

LESSON ONE

―――――――――✂―――――――――

"When my soul fainted within me, I remembered the LORD;
And my prayer went up to You, into Your holy temple."
Jonah 2:7 (NKJV)

How many of us can also say along with the prophet that we have felt our soul faint within us because of some impossible situation in life? And so I welcome you to what I consider to be an extremely important Bible study workshop for the Christian and even for those who are not yet confirmed believers in Jesus Christ. The topic is prayer. I know that we each have so many questions concerning how to pray effectively, how to have our prayers answered, or just how to have a closer communication with the Lord. It is with great joy that I share what I believe the Lord has taught me about the nature and power of prayer. I would encourage you to follow along with the Scriptures presented in this book. Read them in your own Bible—and reread them! Let the Word of God get deep down into your mind and being.

What better place to start our study than with the words of our Lord Jesus concerning prayer in the book of Matthew Chapter 6 verses 5 to 15? These Scriptures will be the focus for a number of our lessons. Now you will recognize that the nucleus of this passage is what we know as the Lord's Prayer. Some call it the Our Father. Many of us memorized the words of the Lord's Prayer when we were children in Sunday school or Catechism class. But the key is not whether we know the words by heart, but rather that we understand them in our hearts. That is the purpose of this study series: to absorb inside our very spirits what the Lord is endeavoring to teach His people about prayer. I believe that, in this section of Matthew,

Jesus shows us *how* we should pray and He gives us an *example* of prayer.

Let's read verses 5 and 6, part of the lead-in to the Lord's Prayer:

Matthew 6:5-6

5 "And when you pray, you shall not be like the hypocrites. For they love to pray standing in the synagogues and on the corners of the streets, that they may be seen by men. Assuredly, I say to you, they have their reward.

6 "But you, when you pray, go into your room, and when you have shut your door, pray to your Father who is in the secret place; and your Father who sees in secret will reward you openly." (NKJV)

In these verses the Lord is cutting right to the core. What is our motivation when we pray? He warns us against praying to be seen by men and to receive their reward—to receive their praises. We should not pray because we want others to think well of us, nor should we just say words to please those around us. Otherwise, what are we really doing? We are not praying to God, rather we are, in effect, praying to those people we are seeking to impress. And so we are not lifting up our prayers to God, but to men.

Therefore Jesus is telling us that prayer is a personal matter between the Lord God and ourselves. Our purpose should be to seek Him and His rewards and that which is right and proper in His eyes! We are not to be concerned, even when praying publicly, about how the words will be received by the individuals who hear us. Our focus and intent should not be on what they are thinking or whether they approve of what we are saying. The prayer is directed to the Almighty, pleasing and acceptable to Him. And that brings us to the first important principal of prayer in the series:

The Lord God who created the heavens and the earth is eternal. He is the Almighty One, the everlasting God, Who exists independent of His creation. Even if you and I were never formed, He still is! Yet for our prayer to be a genuine and powerful prayer, it is imperative that we also come into this knowledge of the truth of His existence and that God is real to us!

"**God must be real to us!**" That sounds very simple, but too often people pray only because they were taught to pray as children. And they may do it almost as a superstition or as a ritual. They are not really sure He is there. Maybe they are hoping He's there. But God is not real to them, and in fact the prayer is not a request being lifted up from their hearts and souls to a real Person, but rather a rite they perform or observe. But for prayer to be effective, for prayer to be real, God must be real to us. We are not praying for other people to see. We are not praying as some type of ceremony. We are praying to communicate with Him. You have to believe in Him whom you cannot see and desire to be alone with Him in the quiet of your room, in the secret place. There is a Scripture in Hebrews Chapter 11 which is revealing. It states in verse 6:

Hebrews 11:6

6   But without faith it is impossible to please Him: for he that cometh to God must believe that He is, and that He is a rewarder of them that diligently seek Him. (KJV)

Let's look at those words: *But without faith* (notice the importance of faith) *it is impossible to please Him*, for he who comes to God must believe that He is—that He exists—and that He is a rewarder of those who diligently seek Him! You have to believe that He is. You have to believe He exists. And notice that it also says that you must believe that He *rewards* those who diligently seek Him. In the main Scripture in Matthew which we read just a moment ago, Jesus tells us in verse 5 that those who pray to be seen by men:

Matthew 6:5b

5   "...Assuredly, I say to you, they have their reward." (NKJV)

But He says in verse 6 that when we correctly pray to our Father in the secret place then:

Matthew 6:6b

6   "...your Father who sees in secret will reward you openly." (NKJV)

And there is a benefit to entering into this relationship with God. The Almighty Creator of all spirits openly rewards those who believe that He is real, and who seek His face, and seek His will. When we pray, we must truly grasp the reality of God's existence! Otherwise, as the Scripture tells us, "it is impossible to please Him."

Before we go any further, one thing should be clarified. Obviously the Lord is not saying that the only place where we can pray is in our bedroom or in some small room off by ourselves. Nor is He speaking in this Scripture against praying in a group. For that matter, in the book of Acts Chapter 1 verse 14, we are told that all the disciples joined together constantly in prayer and in supplication. And later on in Chapter 2 we read how, on the Day of Pentecost, they were again in "one accord" and the Lord blessed their gathering mightily. Then in Chapter 4, after Peter and John are released from prison, we read starting at verse 23:

Acts 4:23-24a
> 23 When they had been released, they went to their own companions and reported all that the chief priests and the elders had said to them.
> 24 And when they heard this, they lifted their voices to God with one accord... (NASB)

So we have here another gathering of the disciples, and they raise their voice to God in one accord—in agreement and with the same mind. And what follows is a beautiful prayer which I would like you to take a moment to read, because it is a great example of prayer.

Acts 4:24b-31
> 24 ...and said, "O Lord, it is You who MADE THE HEAVEN AND THE EARTH AND THE SEA, AND ALL THAT IS IN THEM,
> 25 who by the Holy Spirit, through the mouth of our father David Your servant, said,
>> 'WHY DID THE GENTILES RAGE,
>> AND THE PEOPLES DEVISE FUTILE THINGS?
> 26 'THE KINGS OF THE EARTH TOOK THEIR STAND,
>> AND THE RULERS WERE GATHERED TOGETHER
>> AGAINST THE LORD AND AGAINST HIS CHRIST.'
> 27 "For truly in this city there were gathered together against Your holy servant Jesus, whom You anointed, both Herod

and Pontius Pilate, along with the Gentiles and the peoples of Israel,

28 to do whatever Your hand and Your purpose predestined to occur.

29 "And now, Lord, take note of their threats, and grant that Your bond-servants may speak Your word with all confidence,

30 while You extend Your hand to heal, and signs and wonders take place through the name of Your holy servant Jesus."

31 And when they had prayed, the place where they had gathered together was shaken, and they were all filled with the Holy Spirit and began to speak the word of God with boldness. (NASB)

We see here an assembly of the disciples raising their voices together in one accord in a superb prayer which remembers and is built on the Scriptures. In the prayer, they praise God as the Creator, worshipping and acknowledging who He is. And they pray for power in the name of Jesus to be able to perform the signs that would be needed to accompany the Word going forth. As they do so, the Lord blesses them. They are filled with the Holy Spirit, the place where they are dwelling is shaken, and they are able to speak the Word of God with boldness. Their prayer is indeed answered. Thus it is right and proper in God's sight for believers to gather together and pray together.

In Matthew Chapter 18 and verses 19 to 20, Jesus says:

Matthew 18:19-20

19 "Again I say to you that if two of you agree on earth concerning anything that they ask, it will be done for them by My Father in heaven.

20 "For where two or three are gathered together in My name, I am there in the midst of them." (NKJV)

When brothers and sisters in the Lord bind together in prayer, in love and sincerity, there is a great power—a tremendous power. And I believe that word *sincerity* is a key word to understanding this concept. When we come together in prayer, our concern is for the Lord's opinion, not man's opinion. So, in truth, we are really still in our rooms in our secret place with our Father, since in the room of our hearts we are attentive only to Him. The principle remains the same. Assembled together as disciples of Jesus, there is power because we are gathered in His name, with each one focusing on the Lord—on what He wants. As a group, we are praying to Him and we are not concerned about how we appear nor are we longing to be seen by others— we are not as "the hypocrites." For you see, in that Scripture in Matthew Chapter 6 verse 5, Jesus commands:

Matthew 6:5

5 "And when you pray, you shall not be like the hypocrites. For they love to pray standing in the synagogues and on the corners of the streets, that they may be seen by men. Assuredly, I say to you, they have their reward." (NKJV)

The word hypocrite in the Greek means "an actor." It was someone that would put on a mask and then would play a role on the stage. We are commanded not to be actors. We are not to be pretenders, playing "church" or playing "Christian." Instead we should be honestly praying to our Father, and that is the same whether we are praying to Him in the secret place or whether we are in church praying to Him with others who love Him and are devoted to Him in the same way. Unlike the actor and the hypocrite, who perform a farce, we are called to be truthful and genuine in our prayer—we are called to be sincere. Sincerity is the key.

It is obvious from the Scriptures that the Lord had no patience for hypocrites. He condemned them several times and He spoke the harshest against those who had a show of religion. Prayer must never be a performance. Prayer should be a conversation with the true and only God. We know Him as our Father, we know Him as real, and we love Him.

Let us consider for a moment the opposite condition. We have discussed people that are pretenders—hypocrites—that pray simply to look good to other people. But then there are those that are not hypocrites, but who are likewise much too concerned with other people and how others look at them— so concerned that they are *embarrassed* to pray. They're too flustered and self-conscious to pray out loud, worrying to themselves, "How do I sound?" or "What are they thinking about the words I'm saying?" Their motivating force, rather than being seen by others, is not to be seen by others. Thus they avoid praying audibly in a group altogether. Again, they are too mindful of everyone else. Perhaps you might have felt this way yourself at some time. I know I have. But if you think of being with your Father in the secret place, feeling the love of the Lord as you are concerned for and focused on Him, then the embarrassment fades away. You are doing what is proper and what is right: you are communicating with your Father in Heaven. It is so important to remember and concentrate on the One whom you are addressing and let Him melt away all the other cares.

One last point on this matter: The only role an awareness of others might play in prayer, and this is especially true for those in leadership, is a desire for our petitions to be based on and proclaim the truth of God and His Word in order to bring others into the prayer. We've seen this already in the prayer of the gathered believers in Acts Chapter 4. In this way, those joined together in prayer can truly be in agreement as God's Spirit moves in their assembly, and any unbelievers present will be drawn to God. Moreover, we should of course all be aware of the conditions and needs of our brothers and sisters as we lift our requests up before the Lord. But again, even with such mindfulness, the direction of the prayer is to God, the motivation is truth, and the heart of the one praying is the joy and privilege of speaking to Him.

Why don't we move on now to verses 7 and 8 of Matthew Chapter 6:

Matthew 6:7-8

7 "And when you pray, do not use vain repetitions as the heathen do. For they think that they will be heard for their many words.

8 "Therefore do not be like them. For your Father knows the things you have need of before you ask Him."(NKJV)

Prayer is not a meaningless repetition. Saying many words or repeating expressions as a ritual is a superstition, and it demonstrates a very low opinion of God. It is, as Jesus said, the way the heathen pray. And we read about how the heathen prayed in 1st Kings Chapter 18 verses 16 to 39. Here we have the classic confrontation between the Lord's true prophet, Elijah, and the pagan prophets of the false Canaanite god, Baal. Baal was a type of Satan. And these pagan prophets called on the name of Baal from morning till evening. They frantically danced about, they shouted, they leapt, they even cut themselves with knives and lances, and raised their voices and cried out ever louder as though to try and get their god's attention—and obviously there was no answer because their gods were just stone and wood and the empty shadows of the demonic.

But Elijah prayed a very simple prayer. He prayed it in sincerity. And he prayed it to God who is God—the true Creator of the universe. And in that prayer, Elijah respectfully *talked* to God. Let's read Elijah's prayer in 1st Kings Chapter 18 starting at verse 36:

1 Kings 18:36-37

36 And it came to pass at the time of the offering of the evening sacrifice, that Elijah the prophet came near, and said, "LORD God of Abraham, Isaac, and of Israel, let it be known this day that Thou art God in Israel, and that I am Thy servant, and that I have done all these things at Thy word.

37 Hear me, O LORD, hear me, that this people may know that Thou art the LORD God, and that Thou hast turned their heart back again." (KJV)

God is pleased when we talk with Him. Elijah just simply spoke to his God. He did not repeat formulas as did the prophets of Baal. He did not repeat prayers over and over again. But rather he lifted up a simple prayer—a short prayer—and there was an answer.

1 Kings 18:38-39

38 Then the fire of the LORD fell, and consumed the burnt sacrifice, and the wood, and the stones, and the dust, and licked up the water that was in the trench.

39 And when all the people saw it, they fell on their faces: and they said, "The LORD, He is the God; the LORD, He is the God." (KJV)

God answered. He answered with fire from heaven and He showed Himself to be real. God is our Father. And as our Father, He wants us, His children, to speak to Him naturally in openness and genuineness. He is not some impersonal force to be manipulated by a formula or series of words. God is a person—the Ultimate Person—and He invites us to approach Him in true conversation.

Understand that the prayer is not for God to have knowledge of our situation. We do not need to repeat over and over to increase the chance of Him hearing us. God is greater than that. Jesus said that He knows what we need even before we ask Him (vs. 8). The prayer really is more for us to draw into a loving relationship with Him. We open our hearts to the Lord. He is the One that's all knowing. He is the One that's all love. And when we pray we must desire to come near to Him in truthfulness—not in hypocrisy, not as an act. Rather we hunger to get close to our Lord. When we do this and we say that simple prayer—not babbling, not repeating many words as a ritual—do you know what happens? We come into a very special position of peace and power and the presence of the Lord. And in that place which is different from the rest of the world, in that "secret place," there is spiritual authority. In effect, we open up the windows of heaven and allow Him to release His holy fire. In our case, that fire from heaven is His answer to our prayers. As we enter the reality of His presence, God will show Himself to be very real in our lives.

Too often in the history of the church these principles have been forgotten and prayer has been reduced to a series of repetitions or responsorials that quickly can become void of any true understanding of what is being said or the meaning behind the words. And individuals can all too often get into the poor habit of simply repeating "words" over and over in ritualistic petition. Consider for a moment a child who asks his father a question. I don't know how many of you have had this experience, but sometimes a very young child will ask his parent a question, and, even before the parent begins to give him an answer, the child is on to another question, or he repeats the same question again so that he is unable to hear the answer. The child does not learn because the exchange is not a true communication. Instead his questioning is almost like a silly sing-song chorus, insincere and meaningless. And so it can be with prayer. That brings us to the second important principle:

Prayer must be a communication. It must be a sincere knowledge exchange. We speak to God and then we need to stop and pay attention to Him. We need to listen to Him and trust Him to answer our prayer.

Prayer should never be a chore or a duty or an obligation. Rather, just as we would enjoy having a conversation with a loved one, it should be even more so when we go to the Lord in prayer to speak to Him. And we should have confidence when we go before Him because, as we read in verse 8, Jesus said, "your Father knows the things you have need of before you ask Him." He knows what we need. He's concerned for our needs. And He wants us to ask Him and to approach Him and seek Him for the things we need in our spirits, in our souls, and in our minds, as well as for our physical conditions, including miraculous healings for our bodies. He's concerned for our families. He's concerned for all the elements of our lives. But, for our part, it is vital that we diligently bring each component, each area, each person, and each problem to Him and *speak* to Him.

As we conclude this lesson, I would like to encourage you, that if you should have any doubts, to speak to the Lord today in prayer, in sincerity, in the name of Jesus, and ask Him to heal your mind and heart of the doubts. God is real and He will answer.

LESSON TWO

----------∝----------

In Lesson One we started our Bible study workshop on *The Nature and Power of Prayer* with the words of our Lord Jesus on prayer in Matthew Chapter 6. Let us begin this lesson by reading from where we left off last time at verse 9. You will of course recognize this as the section commonly known as the Lord's Prayer or Our Father:

Matthew 6:9-13
> 9 "In this manner, therefore, pray:
>
> Our Father in heaven,
> Hallowed be Your name.
> 10 Your kingdom come.
> Your will be done
> On earth as it is in heaven.
> 11 Give us this day our daily bread.
> 12 And forgive us our debts,
> As we forgive our debtors.
> 13 And do not lead us into temptation,
> But deliver us from the evil one.
> For Yours is the kingdom and the power and the glory forever.
> Amen." (NKJV)

In verse 9 Jesus says, "In this manner, therefore, pray" or "This is how you should pray." The Lord is not giving us words here just to say over and over in strict repetition—that would be the vain repetitions of the heathen which, as we studied last lesson, Jesus commanded us in verse 7 not to do. There is no inherent benefit to saying the words of the Our Father over and over, almost supersti-tiously. Rather, we have here a format—a template—to illustrate the important elements that should be present when we speak to God and which can guide us in the Spirit as we pray.

Many people, however, are more comfortable praying a liturgical or written out prayer that they can simply repeat. Obviously, the Lord's Prayer has often been incorporated in this way. Or some may even feel that saying the exact words of such an official prayer is the only proper way that they are allowed to pray. They may believe that somehow they are being disrespectful to the Lord if they do not pray in a formalized way, be it the Our Father or some church approved prayer in a book. But Jesus said, "Pray in this manner" or "This is how you should pray"—use these elements in your prayers.

Don't misunderstand. The Our Father is a beautiful prayer, the exact words of which we should memorize and teach our children to memorize. As we understand the fundamentals which the Lord has given us in this prayer, we can have a natural communication with God in our own words. Not only that, but when we do pray together as a group, in the right spirit, sometimes there is not a more appropriate prayer than the exact words of the Our Father which we all know and say together. *But,* as we learned last lesson, the prayer MUST at all times be a sincere communication with God. The danger is in making the Our Father a prayer that is said without even thinking about the words or truly thinking about God. It can then become a mere common place rune or recital rather than the very words of instruction from the Son of God.

Okay. Let us examine the prayer line by line. Jesus addresses God as our Father. Why "Father"? What confidence do we have in calling God our Father? The answer most people would probably give is that God created all people, so He is, in that sense, their Father. And God certainly is the creator of all spirits. In Hebrews 12:9 He is called "the Father of spirits." Job tells us in Job 12:9-10 that in His "hand is the life of every living thing and the breath of all mankind." In Numbers 27:15-16, Moses addresses Him as "the LORD, the God of the spirits of all flesh." And when Paul preached to the Athenians in Acts Chapter 17 starting at verse 22, he said:

Acts 17:22-28

22 Paul then stood up in the meeting of the Areopagus and said: "People of Athens! I see that in every way you are very religious.

23 For as I walked around and looked carefully at your objects of worship, I even found an altar with this inscription: TO AN UNKNOWN GOD. So you are ignorant of the very thing you worship—and this is what I am going to proclaim to you.

24 "The God who made the world and everything in it is the Lord of heaven and earth and does not live in temples built by human hands.

25 And He is not served by human hands, as if He needed anything. Rather, He Himself gives everyone life and breath and everything else.

26 From one man He made all the nations, that they should inhabit the whole earth; and He marked out their appointed times in history and the boundaries of their lands.

27 God did this so that they would seek Him and perhaps reach out for Him and find Him, though He is not far from any one of us.

28 'For in Him we live and move and have our being.' As some of your own poets have said, 'We are His offspring.'" (NIV) *{Capitalization for deity added}*

"We are His offspring." Paul tells the Athenians that God created every nation of men and that we all exist and have our being only in Him. So indeed, in that sense, every individual that ever lived could be considered His child. But I believe that, in the Lord's Prayer, Jesus is speaking of a bond which is much more than this when He directs us to petition God as "our Father." This distinction is important to effective prayer and something that we need to look at closely. We will start by reading from Colossians Chapter 1 verses 19 to 23, and I would ask that you listen carefully, as you study this passage, to the Bible's description of the condition of a person's relationship with God. The apostle Paul starts off in verse 19 speaking about Jesus:

Colossians 1:19-23

19 For it pleased the Father that in Him should all fullness dwell;

20 And, having made peace through the blood of His cross, by Him to reconcile all things to Himself; by Him, I say, whether they are things on earth, or things in heaven.

21 And you, that were formerly alienated and enemies in your mind by wicked works, yet now hath He reconciled,

22 In the body of His flesh through death, to present you holy and unblamable and unreprovable in His sight:

23 If ye continue in the faith grounded and settled, and are not moved away from the hope of the gospel, which ye have heard, and which hath been preached to every creature which is under heaven; of which I Paul am made a minister; (Webster)

Here, Paul makes clear that we were alienated from God because of sin. As it says in Proverbs 20:9, "Who can say, I have made my heart clean, I am pure from my sin?" (KJV) (Or as the *New International Version* translates it: "Who can say, 'I have kept my heart pure; I am clean and without sin'?") If we are honest with ourselves, I don't think any of us could make that statement on our own. The prophet Isaiah writes in Isaiah 53:6 (KJV), "All we like sheep have gone astray; we have turned every one to his own way…" But then Isaiah tells us how our hearts can be made clean and pure, "… and the LORD hath laid on Him the iniquity of us all," of course prophesying what Jesus would accomplish on the cross.

It is a certainty with every person that the softness that was in his heart or her heart as a child is lost as he grows to take control of his life. In his mind and because of his wicked actions, Paul tells us, he becomes an enemy of God, whether he knows it or not, and it is only by Christ's death that he is reconciled to and presented blameless before God. That word *reconcile* is an important one. It means to restore to a state of harmony after a break in relations.

Now let's read from the letter to the Ephesians Chapter 1 verses 3 to 6:

Ephesians 1:3-6
3 Praise be to the God and Father of our Lord Jesus Christ, who has blessed us in the heavenly realms with every spiritual blessing in Christ.

4 For He chose us in Him before the creation of the world to be holy and blameless in His sight. In love

5 He predestined us for adoption to sonship through Jesus Christ, in accordance with His pleasure and will—

6 to the praise of His glorious grace, which He has freely given us in the One He loves. (NIV) *{Emphasis and capitalization for deity added}*

So even though we separated ourselves from God, it was always God's will that we be ADOPTED as His sons and daughters through Jesus Christ, His only begotten Son, whom He loves and who never sinned against Him. And this was God's love for us and the gift He freely gave us. That is why it is written in John 1:12, "But as many as received Him, to them He gave the right to become children of God, even to those who believe in His name," (NASB, *emphasis added*). This is a Scripture that every Christian should know and memorize. And that brings us to the next important principle in our study:

It is because of Jesus that we have confidence to call God our Father. And when we approach God in prayer we know that, as our Father, He loves us and is personally concerned with us. In Jesus we are now truly His children.

Through this wonderful new covenant we enter into a close loving family relationship with God. Remember when Jesus was in the Garden of Gethsemane, how He prayed to the Father. In Mark 14:36 it says:

Mark 14:36

36 And He was saying, "Abba! Father! All things are possible for You; remove this cup from Me; yet not what I will, but what You will." (NASB)

Abba is an Aramaic word that in Jesus' culture would correspond to our word *Daddy* or *Papa*—an affectionate term for one's father. But the tremendous fact is that the dear relationship this term indicates between Jesus and the Father now applies to us as adopted children. Let's read about that in Galatians 4:4-7:

Galatians 4:4-7

4 But when the fullness of the time had come, God sent forth His Son, born of a woman, born under the law,

5 to redeem those who were under the law, that we might receive the adoption as sons.

6 And because you are sons, God has sent forth the Spirit of His Son into your hearts, crying out, "Abba, Father!"

7 Therefore you are no longer a slave but a son, and if a son, then an heir of God through Christ. (NKJV)

Jesus comes to live inside our hearts through the Holy Spirit and we become, in a sense, little children again crying out to our Heavenly Daddy. Consider it! Think about what a wonderful privilege it is that the Scriptures use such a familiar term of endearment. And this is not the only Scripture reference to our *Abba-relationship* to God as Father. In Romans 8:13-17, Paul again speaks about our adoption into God's family:

Romans 8:13-17

13 For if you live according to the flesh you will die; but if by the Spirit you put to death the deeds of the body, you will live.

14 For as many as are led by the Spirit of God, these are sons of God.

15 For you did not receive the spirit of bondage again to fear, but you received the Spirit of adoption by whom we cry out, "Abba, Father."

16 The Spirit Himself bears witness with our spirit that we are children of God,

17 and if children, then heirs — heirs of God and joint heirs with Christ, if indeed we suffer with Him, that we may also be glorified together. (NKJV)

Here again we read about receiving the Holy Spirit because of Jesus and the importance of walking in the Holy Spirit and dying to the old wrong ways, "For as many as are led by the Spirit of God, these are sons of God." The Spirit Himself testifies to our position in God's family through a real experience with the believer. "The Spirit Himself bears witness with our spirit that we are children of God." And the Holy Spirit inside of us leads us to cry out in our hearts to our Father. He communicates to us that we are God's children and He aids us in our communication with God... and *that* is prayer!

We will see how important the Holy Spirit is to our prayer life in the lessons to come. But we will close out this lesson with the words of our Lord Jesus to His disciples at the Last Supper. In the gospel of John, Chapter 16, He tells them:

John 16:27

27 "For the Father Himself loveth you, because ye have loved Me, and have believed that I came from God." (Webster)

When you love Jesus and recognize who He is,
God loves you in a very special way!

LESSON THREE

In our workshop on *The Nature and Power of Prayer*, we've been going line by line through the Lord's Prayer, and in our last study we discussed our confidence in calling God our Father. We saw that it is because of Jesus that we really can call God our Father. When we receive Jesus, when we believe in His name, He gives us the right to become children of God. And this is the glory of the new covenant, the new contract, that God receives freely into His family all those who come to Him the right and prescribed way through Jesus. As it is written in Galatians 3:26-28:

Galatians 3:26-28

26 For you are **all sons** of God through faith in Christ Jesus.
27 For all of you who were baptized into Christ have clothed yourselves with Christ.
28 There is neither Jew nor Greek *(that is, Gentile)*, there is neither slave nor free man, there is neither male nor female; for you are all one in Christ Jesus. (NASB) *{Emphasis and clarification in parenthesis added}*

And that is why we can pray, "Our Father"!

Now let us pick up our study for this lesson in Matthew 6:9 where Jesus gives the full address: "Our Father **in heaven**." In the Scriptures, the Greek and Hebrew words for heaven or heavens can be used to refer to one of three realms, and each of these realms has both a physical and a spiritual element. In ascending order, first there is the atmospheric heaven or sky immediately above us; second, the celestial or stellar heavens of the universe; and third, the abode or dwelling place of God. In 2 Corinthians Chapter 12 verses 2 to 4, Paul tells us that he was caught up to the third heaven:

2 Corinthians 12:2-4
> 2 I know a man in Christ who fourteen years ago was caught up to the third heaven. Whether it was in the body or out of the body I do not know — God knows.
> 3 And I know that this man — whether in the body or apart from the body I do not know, but God knows—
> 4 was caught up to paradise and heard inexpressible things, things that no one is permitted to tell. (NIV)

So when Jesus says, "Our Father in heaven," heaven clearly is the real place where God the Father actually is. Both words for *heaven,* the Hebrew *shamayim* (shaw-mah'-yim) and Greek *ouranos* (oo-ran-os'), mean literally "the heights" or "that which is raised up," and certainly the place where God dwells is so much above earth and above man both literally as well as spiritually that our minds cannot imagine it. As it says in Isaiah 55:8 and 9:

Isaiah 55:8-9
> 8 "For My thoughts are not your thoughts, neither are your ways My ways," saith the LORD.
> 9 "For as the heavens are higher than the earth, so are My ways higher than your ways, and My thoughts than your thoughts." (KJV)

So that we are clear on this, let us read from 1st Kings Chapter 8 starting at verse 27. You may recognize this as part of the prayer which King Solomon gave for the dedication of the great temple in Jerusalem. This temple was to be a place where God would come down and dwell with His people. But Solomon says in verse 27:

1 Kings 8:27-30
> 27 "But will God indeed dwell on the earth? Behold, heaven and the heaven of heavens cannot contain You. How much less this temple which I have built!
> 28 "Yet regard the prayer of Your servant and his supplication, O LORD my God, and listen to the cry and the prayer which Your servant is praying before You today:

29 "that Your eyes may be open toward this temple night and day, toward the place of which You said, 'My name shall be there,' that You may hear the prayer which Your servant makes toward this place.

30 "And may You hear the supplication of Your servant and of Your people Israel, when they pray toward this place. Hear in heaven **Your dwelling place**; and when You hear, forgive." (NKJV) *{Emphasis added}*

Notice in verse 30 that heaven is called the dwelling place of God, even as Jesus called heaven God's throne in the Sermon on the Mount in Matthew 5:34. And yet as Solomon states to God in verse 27, "Behold, heaven and the heaven of heavens cannot contain You." Here Solomon, again referring to the uppermost or third heaven, affirms that even this highest heaven cannot contain God, so how much less the earthly temple. Remember Genesis 1:1? "In the beginning God created the heavens and the earth." (NIV) Even the uppermost heaven was created by God and He is not restricted by it. By His Holy Spirit, His presence is everywhere. In Psalm 139, verses 7 to 10, David sings:

Psalm 139:7-10

7   Where can I go from Your Spirit?
     Or where can I flee from Your presence?

8   If I ascend to heaven, You are there;
     If I make my bed in Sheol *(the nether world)*, behold, You are there.

9   If I take the wings of the dawn,
     If I dwell in the remotest part of the sea,

10 Even there Your hand will lead me,
     And Your right hand will lay hold of me. (NASB) *{NASB footnote added for clarification)*

It is however in the uppermost heaven that God Almighty resides in total glory and majesty. It is His throne: it is as Solomon stated, "His dwelling place." Paul writes in 1 Timothy Chapter 6 that He dwells in unapproachable light. So in the uppermost heaven there is no darkness nor sin but ONLY light, life and love. And that is where appropriately the Lord Jesus directs our prayers: Our Father in heaven. It is as though we are breaking through all the darkness

30

and dirt and confusion down here and propelling straight up through the heavens into the light of the throne room of God. Hebrews 4:16 says, "Let us therefore come boldly to the throne of grace, that we may obtain mercy, and find grace to help in time of need." (Webster) The answer for all our problems and all our needs is at that throne of grace. And by reminding us that our Father is in heaven, I believe Jesus is telling us that, when we pray, we should remember how far His ways are above our ways—how great His power and how pure His love is compared to anything we've seen down here. What might look impossible to us is certainly possible with God. And that knowledge is important to prayer!

I think it is also noteworthy that in Solomon's dedication of the temple in 1st Kings Chapter 8 above, Solomon asks the question in verse 27, "But will God indeed dwell on the earth?" The New Testament gives a resounding YES to that question. In the gospel of John we read:

John 1:1, 14
> 1　In the beginning was the Word, and the Word was with God, and the Word was God.
> 14　And the Word was made flesh, and dwelt among us, (and we beheld His glory, the glory as of the only begotten of the Father,) full of grace and truth. (KJV)

It was not in a temple made of stone that God came to His people, but rather He came to them in the person of the Lord Jesus Christ— the true temple.

Let's move on in our study. In the Lord's Prayer, Jesus goes on to say, "Hallowed be Your name." "Hallowed" means to be devoted to sacred purposes—to be set apart as **holy**. He is saying, "Father, Your name is holy. Father, Your name is revered and set apart as sacred." So this is a statement of praise. And here we have the next important principle in our study of prayer:

Praise is an important part of prayer, and actually it is best if we start prayer with worship and praise to our Father!

In Psalm 71 it says in verse 6:

Psalm 71:6
> 6　By You I have been sustained from my birth;

You are He who took me from my mother's womb;
My praise is continually of You. (NASB)

And again in verse 14:

Psalm 71:14
14 But as for me, I will hope continually,
And will praise You yet more and more. (NASB)

And praise offered up to God is a wonderful way to draw close in joy and worship to the Lord. I believe **we** receive strength when we praise His name. Praise is <u>the</u> perfect way to start our prayers. And this adoration does not have to be elaborate or flowery. Notice how simply and how purely Jesus gives praise to His Father, "Our Father in heaven, hallowed be Your name."

Now you might be asking, "What is the name of God?" And it is an important question. In the Scriptures, names are extremely significant. Not only do they identify the person in the same way as we use names today, but also they often reflect or tell us something about the person's character and nature. And the name of God is critically important. Remember how we read in the temple dedication prayer:

1 Kings 8:29
29 "that Your eyes may be open toward this temple night and day, toward the place of which You said, 'My <u>name</u> shall be there,' that You may hear the prayer which Your servant makes toward this place." (NKJV) *{Emphasis added}*

So that we can better answer the question, let us read from Exodus Chapter 3. Now this is the section where Moses is tending the flock of Jethro, his father-in-law, and he comes to Horeb, the mountain of God. He beholds a bush burning with fire, but the bush is not consumed. Out of the bush, God calls to him and tells Moses to take the sandals off his feet, for the place where he is standing is holy ground. God says to him, "I have surely seen the affliction of My people who are in Egypt, and have heard their cry...and know their sorrows." He tells Moses that He has come down to deliver them out of the hand of the Egyptians and that He is going to send Moses to Pharaoh that he may bring God's people, the children of Israel, out of Egypt. We'll take up the account in verse 13:

Exodus 3:13-15

13 Moses said to God, "Suppose I go to the Israelites and say to them, 'The God of your fathers has sent me to you,' and they ask me, 'What is His name?' Then what shall I tell them?"

14 God said to Moses, "I AM WHO I AM. This is what you are to say to the Israelites: 'I AM has sent me to you.'"

15 God also said to Moses, "Say to the Israelites, 'The LORD, the God of your fathers — the God of Abraham, the God of Isaac and the God of Jacob — has sent me to you.'

"This is My name forever,

the name you shall call Me

from generation to generation." (NIV) *{Capitalization for deity added}*

Notice that the word LORD in verse 15 is written in small capitals in most English translations—that is capital L, followed by a smaller capital O, capital R and capital D. You will see it typed this way throughout the Old Testament. It is the translators' way of rendering the original four- letter Hebrew word or tetragrammaton spelled only with consonants. These four Hebrew consonants are usually transliterated into the English letters YHWH (or sometimes JHWH or JHVH). It is believed that these consonants, YHWH, were pronounced as *Yahweh* by the covenant people of Israel, although there is debate on what vowel sounds actually were used between the consonants.

So then verse 15 would read, "Say to the Israelites, 'Yahweh, the God of your fathers—the God of Abraham, the God of Isaac and the God of Jacob—has sent me to you. This is My name forever, the name you shall call Me from generation to generation.'" Yahweh is derived from the Hebrew verb, "to be", and means simply but profoundly either "He which is" or "I AM". That is why God said to Moses in verse 14, "I AM WHO I AM" or it could be translated, "I AM THAT I AM". Then He continues, "This is what you are to say to the Israelites, 'I AM has sent me to you.'" The name is defined by God Himself in this passage.

In late Old Testament Judaism and especially in the period between the Testaments prior to the time of Jesus, the Hebrew scribes came to regard the name of God as too holy to pronounce and they were afraid to utter, "Yahweh." Instead, when the Scriptures were read aloud, they would say *Adonay or Adonai*—the Hebrew for "My Lord" or "My Master"—in place of the personal name of God. This practice found its way into the Greek translation of the Old Testament known as *The Septuagint* and later into the New Testament. YHWH was replaced in these texts with the Greek word *kurios*, which means one having power or authority, a lord or master (see Matthew 22:44 for a New Testament citing of an Old Testament Scripture). Then in the medieval period, the Jewish scholars known as the Masoretes substituted the vowels from the Hebrew name Adonai (Lord) into the tetrgrammaton, plugging them into YHWH to make YeHoWaH or YaHoVaH. From this artificial replacement we get the familiar name *Jehovah*. (And you will also see Jehovah used in some translations to represent the Hebrew YHWH.) So when the Bible translations substitute the word LORD, with all capital letters, into the text for Yahweh, they are in a sense following this same tradition.

The important thing to remember is that the actual name of God by which He revealed Himself to Moses and Israel derives from His proclamation: "I AM." And we will see in our next lesson that that name has tremendous significance to our prayer life.

LESSON FOUR

————————∽∝∽————————

A s we begin this fourth lesson in the workshop on Prayer, I would like to take a moment to make an observation. To some of you, these series of studies will be a review of Biblical facts that you already know. But to others, this learning program will be the first time that you have experienced line by line Bible teaching and analysis. In these lessons we will be looking at and drawing upon a hefty number of Scripture passages, but I strongly believe, as the Lord tells us in Isaiah 55:11, that when His Word goes forth it does not return to Him void, but it shall accomplish what He pleases, and it shall prosper in the thing for which He sent it. In order for us to be able to walk successfully in the Lord's ways and the Lord's power, given the often difficult situations surrounding us, it is critical to constantly seek His Spirit's anointing *and* study His written Word—the Bible. God strongly warns us in Hosea 4 verse 6:

Hosea 4:6

6   My people are destroyed for lack of knowledge.
Because you have rejected knowledge,
I also will reject you from being My priest.
Since you have forgotten the law of your God,
I also will forget your children. (NASB)

Clearly, we need to know God's Word to survive. Okay, we left off last time in Matthew 6:9, "Our Father in heaven, hallowed be Your name." And we saw how God revealed Himself to the nation of Israel by the name Yahweh—the great I AM! As He said to Moses, "I AM THAT I AM. Thus you shall say to the children of Israel I AM

35

has sent me to you." Let's pick up today's study with a reading from the gospel of Matthew Chapter 1 and verses 20-21:

Matthew 1:20-21

> 20 But while he thought on these things, the angel of the Lord appeared to him in a dream, saying, "Joseph, thou son of David, fear not to take to thee Mary thy wife: for that which is conceived in her is by the Holy Spirit.
>
> 21 And she shall bring forth a Son, and thou shalt call His name JESUS: for He shall save His people from their sins." (Webster)

The name *Jesus* is from the Greek form of the Hebrew name *Yeshua* which we transliterate in our English Old Testament as *Joshua*. Thus Joshua and Jesus are basically the same name. Yeshua means "Yahweh is salvation" or "Yahweh saves." But there was a difference in how this name applied to Jesus from how it applied to the Old Testament Joshua or to all those people who then, out of respect for Joshua, received the same designation. Clearly, there were other men named Jesus at the time the Lord lived. You can read of one such man in Acts 13:6. Joshua had been a prominent figure in Israel's history and children were regularly named after him. And his name was a wonderful name. It designated what God would accomplish, as for example, *God would be salvation* to His people by going before Joshua and the Israelites as they crossed the Jordan to possess the Promised Land.

In that way, the name Jesus was similar to some other Hebrew based names, such as *John*. John comes from the Hebrew *Yohanan*, which means Yahweh is gracious. It was an appropriate name for the angel Gabriel to tell Zacharias to give to his son, John the Baptist, since God was being gracious to his wife Elizabeth and him by giving them a son at an advanced age. Even more importantly, John's ministry would be to testify to the Messiah—to make that jump from the Old Covenant to the New by pointing to the *gift* that God would give in His son Jesus and the gospel of *grace*, so dramatically seen when John exclaims, "Behold, the Lamb of God who takes away the sin of the world!" (John 1:29) (NASB)

However, the way Yeshua or other Yahweh-based names like Yohanan were used to name others was a great deal different from the way the name Jesus was given to the Lord. These names, as they applied to the others, designated what God could do for them and what He could accomplish in their lives and in the lives of His people: *God is their salvation. God is gracious to them.* But let's take a close look at what the angel of the Lord said to Joseph in Matthew 1:21: "…thou shalt call His name JESUS, for He —**HE**— shall save His people from their sins." But Jesus means, "*Yahweh* saves." Who saves? Yahweh saves. Who will save His people from their sins? This child who would be born in Bethlehem will save His people from their sins. That's the reason given by the angel to name him Jesus. So then who is this child? Yahweh in the flesh!

Jesus <u>is</u> God the Savior who brings the ultimate salvation to <u>His</u> people. As it says in Micah 5:2:

Micah 5:2

2   "But you, Bethlehem Ephrathah,
Though you are little among the thousands of Judah,
Yet out of you shall come forth to Me
The One to be Ruler in Israel,
Whose goings forth are from of old,
From everlasting." (NKJV)

And again in Isaiah 9:6:

Isaiah 9:6

6   For unto us a Child is born, unto us a Son is given: and the government shall be upon His shoulder: and His name shall be called Wonderful, Counsellor, The mighty God, The everlasting Father, The Prince of Peace. (KJV)

Many times Jesus proclaimed Himself as the I AM! In John 8:58 He revealed to those debating Him:

John 8:58

58 …"Verily, verily, I say unto you, Before Abraham was, I AM." (KJV)

To Martha, the sister of Lazarus whom He was about to raise from the dead, He said:

John 11:25-26a

25 …"**I am** the resurrection, and the life: he that believeth in Me, though he were dead, yet shall he live:

26 And whosoever liveth and believeth in Me shall never die. …" (KJV) *{Emphasis added}*

To His disciples He said:

John 14:6

6 …"**I am** the way and the truth and the life. No one comes to the Father except through Me." (NIV) *{Emphasis and capitalization for deity added}*

And when they came to arrest Him, in John 18:4-6, He asked them whom they were seeking, and they answered, "Jesus of Nazareth." When Jesus said to them, "I am he" or, literally in the Greek, "I am," they drew back and fell to the ground—the power of His profession of His identity literally knocking them off their feet.

For the nature of Jesus is the same "I AM" nature as that of the Father and the Spirit. That is why Jesus prayed at the Last Supper:

John 17:5-6a

5 "Now, Father, glorify Me together with Yourself, with the glory which I had with You before the world was.

6 "I have <u>manifested Your name</u> to the men whom You gave Me out of the world; …" (NASB) *{Emphasis added}*

He manifested the name of God by showing us the character of God. For Jesus is the exact representation of the Father. He is the I AM as a man. We are told in the Scriptures that He is the image of the invisible God and that He is the brightness of God's glory and the express image of His person (Colossians 1:15, 2 Corinthians 4:4, Hebrews 1:3). When we see Him we see the Father. And as the perfect man—the only good, sinless man—He alone can make atonement for our sins. Truly He is *Jesus,* meaning "I AM Salvation."

And in the majority manuscripts of the New Testament, verse 11 of that prayer is rendered:

John 17:11

11 "I will remain in the world no longer, but they are still in the world, and I am coming to You. Holy Father, protect them by the power of Your name, **the name You gave Me**, so that they may be one as We are one." (NIV) *{Emphasis and capitalization for deity added}*

Later on in this series we will speak about the importance of praying in the name of Jesus. But for our study up to this point, it is important that we understand what the name of God means for us. God IS! And we are NOT! This is the reason we should praise Him. When we praise Him we are recognizing the **only** source of goodness—of light—of life—of love. And God IS! He never changes. He always is. He's the Eternal, the beginning and the end. He's the only real God and the Author of all that exists. And He is here and now working in our lives, just as He was active in the lives of the Israelites coming out of Egypt.

That's a crucial, crucial point! Many people understand and know God as the Almighty. But they have so much difficulty believing that He is intimately concerned for every aspect of their lives down here. To them God is someone they go to after they die, and they have a hard time accepting that He can intervene and wants to intervene in what goes on in the everyday lives of those who are truly, truly His. And that was really the distinction between how He dealt with Abraham, Isaac and Jacob and how He would deal with Moses and the Israelites. He tells Moses in Exodus 6:2-3 that the patriarchs knew Him as God Almighty but that they would know Him now by the name Yahweh; meaning, I believe, that **now** all the promises made to the patriarchs would actually be manifested—actually happen— actually come about in the earth. He IS and He fulfills His promises, and they would receive deliverance from Egypt and they would possess the Promised Land.

God IS! He never fails. He's all sufficient. He needs no one else. And He is self-fulfilled. He is what He wills. It is right and His nature to be merciful and righteous, and HE IS—nothing can hinder Him. We on the other hand fail without Him. It is like a lamp that quickly dims when disconnected from its source of power. I believe many people try and fool themselves that they do not need a deep personal relationship with God to achieve that which is virtuous and worthy. They think that somehow, on their own, through some sort of positive thinking or the right educational degree or the right self-help program, they can make their lives work. Paul summarizes perfectly in Romans Chapter 7 the human condition when we try on our own to be good. He says:

Romans 7:18-19
> 18 For I know that in me (that is, in my flesh,) dwelleth no good thing: for to will is present with me; but how to perform that which is good, I find not.
> 19 For the good that I would, I do not; but the evil which I would not, that I do. (Webster)

Then he says:

Romans 7:24-25a
> 24 O wretched man that I am! Who will deliver me from this body of death?
> 25 I thank God — through Jesus Christ our Lord! ... (NKJV)

We are delivered because God IS! God **is** love. He **is** goodness. And so Jesus accomplished for us what we could not. And God **is** all powerful! As Jeremiah prayed:

Jeremiah 32:17
> 17 'Ah Lord GOD! behold, Thou hast made the heaven and the earth by Thy great power and out-stretched arm, and there is nothing too hard for Thee:' (Webster)

And as Jesus taught:

Mark 10:27
> 27 ..."With men it is impossible, but not with God: for with God all things are possible." (KJV)

It is extremely important to understand this when we pray. Why? Because Jesus said:

John 16:27
> 27 "For the Father Himself loveth you, because ye have loved Me, and have believed that I came from God." (Webster)

All that love, all that power, all that life is concerned for YOU in a very special way because of your relationship to His Son Jesus.

TREMENDOUS! Truly Father, Your name is HOLY. Hallowed be Your name!

Now many of you reading this book are Christians, and you know the power of God and you've praised and worshipped His holy Name. But for others of you, this might be the first time that you have ever really heard about the power of God and the love that God has for you. It might be the first time you've truly heard about Jesus or really understood what it meant for Him to give up His life for you. There is a Scripture in Philippians Chapter 2 where the apostle Paul tells us that, though Jesus Christ was in very form God, He made Himself of no reputation and He took the form of a servant and came down in the likeness of men. And he continues:

Philippians 2:8-11
8   Being found in appearance as a man, He humbled Himself by becoming obedient to the point of death, even death on a cross.
9   For this reason also, God highly exalted Him, and bestowed on Him the name which is above every name,
10 so that at the name of Jesus EVERY KNEE WILL BOW, of those who are in heaven and on earth and under the earth,
11 and that every tongue will confess that Jesus Christ is Lord, to the glory of God the Father. (NASB)

Perhaps you've never read a "religious" book before. Perhaps this workshop was given to you by a friend or relative. I don't believe it is an accident that you are reading these words. Rather, God is using this book to tell you that it is time for you to bow your knee and confess Jesus Christ as Lord and to ask Him to come into your heart and change you. It is time to ask Him to bring that power of the great I AM into your life to save you, make you a new person, and reconcile you unto the Father. God loves you and He cares for you and this is the gift He has for you, in Jesus name.

LESSON FIVE

————————◇————————

In our Bible workshop on *The Nature and Power of Prayer*, we have been going line by line through the Lord's Prayer in Matthew Chapter 6 to find out how our Lord Jesus wants us to pray. I personally find it highly enlightening to perform such an exact study and I hope you do also. When we go in depth into the Bible, we can truly begin to see how much God has for us in His Holy Word. And with Scripture, it seems, even the simplest verses are chock full of life giving truths. Today's lesson is particularly fascinating because in this, the 5th part of our series, we'll be talking about **the kingdom of God.**

In Matthew 6:10 Jesus prays to the Father, "Your kingdom come." To appreciate this declaration let's go back in the Bible to the book of Genesis and take a look at *beginnings:*

Genesis 1:1-5

1   In the beginning God created the heavens and the earth.
2   Now the earth was formless and empty, darkness was over the surface of the deep, and the Spirit of God was hovering over the waters.
3   And God said, "Let there be light," and there was light.
4   God saw that the light was good, and He separated the light from the darkness.
5   God called the light "day," and the darkness He called "night." And there was evening, and there was morning—the first day.
    (NIV) *{Capitalization for deity added}*

Here we see that the heavens and the earth were made separate. Back in Lesson Three we discussed the heavens. And in that

42

study we saw that in the heaven of heavens, that is the uppermost or third heaven, God Almighty resides in total glory and **majesty**. There is no darkness or sin there, but only the light, life and love of the Father.

Not only were the heavens and earth created separate, but we observe from this passage in Genesis that the light, which is declared as good, was separated from the darkness and there was day and night. And that is extremely important to understanding the world we live in, because in our world, in our realm, we taste both light and darkness and we make a choice. As creatures made in the image of our God, we have a <u>free will</u>. Have you ever thought about what a miracle it is that you exist and that you are a distinct person capable of feeling and believing, of thinking and wondering, and that you are able to and constantly do make decisions?

It is a key question. All too often people are so busy with daily routines and the fascinations that can preoccupy our time that facing the primary fact of the wonder of their existence and asking the question, "Why am I here?" is suppressed. Sometimes it is suppressed because the person does not want to face the tremendous implications that the question poses. And I think many deep down know that the answer given by modern society—that is, that they are merely a machine and the result of millions of years of random accidents and mishaps—is nonsense. The Scripture says:

Psalm 139:14

> 14 I will praise Thee; for I am fearfully and wonderfully made: marvellous are Thy works; and that my soul knoweth right well. (KJV)

And you need to hear this. You are not an accidental assemblage of parts. You are a wondrously created individual of great value to your heavenly Father and your existence is filled with tremendous purpose. Deep in your soul you know this. God has made you in His image and as a distinct individual—as a distinct spirit—you can choose. We each can choose light or we can choose darkness.

The stage is set in Eden. In all this beauty and perfection, man is made *ruler* of this world as he is in submission to God. We read in Genesis Chapter 1:

Genesis 1:26-27

> 26 And God said, "Let Us make man in Our image, after Our
> likeness: and let them have dominion over the fish of the sea,
> and over the fowl of the air, and over the cattle, and over all
> the earth, and over every creeping thing that creepeth upon
> the earth."
> 27 So God created man in His own image, in the image of God
> created He him; male and female created He them. (KJV)

Mankind was given dominion of this beautiful planet. But we all know the account of how Adam chose the rebellion which Satan offered to Eve and him. And so he actually made Satan **his** king, and turned the dominion of the world over to the evil one. Now I realize at this point that some of you are thinking, "He really believes there is a devil?" The Scriptures from Genesis to Revelation tell us that there is indeed a devil and there are demons. And unlike the court of human opinion, God's Word never changes. I remember back in the very early 1980's, when my wife and I were newly saved, how careful you had to be when you spoke about an angelic realm. Having come out of a secular, cold scientific period in American society, even Christians who spoke openly about God were hesitant sometimes to speak about the reality of angels as the Bible had always taught. Then came the mid 1990's and almost everybody, from all types of different belief systems, became caught up with angels. It became impossible to turn around without seeing angel pins, angel earrings, angel books and magazine articles about angels. Belief in angels became a fad—and sometimes to the detriment of faith in the Lord. Often I have come across people that have faith in some sort of angelic contact but not faith in the Lord of the Scriptures.

Still, when people are interviewed today, it seems a majority believe angels exist and it has become acceptable to believe in angels—at least benevolent angels. But the Bible always taught the existence of angels, even back when it would have been a source of ridicule. And the Bible also states that there are fallen angels or demons. In Matthew 25:41, Jesus tells us that the everlasting fire was prepared for the devil and the devil's angels. And in 2 Corinthians Chapter 11 and verse 14, Paul, the apostle, informs us that Satan transforms himself into or masquerades as an angel of light.

It is to this same Satan that Adam gave the dominion of this planet through his disobedience to God. Adam and Eve should have ruled over the creation in submission to God Almighty, but instead, by listening to the Evil One, Satan became their king and, in a sense, the ruler of this realm—the ruler of this world. They transferred their dominion to him, and this world became a kingdom of darkness.

Let's take a moment to read from the gospel of Luke, Chapter 4 and verses 5 to 8. This is the chronicle of Satan tempting Jesus in the wilderness.

Luke 4:5-8

5   And the devil taking Him up upon a high mountain, showed to Him all the kingdoms of the world in a moment of time.

6   And the devil said to Him, "All this power will I give Thee, and the glory of them: <u>for that is delivered to me</u>, and to whomsoever I will, I give it.

7   "If Thou therefore wilt worship me, all shall be Thine."

8   And Jesus answered and said to him, "Get thee behind Me, Satan: for it is written, 'Thou shalt worship the Lord thy God, and Him only shalt thou serve.'" (Webster) *{Emphasis added}*

Notice in this Scripture that Jesus does not contest Satan's dominion over the kingdoms of the world. In John 12:31, 14:30, and 16:11 Jesus even calls Satan "the ruler of this world." And Paul refers to Satan in 2 Corinthians 4:4 as "the god of this world" or "of this age." In Ephesians 2:2 he reminds the believers that before their salvation they had "formerly walked according to the course of this world, according to the prince of the power of the air, of the spirit that is now working in the sons of disobedience." (NASB) That expression, *the prince of the power of the air,* could also be translated "the ruler of the kingdom of the air."

You begin to get an image of an almost demonic blanket shrouding this world, with Satan, the king of the sons of disobedience, all too often exercising his dominion. And when we begin to grasp this, it explains why so many things are the way they are all around us. But let's be assured that, in truth, the Lord God is still over all! David wrote in Psalm 24:1:

Psalm 24:1

1   The earth is the LORD's, and the fulness thereof; the world, and they that dwell therein. (KJV)

And because God is the Creator, all belong to Him. As David also prayed in 1ˢᵗ Chronicles 29 starting at verse 10:

1 Chronicles 29:10-13

> 10 ..."Blessed be Thou, LORD God of Israel our Father, for ever and ever.
> 11 Thine, O LORD, is the greatness, and the power, and the glory, and the victory, and the majesty: <u>for all that is in the heaven and on the earth is Thine</u>; Thine is the kingdom, O LORD, and Thou art exalted as head above all.
> 12 Both riches and honor come from Thee, and Thou reignest over all; and in Thy hand is power and might; and in Thy hand it is to make great, and to give strength to all.
> 13 Now therefore, our God, we thank Thee, and praise Thy glorious name." (Webster) *{Emphasis added}*

While the kingdoms of this world have most often followed Satan, still God is ultimately in control of all that goes on. In Daniel 2:21, Daniel says that God "removes kings and sets up kings," and in Daniel 4:25 he tells Nebuchadnezzar that "the Most High is ruler over the kingdom of men, and gives it to whomever He chooses." Psalm 89:11 reads:

Psalm 89:11

> 11 The heavens are Yours, the earth also is Yours;
> The world and all it contains, You have founded them. (NASB)

And yet we must understand that a kingdom can be defined as a king and his subjects. Man has made Satan king of the kingdom of the world. He is the one in the world, and the whole world, apart from Christ, is under the evil one's control. If someone does not believe this, simply turn on your TV or radio or read some of the newspaper or online headlines today. Darkness has been chosen over light. In 1ˢᵗ John 5:19 we read:

1 John 5:19

> 19 We know that we are of God, and that the whole world lies in the power of the evil one. (NASB)

And in Revelation 12:9 we are told that:

Revelation 12:9a

> 9 And the great dragon was thrown down, the serpent of old who is called the devil and Satan, <u>who deceives the whole world</u>; ... (NASB) *{Emphasis added}*

The kingdom of this world has been under the devil and under darkness. Satan has been sinning from the beginning, leading man to sin and bringing the curse of decay and corruption upon God's creation. That is why we must pray, "Father Your kingdom <u>come</u>— Your kingdom of heaven—Your kingdom of Light." In Genesis, once our first parents, Adam and Eve, had followed Satan's temptation, God said to Adam in Chapter 3 verse 17:

Genesis 3:17

> 17 ..."Because you have listened to the voice of your wife, and have eaten from the tree about which I commanded you, saying, 'You shall not eat from it';
> Cursed is the ground because of you;
> In toil you will eat of it
> All the days of your life." (NASB)

It is really because of man's rebellion that life in this world is so hard. Satan certainly won a victory over God's creation. We thought we didn't need God—that we could be like God on our own. And it is as though the Lord pulls back His hand of blessing just a little, as if to say, "Here now is the world you wanted apart from Me. You keep it! Can you keep yourselves from decay and aging? Can you keep your spirit and mind whole apart from Me? Will this earth easily yield to your command?"

The answer of course is **no**. Life is toil. Cursed is the ground Adam for your sake. Not only that, but through the rebellion, all types of demonic spirits have been given authority in the affairs of mankind. Remember that expression for Satan: *the prince of the power of the air*? Well, Paul describes in Ephesians 6:10-12 a whole hierarchy of fallen angels that seem to be lifted up in positions of influence in the heavenly realms. Of course, we are not speaking about the uppermost heaven but rather the interface of the lower heavens with the spiritual realm—that blanket surrounding the world which I mentioned before. Paul writes:

47

Ephesians 6:10-13

10 Finally, my brethren, be strong in the Lord and in the power of His might.

11 Put on the whole armor of God, that you may be able to stand against the wiles of the devil.

12 For we do not wrestle against flesh and blood, but against principalities, against powers, against the rulers of the darkness of this age, against spiritual hosts of wickedness in the heavenly places.

13 Therefore take up the whole armor of God, that you may be able to withstand in the evil day, and having done all, to stand. (NKJV)

It is wonderful to know that, in spite of all the darkness and evil, we can stand in the power of the Lord. In 1st John 3:8 it reads:

1 John 3:8b

8 …For this purpose the Son of God was manifested, that He might destroy the works of the devil. (KJV)

And Jesus said in the gospel of John Chapter 12:

John 12:31-32

31 "Now judgment is upon this world; now the ruler of this world will be cast out.

32 "And I, if I am lifted up from the earth, will draw all men to Myself." (NASB)

Therefore, when we talk about God's kingdom coming on earth as it is in heaven, we are looking to a dramatic turnaround in the way this world operates—from the angelic authorities to the people made in the image of God to the physical creation itself—all because of what Jesus did on the cross, when He was lifted up and defeated the evil one. And a proper understanding of the kingdom of God is imperative to prayer. In our next few lessons, we will contrast the kingdom of the world to the kingdom of heaven and discuss when exactly the kingdom of God comes.

LESSON SIX

———————∝———————

I n our last lesson, we began to speak about that part of the Our Father where Jesus teaches us to pray, "Your kingdom come." And we said that a proper understanding of the kingdom of God was imperative to our prayers being Scriptural, pleasing, and powerful. Let us take a moment to contrast the kingdom of heaven with the kingdom of this world:

We learned last time that the kingdom of the world is a kingdom of *darkness*. And we have already spoken about the unapproachable light of the heaven of heavens, so the kingdom of heaven is a kingdom of *light* and holiness.

In Lesson Five we showed from Scriptures such as 2nd Corinthians 4:4 that Satan is the god of the kingdom of the world. But God Almighty is the God of the kingdom of heaven. And God IS that He IS. His name is Yahweh, the great I AM. But Satan is NOT. All that the devil has for mankind is emptiness and despair. And although Satan is strong and is called "the strong man" in Mark 3:27, he is **not** all powerful. For Jesus tells us in that same verse that this strong man can be bound, and in Revelation 12:8 we read that ultimately Satan will not prevail, or literally, that he was "not strong enough." 1st John 4:4 is a wonderful verse:

1 John 4:4

4   Ye are of God, little children, and have overcome them: because greater is He that is in you, than he that is in the world. (KJV)

God certainly is greater than Satan. And the kingdom of heaven is greater than the kingdom of the world. While God is the Creator of mankind and made man in His image, Satan cannot create anything.

Rather he is the Murderer and Destroyer of man. The only way he can make one in his image is to take the individual who God originally created and degenerate that person by leading him or her into sin until the heart becomes hard like his own. And we read last time from Revelation 12:9 how Satan deceives and leads astray the whole world. The apostle Peter tells us in 1st Peter 5:8:

1 Peter 5:8

> 8 Be of sober spirit, be on the alert. Your adversary, the devil, prowls around like a roaring lion, seeking someone to devour. (NASB)

So Jesus rightly calls Satan the evil one in the Lord's Prayer and elsewhere in the gospels. But God is the Good and Holy One. As we read in Luke 18:19, "...No one is good except One, that is, God." And Jesus, in Luke 1:35, is called the Holy One by the angel Gabriel.

Moreover, God is our Savior. Remember our study back in Lesson Four when we looked at the meaning of the name of Jesus (*Yahweh is Salvation*)? In Isaiah 63:16 the prophet writes:

Isaiah 63:16b

> 16 ...You, O Lord, are our Father;
> Our Redeemer from Everlasting is Your name. (NKJV)

But Satan is the deceiver, the adversary, and the accuser. Actually, that's what the name *Satan* means in the Hebrew—"the Adversary" or "the Opposer"—just as the Greek word we translate *devil* means "an accuser" or "a slanderer." In 2 Corinthians 4:4, Paul tells us that Satan, the god of this age, has blinded the minds of those who do not believe, so that the light of the gospel of the glory of Christ, who is the image of God, should not shine on them. And Jesus says of him in John 8:44:

John 8:44

> 44 "...He was a murderer from the beginning, not holding to the truth, for there is no truth in him. When he lies, he speaks his native language, for he is a liar and the father of lies." (NIV)

Throughout the Scriptures we see how Satan leads men to sin and **then** accuses them before God. In Revelation Chapter 12, in the section which chronicles how one day Satan will be cast out of the heavenly realms and down to the earth, it says in verse 10:

Revelation 12:10
> 10 Then I heard a loud voice in heaven, saying,
> "Now the salvation, and the power, and the kingdom of our God and the authority of His Christ have come, for the <u>accuser</u> of our brethren has been thrown down, he who accuses them before our God day and night." (NASB) *{Emphasis added}*

A case in point is given in the Old Testament book of Job, where we read how Satan maligns Job in his presentation before God. In Job 1:9-11 it says:

Job 1:9-11
> 9 Then Satan answered the LORD, "Does Job fear God for nothing?
> 10 "Have You not made a hedge about him and his house and all that he has, on every side? You have blessed the work of his hands, and his possessions have increased in the land.
> 11 "But put forth Your hand now and touch all that he has; he will surely curse You to Your face." (NASB)

In the same way, in the book of Zechariah, Satan tries to use the sins of the high priest, Joshua, against him at the time of the rebuilding of the temple:

Zechariah 3:1-5
> 1 Then he showed me Joshua the high priest standing before the angel of the LORD, and Satan standing at his right side <u>to accuse him</u>.
> 2 The LORD said to Satan, "The LORD rebuke you, Satan! The LORD, who has chosen Jerusalem, rebuke you! Is not this man a burning stick snatched from the fire?"
> 3 Now Joshua was dressed in filthy clothes as he stood before the angel.
> 4 The angel said to those who were standing before him, "Take off his filthy clothes."
> Then he said to Joshua, "See, I have taken away your sin, and I will put fine garments on you."

5   Then I said, "Put a clean turban on his head." So they put a clean turban on his head and clothed him, while the angel of the LORD stood by. (NIV) *{Emphasis added}*

In this Scripture, we have the great message of the gospel of God's grace. Even though our garments may be filthy—that is, even though we have sinned and have lived in the past as part of the kingdom of the world—the Lord can remove those iniquities and clothe us in clean robes and wrap righteousness around our heads. Amen. Satan is strong, but he is not strong enough! He cannot keep us imprisoned in his kingdom simply by being an adversary, as in a court of law, constantly bringing our past sins up before God, the Judge. And that's because, in that court room, we have on our side a powerful lawyer. John teaches us in 1st John 2:1:

1 John 2:1
1   My little children, I am writing these things to you so that you may not sin. And if anyone sins, we have an Advocate with the Father, Jesus Christ the righteous; (NASB)

Even as Satan is looking to destroy us, God's own Son is our just advocate as we read in Hebrews 7:25:

Hebrews 7:25
25 Therefore He is able to save completely those who come to God through Him, because He always lives to intercede for them. (NIV) *{Emphasis and capitalization for deity added}*

What a contrast we have between Satan and the Lord Jesus, and what a contrast between the kingdom of the world and the kingdom of heaven. It is vitally important, to prayer and to our understanding of the things that go on around us, not to confuse the nature of Satan with the nature of God.

And here is an excellent definition of *salvation*: **Being brought out of the kingdom of darkness and into the kingdom of light.** Colossians 1:12-14 tells us how this happens:

Colossians 1:12-14

12 giving thanks to the Father who has qualified us to be partakers of the inheritance of the saints in the light.

13 He has delivered us from the power of darkness and conveyed us into the kingdom of the Son of His love,

14 in whom we have redemption through His blood, the forgiveness of sins. (NKJV)

Remember in our last lesson when we spoke about that hierarchy of fallen angels interfacing with this world? We read in Colossians 2:15 that on the cross, Jesus disarmed principalities and powers and made a public spectacle of them, triumphing over them in it. What seemed to the world like a moment of weakness was instead the strength and the power of the kingdom of heaven. Rejected by the world, abandoned by His friends, separated from the Father, suffering agonizing pain and probably the most horrific of demonic attacks, with the weight of all the sins of the world upon His shoulders, still on that cross Jesus did not sin. The purity of His heart in His weakness was stronger than all the combined evil of man and of Satan's forces in their strength. And so He won the victory. And we can rejoice as the kingdom of heaven goes forward in the power of that victory, even as Jesus rejoiced over the victory in Luke Chapter 10:

Luke 10:17-21

17 The seventy returned with joy, saying, "Lord, even the demons are subject to us in Your name."

18 And He said to them, "I was watching Satan fall from heaven like lightning.

19 "Behold, I have given you authority to tread on serpents and scorpions, and over all the power of the enemy, and nothing will injure you.

20 "Nevertheless do not rejoice in this, that the spirits are subject to you, but rejoice that your names are recorded in heaven."

21 At that very time He rejoiced greatly in the Holy Spirit, and said, "I praise You, O Father, Lord of heaven and earth, that You have hidden these things from the wise and intelligent and have revealed them to infants. Yes, Father, for this way was well-pleasing in Your sight." (NASB)

The seventy saw the power of the kingdom of heaven, just as Paul tells us in 1ˢᵗ Corinthians 4:20:

1 Corinthians 4:20

> 20 For the kingdom of God is not a matter of talk but of power. (NIV)

But to walk in the power of the coming kingdom we must become, as you read in the Scripture up above, like little children. These are the words of Jesus in Luke 18:17:

Luke 18:17

> 17 "Verily I say to you, Whoever shall not receive the kingdom of God as a little child, shall in no wise enter into it." (Webster)

We have to be born again and trust our heavenly Father. We have to accept in faith the plan of His salvation in what only Jesus could do for us on the cross. We have to desire our hearts to be softened and made pure, to leave the darkness and the world behind and enter the kingdom of light.

But that brings up a very important question. We pray, "Our Father in heaven, hallowed be Your name. Your kingdom come." When exactly does the kingdom of God come? You have probably heard much conflicting teaching on this and the question needs to be answered so that we know exactly what we are praying. Let us consider the morning of the crucifixion for a moment. When Israel's leaders handed Jesus over to Pilate, the Roman governor asked Jesus if He was the king of the Jews. Pilate could not understand what Jesus could have done to have His own people desire His execution. We read the Lord's answer in John 18:36-37:

John 18:36-37

> 36 Jesus answered, "My kingdom is not of this world. If My kingdom were of this world, My servants would fight, so that I should not be delivered to the Jews; but now My kingdom is not from here."
>
> 37 Pilate therefore said to Him, "Are You a king then?"
> Jesus answered, "You say rightly that I am a king. For this cause I was born, and for this cause I have come into the

world, that I should bear witness to the truth. Everyone who
is of the truth hears My voice." (NKJV)

Because Jesus' kingdom is **not** of this world, He would be
rejected by this world with a violent assault. Though there was no
basis for any charge against Him, His very presence, the claims
He made, and the teachings He gave were enough to arouse the
world's anger. It is the same many times today when the gospel is
presented. And even those who were His disciples deserted Him
in fear—the fear that so characterizes our human nature. No voice
could be found in His defense even after so many had been helped
and so many had been healed. There was not one servant from
this world that would stand with Him. And remember, a kingdom is
a king and his subjects. That's why Jesus said His kingdom was not
of this world.

Yet also notice that Jesus answered, "You say rightly that I am
a king. For this cause I was born, and for this cause I have come
into the world." The King of the kingdom of heaven had to first be
sent into this world, for the kingdom of God to come. The King of the
kingdom of light had to arrive to defeat and save from the kingdom of
darkness. Unfortunately, not everyone will yield to and receive that
light. In John Chapter 3 verses 19 to 21 the Lord taught:

John 3:19-21
19 "This is the judgment, that the Light has come into the world,
    and men loved the darkness rather than the Light, for their
    deeds were evil.
20 "For everyone who does evil hates the Light, and does not
    come to the Light for fear that his deeds will be exposed.
21 "But he who practices the truth comes to the Light, so that
    his deeds may be manifested as having been wrought in
    God." (NASB)

In our next lesson we will see how the true subjects of the
kingdom are made and will answer the question, "When does the
kingdom of heaven come to earth?"

LESSON SEVEN

————————✄————————

I pray the Lord blesses you in a very special way as you begin this Bible workshop—the seventh lesson in the study series on *The Nature and Power of Prayer*. We have been going line by line through the Lord's Prayer as Jesus presented it in Matthew Chapter 6. And in the previous two lessons we have examined that portion where we are instructed to pray, "Your kingdom come." I ended up last time with the question, "When does the kingdom of heaven come to earth?" There are so many different teachings on this subject and it can be very confusing. But I think the key to a proper understanding is to remember that a kingdom is foremost a king and his subjects, and *then* that there is a land or a realm that they occupy. The kingdom, based on that king and based on the principles under which his subjects operate, will take on certain characteristics, as we saw last time when we contrasted the kingdom of the world with the kingdom of heaven. And, when we look at the central elements to the kingdom being the king and his subjects, we see why Jesus said in John 18:36:

John 18:36

> 36 Jesus answered, "My kingdom is not of this world. If My kingdom were of this world, My servants would fight, so that I should not be delivered to the Jews; but now My kingdom is not from here." (NKJV)

We considered last time that when the King of the kingdom of heaven came to earth there were as yet no subjects of that kingdom to stand with Him, leaving the kingdom of this world to cast Him out with violence. Clearly His kingdom was not of this world.

Nevertheless, when John the Baptist came as a forerunner of Jesus, it says in Matthew 3 verse 2 that he came preaching, "Repent, for the kingdom of heaven is at hand." (NASB) Moreover, we read in Mark 1 verses 14-15:

Mark 1:14-15
> 14 Now after that John was put in prison, Jesus came into Galilee, preaching the gospel of the kingdom of God,
> 15 And saying, "The time is fulfilled, and the kingdom of God is at hand: repent ye, and believe the gospel." (KJV)

How then was the kingdom of God at hand? It was as close as the man Christ Jesus who was living right among them. We are told in Romans 14:17 that the kingdom of God is "righteousness and peace and joy in the Holy Spirit." Here standing before them was the Prince of Peace, the Only Righteous and Holy One in all human history. Here was the Messiah to whom the Father gave the Holy Spirit without limit. And He manifested the power and joy of the kingdom of heaven. Jesus healed the people and freed them from the power which Satan and his demons had over them. And so He said, in Matthew 12:28:

Matthew 12:28
> 28 "But if I cast out demons by the Spirit of God, then the kingdom of God has come upon you." (NASB)

In addition, He taught them the principles of the kingdom. We read in the gospels the different parables that Jesus used to show them what the kingdom of heaven is like. So then, the kingdom came with Jesus. More precisely:

The kingdom of heaven came, comes, and will come.

By this point, I probably have some of you perplexed, but stay with me as I explain this important principle further. The kingdom of heaven came with the King. It came to earth when the King from above, the King from heaven, came down to earth and was born in Bethlehem, grew up in Nazareth, and preached to Israel doing many mighty works. Then He died for us on Calvary.

But a kingdom is a king and his subjects. And so, while the kingdom came with the King, there were still not any true subjects. I think of Peter, who in Matthew 26:35 said, "Even if I have to die with You, I will not deny You," (NASB) and yet a short time later he denied Jesus three times, the last time with cursing and swearing. However, at the Last Supper Jesus had told them in John 16:7 that it was to their advantage if He went away, because then He could send the Helper, the Holy Spirit, to them. So we see Peter on the shores of Galilee, a repentant man, facing his risen Lord who had died so that Peter's sins would be forgiven. And we also see him on the day of Pentecost, having now received the Holy Spirit which Jesus promised, a new person who, with boldness and joy, stands up without fear before thousands to preach the gospel of salvation. *For when the Lord Jesus comes into a believer's heart, only then is a subject of the kingdom made!* And that's still going on today. This is what we mean when we say the kingdom comes.

Jesus said, in John Chapter 3 verse 3:

John 3:3

3   ..."Verily, verily, I say unto thee, Except a man be born again, he cannot see the kingdom of God." (KJV)

And down in verse 5 He states:

John 3:5

5   ..."Verily, verily, I say unto thee, Except a man be born of water and of the Spirit, he <u>cannot enter into</u> the kingdom of God." (KJV) *{Emphasis added}*

Reading from Paul's letter to Titus will make this clearer:

Titus 3:4-7

4   But when the kindness and love of God our Savior towards man appeared,

5   <u>Not by works of righteousness which we have done</u>, but according to His mercy <u>He saved us, by the washing of regeneration, and renewing of the Holy Spirit</u>;

6   Which He shed *(poured out)* on us abundantly, through Jesus Christ our Savior;

7   That being justified by His grace, we should be made heirs according to the hope of eternal life. (Webster) *{Emphasis and clarification in parenthesis added}*

That washing of regeneration—that **water** we need to be born of—flows from the blood which Jesus shed. We are told in Revelation 1:5-6 that:

Revelation 1:5-6a

5   …Jesus Christ, the faithful witness, the firstborn from the dead, and the ruler over the kings of the earth… loved us and washed us from our sins in His own blood,

6   and has made us kings and priests to His God and Father… (NKJV)

Therefore, by God's mercy, we are washed in the blood of Jesus and renewed by His Holy Spirit. We remember how the apostle John recorded that when the side of Jesus was pierced with a spear, immediately blood and water came out. When we go into the waters of baptism, repenting and calling on the name of Jesus, it is as though we are immersed in the sacrifice He made and the blood He shed to save us. As we are so washed and as we are renewed by the Holy Spirit, we become new creatures, born again, and now members of the kingdom of God. And so the kingdom of God is coming to earth as each subject is made.

Furthermore, the kingdom of God is a matter of righteousness, peace and joy in the Holy Spirit (Romans 14:17). It is important to understand that, unlike an earthly kingdom, you cannot force people to be subjects of the kingdom of heaven, since, by definition, they would not be subjects at all. That ties into the free will choices we spoke about two lessons back. True subjects hunger and thirst for the righteousness provided by their Lord who saved them. This is why Jesus told the Pharisees in Luke 17:20 that the kingdom of God does not come visibly:

Luke 17:20-21

20   Now when He was asked by the Pharisees when the kingdom of God would come, He answered them and said, "The kingdom of God does not come with observation;

21 "nor will they say, 'See here!' or 'See there!' For indeed, the kingdom of God is within you." (NKJV)

That expression "within you" could also be translated, "in the midst of you." The Pharisees were looking for the kingdom to come with grand power and might and great signs from above. They were looking for Israel to be supernaturally reestablished, with themselves in powerful positions. Yet even after all of Jesus' miracles of compassion, they missed the very King of the kingdom in their midst. They did not recognize Him, and so they showed themselves to be no more members of the kingdom than their Roman oppressors.

In this verse then, Jesus is telling them not to look for the kingdom to come around them as some external event or happening. Rather, the kingdom of heaven comes within! Not that it was already within the hardened hearts of the Pharisees. But instead they, like everyone else, would need to accept in their hearts the gentle King presented to them, to be able even to see the kingdom of God. Disciples—subjects of the kingdom—must be made first before any visible manifestation. And that comes by faith. And when we pray, "Our Father in heaven, hallowed be Your name. Your kingdom come," we are on the first level, petitioning the Father to bring subjects into His kingdom. We are asking Him to reach people with the gospel of Jesus and to soften their hearts so as to give them an opportunity—a moment to understand and receive Messiah, the King, who will save them out of the kingdom of darkness and into the kingdom of light.

You know, after His resurrection and right before His ascension, Jesus' disciples were also concerned with the restoration of the kingdom to Israel:

Acts 1:6-8

6 Then they gathered around Him and asked Him, "Lord, are You at this time going to restore the kingdom to Israel?"

7 He said to them: "It is not for you to know the times or dates the Father has set by His own authority.

8 But you will receive power when the Holy Spirit comes on you; and you will be My witnesses in Jerusalem, and in all Judea and Samaria, and to the ends of the earth." (NIV) *{Capitalization for deity added}*

Notice that Jesus does not deny that the kingdom would be restored to Israel and we'll talk more about that in our next lesson. It is obvious from this Scripture that He agrees that the kingdom coming to Israel is in the Father's plan. But it was not for them to know when it would happen. Instead they were to go out and be His witnesses. In Matthew 28:19-20, He tells them to:

Matthew 28:19-20a

19 "Therefore go and make disciples of all nations, baptizing them in the name of the Father and of the Son and of the Holy Spirit,

20 and teaching them to obey everything I have commanded you..." (NIV)

These are not disciples made by flashes of lightning and claps of thunder. Instead they were subjects made by faith. The kingdom of God is a matter of **FAITH** and it creates true subjects of repentance and love, rather than robots of fear. It was for this reason that Jesus came in meekness as a servant and, after His resurrection from the dead, ascended into heaven that those who would love Him would choose—**choose**—to be subjects rather than being forced to be subjects. Consider this: you really know that your children are in agreement with you, if, when you are not there with them, they do the right thing which you've taught them to do. And that is one reason for the ascension: that subjects of truth and choice can be made—that the children of God may be revealed.

Then the subjects in turn can have victory in their lives in Jesus. And that's the second level we are praying when we pray, "Your kingdom come." We are asking the Lord to give the kingdom power and the kingdom joy now to those who are in Jesus, that they would be the city on the hill which the Lord described. We are requesting that they would be the light of the world, even as He is the true light.

In the Pentecost sermon in Acts Chapter 2, Peter tells us that David is speaking about the ascension of Christ when he writes in Psalm 110:

Psalm 110:1

1 The LORD said unto my Lord, "Sit Thou at My right hand, until I make Thine enemies Thy footstool." (KJV)

From the time of the Lord's ascension and continuing today, subjects of the kingdom are made one by one as people's lives are snatched out of the hands of the enemy. Jesus then changes their lives, even as Peter was changed, and gives them the kingdom peace and power they so desperately need in this world. The work of Satan and his demons is frustrated. Thus the enemies of Jesus are made His footstool, as we read in Romans 16:20 concerning we who believe:

Romans 16:20

20 And the God of peace will crush Satan under your feet shortly. The grace of our Lord Jesus Christ be with you. Amen. (NKJV) *{Emphasis added}*

Amen! Every demon and principality, every thought and argument that exalts itself above God (2 Corinthians 10:4-5) is brought down under the feet of Jesus—even the feet of His body, which is the church. We certainly can have victory in Jesus.

Now we said before that the kingdom came, comes, and will come. What about that last part, "the kingdom of heaven will come"? Understand that while the Pharisees needed to hear that the kingdom of God does not come to them by observation, the narrative in Luke 17 does not stop there. Jesus goes on to speak to His disciples, showing them that the kingdom of heaven does indeed, at some point, come visibly with power and great glory to the earth—when the King returns. And we'll speak about that in our next lesson. But let us close this study with a reading from Matthew Chapter 25:

Matthew 25:31-34

31 "...when the Son of Man comes in His glory, and all the angels with Him, then He will sit on His glorious throne.

32 "All the nations will be gathered before Him; and He will separate them from one another, as the shepherd separates the sheep from the goats;

33 and He will put the sheep on His right, and the goats on the left.

34 "Then the King will say to those on His right, 'Come, you who are blessed of My Father, inherit the kingdom prepared for you from the foundation of the world.'" (NASB)

LESSON EIGHT

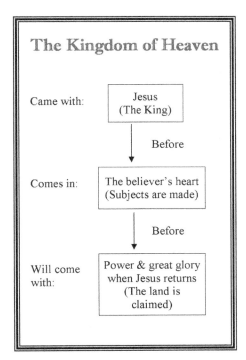

The Kingdom of Heaven

Came with: Jesus (The King)

↓ Before

Comes in: The believer's heart (Subjects are made)

↓ Before

Will come with: Power & great glory when Jesus returns (The land is claimed)

We have been studying that part of the Lord's Prayer where Jesus teaches us to pray, "Your kingdom come." In our last lesson, we saw that the kingdom of heaven came to earth with Jesus, the King; that it comes right now into each believer's heart as subjects of the kingdom are made and victories are won in the name of Jesus; and that at some point it will come in power and great glory. And it's this last part that we want to examine today, for a day is coming when the kingdom *will* come visibly to this earth, when the King returns, this time in all His glory and majesty. But for those of our generation who have rejected His call, it will be too late to become members of that kingdom.

Consider the Scripture in Malachi 4:1 which says:

Malachi 4:1

1   "Surely the day is coming; it will burn like a furnace. All the arrogant and every evildoer will be stubble, and the day that is coming will set them on fire," says the LORD Almighty. "Not a root or a branch will be left to them." (NIV)

Earlier in Malachi, in Chapter 3 verse 2, the Lord speaks to the prophet about the day of Messiah. He says:

Malachi 3:2

2   But who can endure the day of His coming? Who can stand when He appears? For He will be like a refiner's fire or a launderer's soap. (NIV) *{Capitalization for deity added}*

Throughout the Scriptures we see that our God is a consuming fire of holiness. So then, how can we, all sinners, endure that awesome day when the kingdom of heaven comes in its fullness? It was the gracious gift of the Father that Jesus, very God in the flesh, could come as a human and live among people, and that those around could survive in His presence and speak and walk with Him. But on the Mount of Transfiguration, the true nature of Jesus was revealed, witnessed by the three men who were the closest to Him and had faith in Him:

Matthew 17:1-2; 5-9

1   And after six days, Jesus taketh Peter, James, and John his brother, and bringeth them upon a high mountain apart.
2   And He was transfigured before them: and His face shone as the sun, and His raiment was white as the light. (Webster)

Then down at verse 5 it reads:

5   While he *(Peter)* was yet speaking, behold, a bright cloud overshadowed them: and behold, a voice out of the cloud, which said, "This is My beloved Son, in whom I am well pleased: hear ye Him."
6   And when the disciples heard it, they fell on their face, and were in great fear.
7   And Jesus came and touched them, and said, "Arise, and be not afraid."

8   And when they had lifted up their eyes, they saw no man, save Jesus only.

9   And as they were descending the mountain, Jesus charged them, saying, "Tell the vision to no man, until the Son of Man be raised again from the dead." (Webster)

In 2nd Peter Chapter 1 verses 16 to18, Peter tells us:

2 Peter 1:16-18

16   For we have not followed cunningly devised fables, when we made known to you the power and coming of our Lord Jesus Christ, but were eye-witnesses of His majesty.

17   For He received from God the Father honor and glory, when there came such a voice to Him from the Excellent Glory, "This is My beloved Son, in whom I am well pleased."

18   And this voice which came from heaven we heard, when we were with Him on the holy mount. (Webster)

The apostle Peter is saying that their description of the majesty of Jesus, which they witnessed on the Mount of Transfiguration, was to make "known to you"—that is, make known to **us**—"the power and coming of our Lord Jesus Christ." They were privileged to see the true person of Jesus, His glory and power and majesty, which was hidden from the world in His first coming. And actually, they received a preview of the way He will appear when He returns. As we are told in the book of Revelation, He returns King of kings and Lord of lords. Jesus teaches in Matthew 24:30-31 about that day. He says:

Matthew 24:30-31

30   "And then shall appear the sign of the Son of Man in heaven: and then shall all the tribes of the earth mourn, and they shall see the Son of Man coming in the clouds of heaven with power and great glory.

31   "And He shall send His angels with a great sound of a trumpet, and they shall gather together His elect from the four winds, from one end of heaven to the other." (KJV)

If you remember, in our last lesson we studied from Luke Chapter 17 verses 20 and 21 how Jesus told the Pharisees that the kingdom of God does not come with observation. First there had to be the true and quiet reception in their hearts of the King who was standing right in their midst. They needed the kingdom of God to come within them—to be born again! This is something that happens individually to each person. It is not a kingdom in the sense of a location where you can say, "See it is over here." But immediately after telling them this, we read in Luke 17:22-30:

Luke 17:22-30

22 Then He said to His disciples, "The time is coming when you will long to see one of the days of the Son of Man, but you will not see it.

23 People will tell you, 'There he is!' or 'Here he is!' Do not go running off after them.

24 For the Son of Man in His day will be like the lightning, which flashes and lights up the sky from one end to the other.

25 But first He must suffer many things and be rejected by this generation.

26 "Just as it was in the days of Noah, so also will it be in the days of the Son of Man.

27 People were eating, drinking, marrying and being given in marriage up to the day Noah entered the ark. Then the flood came and destroyed them all.

28 "It was the same in the days of Lot. People were eating and drinking, buying and selling, planting and building.

29 But the day Lot left Sodom, fire and sulfur rained down from heaven and destroyed them all.

30 "It will be just like this on the day the Son of Man is revealed." (NIV) *{Capitalization for deity added}*

The Lord Jesus taught about a literal day when He would return to establish a literal kingdom, when the kingdom of God would come to earth and people would be able to see it. And notice, this is not going to be some ordinary movement of men, where someone can say, "Look over there, that's the kingdom," and it is not going to happen by following some charismatic earthly leader. Instead, when Jesus comes back, it is like the lightning that flashes and lights up the sky from one end to the other. Or as we read earlier in Matthew Chapter 24, "Then shall appear the sign of the Son of Man in heaven: and then shall all the tribes of the earth mourn, and they shall see the Son of Man coming in the clouds of heaven with power and great glory." He doesn't come back as He came the first time, as a baby born in a manger and as a servant to die. He comes back a King to rule! And many of the Pharisees were actually looking for Messiah to come in this way the first time. But they did not understand the answer to the question we put forth at the start of the lesson: How can we, all sinners, endure the awesome day when the kingdom of heaven comes in its fullness? *"Who can endure the day of His coming? Who can stand when He appears?"*

The answer, of course, is no one can. Because of sin and rebellion, the coming of Christ in all His power would be a fearful thing to everyone. No one could stand. No one could endure if it wasn't for the sacrifice Jesus made first. Without His salvation, the most upright Pharisee could not stand any better than the worst sinner in Israel. So then, before the Lord could come as the reigning King, we had to first be made His people, standing just or righteous before Him by **faith** and receiving His kingdom by free will into our hearts. As it is written in Habakkuk 2:4:

Habakkuk 2:4
    4   "Behold, as for the proud one,
          His soul is not right within him;
          But the righteous will live by his faith." (NASB)

And before we could be made His people, the Lord Jesus would have to come to this world as one of us to offer Himself the perfect sacrifice to save us from our sins and provide the basis for our faith. First the King came to provide salvation, then the subjects of the kingdom are made by faith, and then the King will come back to take the land and establish the visible kingdom. Ultimately there will be a glorious new heaven and a new earth. But even before this, the Bible speaks about the day when Jesus will return to this earth to set up the Messianic Kingdom or the Messianic millennium—a 1000 year kingdom promised through the Hebrew prophets and confirmed in the Book of Revelation.

So when we pray "Your kingdom come," not only are we praying and petitioning for subjects of the kingdom to be made, and not only are we looking for kingdom victories for God's people in this age, but we are anticipating and even longing for the return of our Lord Jesus. That word *longing* is a very good one. While the day of the Lord is a fearful thing to many, Paul says in 2ⁿᵈ Timothy:

2 Timothy 4:8

> 8   Henceforth there is laid up for me a crown of righteousness, which the Lord, the righteous Judge, will give me at that day: and not to me only, but to all them also that *love* His appearing. (Webster) *{Emphasis added}*

Believers are to love the day of His appearing and pray for it. Actually, that's how the Bible closes. In Revelation 22:20, after Jesus says, "Surely I am coming quickly," John's prayer is:

Revelation 22:20b

> 20 ..."Amen. Even so, come, Lord Jesus." (KJV)

And we should all pray in the same way as John prayed, with a loud and firm *Amen!*

Now you might be asking, "Does the Bible give us some idea of when Jesus will return to set up the kingdom?" The answer is yes. There are many signs and event markers laid out and foretold in the Scriptures; however, Jesus also taught that no one knows the day or the hour. Actually we could dedicate another whole study series just to last day events. But for the purpose of our study of prayer, I want to focus on one essential requirement. To do so we have to go to the gospel of Luke Chapter 13:

Luke 13:34-35

> 34 "Jerusalem, Jerusalem, you who kill the prophets and stone those sent to you, how often I have longed to gather your children together, as a hen gathers her chicks under her wings, and you were not willing.
> 35 Look, your house is left to you desolate. I tell you, you will not see Me again until you say, 'Blessed is He who comes in the name of the Lord.'" (NIV) *{Capitalization for deity added}*

From the Lord's own words, the city that will have to declare Jesus as Messiah, in order for Him to return, is **Jerusalem!** Now look in Acts Chapter 3 after the man who was lame from birth is healed at the temple by the apostles Peter and John. Peter addresses the people, who have gathered and are amazed at the miracle, saying:

Acts 3:12-13a

12 ..."Fellow Israelites, why does this surprise you? Why do you
stare at us as if by our own power or godliness we had made
this man walk?

13 The God of Abraham, Isaac and Jacob, the God of our fathers,
has glorified His servant Jesus..." (NIV) *{Capitalization for
deity added}*

To whom is Peter speaking? Clearly, he is speaking to the people
of Israel. He goes on to tell them that it was the name of Jesus, and
faith in His name, which has made the lame man strong and given
him complete healing for all of them to see. And then Peter appeals
to them in verses 19-20:

Acts 3:19-20

19 "Repent, then, and turn to God, so that your sins may be
wiped out, that times of refreshing may come from the Lord,

20 and that He may send the Messiah, who has been appointed
for you—even Jesus." (NIV) *{Emphasis and capitalization for
deity added}*

Do you see the important principle taught in these two Scriptures?

When Israel turns to God through Jesus, the Lord can return.

In Chapter 11 of Revelation we read about a future day when the
survivors of Jerusalem accept the testimony of Jesus and give glory
to the God of heaven. And then in verse 15 it says:

Revelation 11:15

15 The seventh angel sounded his trumpet, and there were loud
voices in heaven, which said:
"The kingdom of the world has become the kingdom of our
Lord and of His Messiah, and He will reign for ever and ever."
(NIV) *{Capitalization for deity added}*

When the people of Israel accept Jesus as the Messiah, the
kingdom of the world no longer belongs to Satan but becomes the
kingdom of God, and the King of the Jews can return and rule on
David's throne.

We must understand that the nation Israel and the Jewish people are at the center of God's plan, His blueprint of salvation, for mankind. And Jesus of Nazareth is, and must be recognized by His own people as, their promised King.

John 19:19-22

19 And Pilate wrote a title, and put it on the cross. And the writing was, JESUS OF NAZARETH THE KING OF THE JEWS.

20 Many of the Jews then read this title: for the place where Jesus was crucified was nigh *(near)* to the city: and it was written in Hebrew, Greek, and Latin.

21 Then said the chief priests of the Jews to Pilate, "Write not, 'The King of the Jews'; but that 'He said, "I am King of the Jews."'"

22 Pilate answered, "What I have written, I have written." (Webster) *{Clarification in parenthesis added}*

Blessed will be that day when Israel, both the leadership and the people, proclaim Jesus of Nazareth as the King of the Jews! Paul tells us in Romans 11:15 that, if the Jewish nation's separation from God because of their refusal to accept Jesus meant the reconciling of the Gentile world to God, "…what will their acceptance be but life from the dead?" That is why it is so important for us to pray for the descendants of Abraham and for Jerusalem. As the psalmist wrote in Psalm 122 verse 6:

Psalm 122:6

6 Pray for the peace of Jerusalem:
"May they prosper who love you." (NASB)

Amen!

LESSON NINE

――――――∝――――――

W elcome back to our Bible study. For the last few lessons, we have been looking at that part of the Lord's Prayer where Jesus teaches us to pray, "Your kingdom come." And we have been discussing in detail the kingdom of God. In this lesson, we want to expand the study to include the next part of Matthew 6:10 where Jesus prays to the Father,

Matthew 6:10

10 "…Your will be done on earth as it is in heaven." (NKJV)

There are so many questions raised when we talk about the will of God. But first let us just take a moment to review what we studied last time. We looked ahead at that future day when the kingdom of heaven would come to earth in power and glory and majesty, when the king, Jesus, returns. But we saw how first it was necessary for Messiah to come as a servant and die for us, to bring redemption and allow for subjects of the kingdom to be made through faith in Him. That is why we read in Colossians 1 verses 19 and 20 the following statement about Jesus:

Colossians 1:19-20

19 For it pleased the Father that in Him should all fullness dwell;

20 And, having made peace through the blood of His cross, by Him to reconcile all things to Himself; by Him, I say, whether they are things on earth, or things in heaven. (Webster)

This was the plan of God. For from the beginning, before you or I or anyone ever sinned, God had the solution to sin—the Lord Jesus! The gospel of John Chapter 1 and verse 1 declares of Him:

John 1:1

1   In the beginning was the Word, and the Word was with God, and the Word was God. (KJV)

And in Revelation 13:8 He is called:

Revelation 13:8b

8   …the Lamb slain from the foundation of the world. (KJV)

So from the very beginning, God had the solution in Himself to mankind's rebellion, that is, in the Word—His Son Jesus who was meant to die for us from the foundation of the world. And Jesus knew that there would be a gap of time between this work of salvation that He would perform on the cross and His return in power to claim this realm back for God, establishing the visible Kingdom. In Luke Chapter 19 starting at verse 11 we read:

Luke 19:11-13

11   While they were listening to this, He went on to tell them a parable, because He was near Jerusalem and the people thought that the kingdom of God was going to appear at once.
12   He said: "A man of noble birth went to a distant country to have himself appointed king and then to return.
13   So he called ten of his servants and gave them ten minas. 'Put this money to work,' he said, 'until I come back.'" (NIV) *{Capitalization for deity added}*

Or as the *New American Standard Bible* puts it, "Do business with this until I come back." Obviously, in that parable the nobleman is a type of Jesus who ascends to the right hand of the Father and then returns to claim the kingdom. And the servants are the believers who are called to do the Master's business until He does return. We know from the rest of that parable, sometimes called the parable of the minas, that believers have a responsibility to be zealous for the work of the kingdom of heaven, while we wait for the Master to return. But we will speak more about that in our next lesson. What we must understand at this point is that this great plan of salvation was the perfect and pleasing will of God from the foundation of the world; that Jesus performed it on Calvary; that there would be a time of Messiah's separation from this world; and then, at the fullness of times, He will return for the ultimate restoration. This is God's will and design.

We have talked quite a bit in our past lessons about man's free will; but even so, God is still in control! And He works out everything in conformity with the purpose of His will. This is what we know from the Scriptures as *predestination*. Now predestination can be a scary word to some. It brings up images of a hyper-Calvinistic god who for no apparent reason decides to pick some and reject others, with nothing the individual can do to change it. No wonder it's scary: it is a false image of God. I think if we read a key Scripture on this, Ephesians 1:2-12, we'll be able to see more clearly what the Bible means by "predestined." I would ask you to notice when **the will of God** is mentioned in these verses. Let's start by reading the first part from verse 2 into verse 6.

Ephesians 1:2-6

2 Grace and peace to you from God our Father and the Lord Jesus Christ.

3 Praise be to the God and Father of our Lord Jesus Christ, who has blessed us in the heavenly realms with every spiritual blessing in Christ.

4 For He chose us in Him before the creation of the world to be holy and blameless in His sight. In love

5 He predestined us for adoption to sonship through Jesus Christ, in accordance with His pleasure and will—

6 to the praise of His glorious grace, which He has freely given us in the One He loves. (NIV) *{Emphasis and capitalization for deity added}*

Once again we see that it was God's plan before the creation of the world that those who believe in Christ would be presented before Him holy and blameless. This is His glorious grace. This is the free gift of salvation He gives us in Jesus. And notice in verse 4 the pleasure and will of God behind predestination: IN LOVE He pre-destined—that is, in love He determined beforehand—for us to be adopted as His sons through Jesus. That word love is an important one. It obliterates the harsh hyper-Calvinistic image of God we described before. For we know from 2nd Peter Chapter 3 verse 9:

2 Peter 3:9

9 The Lord is... long-suffering toward us, <u>not willing</u> that any should perish, but that all should come to repentance. (Webster) *{Emphasis added}*

And 1st Timothy Chapter 2 and verse 4 tells us that "God our Savior" (verse 3):

1 Timothy 2:4

4 ...desires all men to be saved and to come to the knowledge of the truth. (NASB)

Now look at Romans Chapter 8 verses 28-30 where Paul writes:

Romans 8:28-30

28 And we know that God causes all things to work together for good to those who love God, to those who are called according to His purpose.
29 For those whom He foreknew, He also predestined to become conformed to the image of His Son, so that He would be the firstborn among many brethren;
30 and these whom He predestined, He also called; and these whom He called, He also justified; and these whom He justified, He also glorified. (NASB)

In verse 29 we see that God predestines, to be conformed to the image of Jesus, those whom He foreknows. What does He foreknow? He foreknows that they will love Him (verse 28)! And again we have that word love. Those who will love God are the ones who are called according to His purpose. It is not that we love God first. For that matter, on our own we don't seek God; we don't care about the things of God. But the Lord does the whole work. He loved us and died for us. And He calls to us through His Holy Spirit. He softens us and gives us an opportunity to receive His salvation, desiring that none should perish. He will touch our heart and do everything possible for us to accept His Son, stopping only to the point that we would no longer have free will; otherwise, love would not be love! Love is the response of a free agent, not an automaton. And because God is all-knowing, He foreknows. He knows in advance those who will return that love once He has done everything. What does it say? He works all things together for good to those who love God. They are His chosen. And He predetermines them to be conformed into the image of His Son. He works everything out for them and their salvation. The very next verse in Romans is a powerful one and a favorite of mine:

Romans 8:31

> 31 What shall we then say to these things? If God is for us, who can be against us? (Webster)

Amen! He is in control of everything. So then, the Father's purpose in predestination is not to deprive man of his free will. Rather, because of free will, He provides by foreknowledge a solution to our rebellion and the mess we create. Man might have chosen Satan as his ruler, but God is in ultimate control! Though we don't deserve it, He has had a plan for our lives from the very beginning to bring us back to Him through His Son.

We are taught to pray in this portion of the Our Father, "Your will be done on earth as it is in heaven." And I think of Jesus in the garden of Gethsemane the night before His crucifixion, His sweat like great drops of blood falling to the ground. In Mark 14:36 we read His prayer:

Mark 14:36

> 36 And He was saying, "Abba! Father! All things are possible for You; remove this cup from Me; yet not what I will, but what You will." (NASB)

Assuredly, all things are possible with God. But the cup of the agony which Jesus was about to suffer was the only solution—God's "I AM" solution to the impossibility created by man's freewill choice of rebellion. When asked by His disciples in Matthew 19:25, "Who then can be saved," Jesus looked at them and said:

Matthew 19:26

> 26 ..."With men this is impossible; but with God all things are possible." (KJV)

Jesus, as God in the flesh, provided the impossible. Let's finish reading that section in Ephesians Chapter 1 picking up at verse 7. And again, notice when the **will of God** is mentioned:

Ephesians 1:7-12

> 7 In Him we have redemption through His blood, the forgiveness of sins, according to the riches of His grace
> 8 which He made to abound toward us in all wisdom and prudence,
> 9 having made known to us the mystery of <u>His will</u>, according to His good pleasure which He purposed in Himself,
> 10 that in the dispensation of the fullness of the times He might gather together in one all things in Christ, both which are in heaven and which are on earth — in Him.
> 11 In Him also we have obtained an inheritance, being predestined according to the purpose of Him who works all things according to the counsel of <u>His will</u>,
> 12 that we who first trusted in Christ should be to the praise of His glory. (NKJV) *{Emphasis added}*

In the wisdom and prudence of God, forgiveness and grace abound to His chosen ones. He makes known to us the great mystery of His will in Jesus. And this plan of salvation is His good pleasure—His perfect pleasing will. And you might ask at this point, "Is there any other type of will of God?" The answer is, "Yes there is." Not everything that happens in this dark world is the heart's desire of God. But He allows it, and we call this His *conditional will*. He allows it so that we may have free will—that we might choose. But let's be very clear: God is never tricked nor does He miss anything. Jesus said in Matthew 10:29:

Matthew 10:29

> 29 "Are not two sparrows sold for a copper coin? And not one of them falls to the ground apart from your Father's will." (NKJV)

Therefore nothing happens apart from the Father's will—His conditional will. But not everything that happens is His heart's desire—His pleasing will. Sometimes His good and pleasing will is called His *positional will*. This is the righteous and holy will of God—what God wants us to do as opposed to what He allows us to do in this world. And we studied how, in the uppermost heaven where the Father resides in the totality of His majesty, His positional will is always done. Thus when we pray, "Your kingdom come, Your will be done on earth as it is in heaven," we are in essence praying, "Father, may Your heart's desire always be realized on earth, just as it is in Your heaven, and we look forward to that day of the kingdom when it will."

There is something amazing here that we need to understand. In this realm, we see all the free will choices of humans and angels and demons, which God allows for a time. And more often than not, the choices people make are outside the heart's desire will of the Father. Yet we just read in Ephesians 1:11 that He works all things according to the counsel of His will. Consider the unimaginable greatness of the mind of God. He is in ultimate control, and He will work everything out according to the mystery of His plan in Christ Jesus. In the end, God's perfect pleasing will **will** be accomplished. His will **will** be done on earth as it is in heaven.

The intelligence of our God is incomparable! We read in Ephesians 1:10 how, when the times will have reached their fulfillment, He will bring together in one all things in Christ, both which are in heaven and which are on the earth. We saw a similar statement at the beginning of the lesson in the reading from Colossians Chapter 1. From that Scripture and elsewhere in the Bible it is clear that, in the Father's plan, the shed blood of Jesus ultimately purchases back to God even the universe—the very creation itself. It is the pleasure of the Father to reconcile all things to Himself, whether things on earth or things in heaven through Jesus. The creation will be freed from that curse of decay we discussed several lessons back, when Adam and Eve sinned. Paul teaches in Romans 8:19-22:

Romans 8:19-22
19 For the creation waits in eager expectation for the children of God to be revealed.
20 For the creation was subjected to frustration, not by its own choice, but by the will of the One who subjected it, in hope

21 that the creation itself will be liberated from its bondage to decay and brought into the freedom and glory of the children of God.

22 We know that the whole creation has been groaning as in the pains of childbirth right up to the present time. (NIV) *{Capitalization for deity added}*

In the Father's will, the decay and corruption we see around us will end at the reconciliation. And we'll talk more about that in Lesson Ten.

LESSON TEN

———————∝———————

We have been looking at that part of the Lord's Prayer where Jesus teaches us to pray, "Your kingdom come. Your will be done on earth as it is in heaven." And we have discussed the kingdom of heaven for several lessons. It is essential for us to understand that we who are Jesus' disciples are a part of the battle to usher in the kingdom of heaven, especially on the level of making subjects for the King. In Matthew 16 verse 15, Jesus asked His disciples:

Matthew 16:15-16
> 15 …"But who do you say that I am?"
> 16 Simon Peter answered, "You are the Christ, the Son of the living God." (NASB)

When Peter made this declaration, Jesus gave to him, and in so doing gave to **all** who make a like confession (a confession that is genuine, made with all our being, and in submission to our Master and Lord), a special position. He said:

Matthew 16:19
> 19 "I will give you the keys of the kingdom of heaven; whatever you bind on earth will be bound in heaven, and whatever you loose on earth will be loosed in heaven." (NIV)

Again at the Last Supper, in Luke 22:29, Jesus told His close disciples:

Luke 22:29
> 29 "And I confer on you a kingdom, just as My Father conferred one on Me," (NIV) *{Capitalization for deity added}*

Therefore, there is a real privilege and responsibility in being a disciple of the Lord. We are to be, as we mentioned in the last lesson with the parable of the minas, zealous for the business of our Master. And we should bring back to Him as many as we are able, by using wisely and earnestly in His service the talents and gifts, the time and provisions He has given us. He gives us the keys and the anointing to supernaturally open up the kingdom of heaven to others.

You might well ask, "What will the kingdom of heaven be like when it is fully realized?" In the last lesson, we read in Colossians 1:20 how God reconciles all things to Himself by Jesus, whether things on earth or things in heaven, through the blood of His cross. Likewise, in Ephesians 1:10 we studied:

Ephesians 1:10
> 10 that in the dispensation of the fullness of the times He might gather together in one all things in Christ, both which are in heaven and which are on earth — in Him. (NKJV)

And we closed the lesson examining from the book of Romans how in God's plan the creation itself will be freed from its bondage to decay:

Romans 8:20-21
> 20 For the creation was subjected to frustration, not by its own choice, but by the will of the One who subjected it, in hope
> 21 that the creation itself will be liberated from its bondage to decay and brought into the freedom and glory of the children of God. (NIV) *{Capitalization for deity added}*

We learn from the book of Revelation how, after Jesus returns and after that 1000 year Messianic Kingdom which we previously discussed in Lesson Eight, there will be *a new heaven and a new earth*. If you remember in Genesis 1:1 it says:

Genesis 1:1
> 1 In the beginning God created the heavens and the earth. (NIV)

We spoke about the heavens early on in our study and we saw that in this Genesis creation (the creation in which we now live) there is a separation between the heavens and the earth. Think back to that Scripture in Isaiah 55 where the Lord says:

Isaiah 55:9
>   9   "For as the heavens are higher than the earth, so are My ways higher than your ways, and My thoughts than your thoughts." (KJV)

Daily, our telescopes are confirming the enormity and "height" of the second heaven, our stellar universe. How much more then is there, both physically and spiritually, an insurmountable gulf between the uppermost heaven of God's majesty and the clay of this world? But in the re-creation, when all things are made new, even the heavens and earth are reconciled. At that time, the majesty and glory and power and perfect will of the Father will engulf everything, as the dwelling of God will be with men. And this connection is seen so clearly in the New Jerusalem, the holy city, that comes down out of heaven from God. Let us take a moment and read those wonderful passages in Revelation Chapters 21 and 22:

Revelation 21:1-5a
>   1   And I saw a new heaven and a new earth: for the first heaven and the first earth were passed away; and there was no more sea.
>   2   And I John saw the holy city, New Jerusalem, coming down from God out of heaven, prepared as a bride adorned for her husband.
>   3   And I heard a great voice out of heaven saying, "Behold, the tabernacle of God is with men, and He will dwell with them, and they shall be His people, and God Himself shall be with them, and be their God.
>   4   "And God shall wipe away all tears from their eyes; and there shall be no more death, neither sorrow, nor crying, neither shall there be any more pain: for the former things are passed away."
>   5   And He that sat upon the throne said, "Behold, I make all things new."... (KJV)

Then down at verse 21 we read:

Revelation 21:21-22:5

21 And the twelve gates were twelve pearls; every several gate was of one pearl: and the street of the city was pure gold, as it were transparent glass.

22 And I saw no temple therein: for the Lord God Almighty and the Lamb are the temple of it.

23 And the city had no need of the sun, neither of the moon, to shine in it: for the glory of God did lighten it, and the Lamb is the light thereof.

24 And the nations of them which are saved shall walk in the light of it: and the kings of the earth do bring their glory and honour into it.

25 And the gates of it shall not be shut at all by day: for there shall be no night there.

26 And they shall bring the glory and honour of the nations into it.

27 And there shall in no wise enter into it any thing that defileth, neither whatsoever worketh abomination, or maketh a lie: but they which are written in the Lamb's book of life.

CHAPTER 22

1 And he shewed me a pure river of water of life, clear as crystal, proceeding out of the throne of God and of the Lamb.

2 In the midst of the street of it, and on either side of the river, was there the tree of life, which bare twelve manner of fruits, and yielded her fruit every month: and the leaves of the tree were for the healing of the nations.

3 And there shall be no more curse: but the throne of God and of the Lamb shall be in it; and His servants shall serve Him:

4 And they shall see His face; and His name shall be in their foreheads.

5 And there shall be no night there; and they need no candle, neither light of the sun; for the Lord God giveth them light: and they shall reign for ever and ever. (KJV)

What a beautiful and marvelous time that will be. The presence of the Father will surround us, everything being completely in His love and His will. We will speak and fellowship face to face with our Lord Jesus. And as God speaks to us, I believe the Holy Spirit, who will live inside us forever, will be echoing His very words and will into our hearts. We will be in God and with God and God will live inside of us. Is it any wonder that we pray, "Your kingdom come" or as the Bible ends, "Amen. Even so, come, Lord Jesus." (KJV)

Okay. Let us pick up our discussion from the previous lesson about the will of God. We made an important distinction last time between the conditional will of God—that is, what He allows on certain terms in this world—and His positional will—that is, His absolute attitude and stand. It is a terribly important point because, while everything that happens in this world must be allowed by God to happen, not everything that happens is His heart's desire. Otherwise, why would Jesus tell us to pray, "Your will be done on earth <u>as it is in heaven</u>"? His positional will—His good pleasure—is not always, and in truth, sometimes very rarely done on earth. We certainly see that from all the horror and rebellion around us in this world. And it is necessary to understand this truth so as not to get caught in the trap some get into when they automatically think that, just because something happens, it must be the will of God. They look at conditions and see them as indicators of God's wishes. Now that would be fine if Satan and demons and other humans and even we ourselves had no input into this world, but we do. And just because God may give us a length of rope to run around on and exercise our free will, this doesn't mean He is in agreement with the choices we make or the situations that result.

Those that confuse the two develop a low opinion of God, because they mistake the desires and schemes of Satan for God's position. Not only that, but they can become quickly defeated because they are walking by sight not faith. Since they assume that what they see happening around them must be God's will, they do not have the faith to believe Him for the good things He has promised in His Scriptures nor trust in who He really is and the good He actually wants. God has given us a revelation of His true nature in Jesus, but they cannot see it because they assume that everything that takes place occurs because God wants and desires it to occur. And so Satan wins a double victory. He destroys people's lives and then gets them to accept that destruction as the will of God for them.

You should know that when we talk about the positional will or the absolute heart's desire of God, there are tremendous promises in the Scriptures. Look at 1st John Chapter 5 verses 13 to 15:

1 John 5:13-15

13 These things I have written to you who believe in the name of the Son of God, that you may know that you have eternal life, and that you may continue to believe in the name of the Son of God.

14 Now this is the confidence that we have in Him, that if we ask anything according to His will, He hears us.

15 And if we know that He hears us, whatever we ask, we know that we have the petitions that we have asked of Him. (NKJV)

What a marvelous confidence we have in our Lord Jesus. And notice that if we are *not* asking God according to His will—that is, if we are asking while in the kingdom of darkness, or if we are a member of the kingdom of light but are asking a request that really is of the kingdom of darkness—we shouldn't expect God to entertain our prayer or answer it. But if we are asking according to His will, the perfect will of the kingdom of light, He hears us and we have whatever was asked of Him! This brings us to the next important principle in our series:

The greatest barrier to God's will in an individual's life is their will opposed to Him!

That deserves repeating. The greatest barrier to God's will in an individual's life is their will opposed to Him. You see, you must agree that you want His heart's desire, and there should be no fear in this since we are told in James 1:17 that:

James 1:17

17 Every good gift and every perfect gift is from above, and comes down from the Father of lights, with whom there is no variation or shadow of turning. (NKJV)

Likewise, 1st John 4:16 tells us that God is love. So there should be no fear in wanting His perfect, pleasing will. And once you agree that you want His heart's desire, *for your part* the barrier is removed and you have allowed the kingdom of heaven to come to earth *in you*. No longer are you a hindrance but instead you are now a vessel through which and to whom your heavenly Father wishes to pour out blessings and answers to prayer. This does not mean that the wills of others are not also involved. They certainly are. But for your part, you are in agreement with God and expect God to accomplish that which He desires. And as His child, as His disciple, as a soldier in the battle for the kingdom, will He not wish to pour out abundantly? Amen!

In addition, it is imperative that when we pray according to God's will, as we just read in 1ˢᵗ John, that we believe Him for what we have asked. There is another promise in James Chapter 1 in verses 5 to 8:

James 1:5-8

5 If any of you lacks wisdom, you should ask God, who gives generously to all without finding fault, and it will be given to you.

6 But when you ask, you must believe and not doubt, because the one who doubts is like a wave of the sea, blown and tossed by the wind.

7 That person should not expect to receive anything from the Lord.

8 Such a person is double-minded and unstable in all they do. (NIV)

So here we have a promise that if we pray to God for wisdom (and I'm sure we have all at some time needed wisdom to know how to handle a situation), God will give us wisdom liberally and without expressing disapproval. James declares, "It will be given to you." But if we doubt, if we don't ask in faith anticipating to receive from God, James says, "That person should not expect to receive anything from the Lord."

If you think about it, double-mindedness is a characteristic of instability. One minute a person is saying they believe in God, but the next minute, by their attitude, they show that they really doubt His existence, or His ability to interact with us, or His nature to want to give help to His children even as any human father would want to help. In Mark Chapter 11:22-24, Jesus teaches about prayer and faith. He says:

Mark 11:22-24

22 And Jesus answered saying to them, "Have faith in God.

23 "Truly I say to you, whoever says to this mountain, 'Be taken up and cast into the sea,' and does not doubt in his heart,

but believes that what he says is going to happen, it will be granted him.

24 "Therefore I say to you, all things for which you pray and ask, believe that you have received them, and they will be granted you." (NASB)

What a wonderful promise! However, since we know this only applies as we are praying as subjects of the kingdom of light—praying according to God's will as we read in 1st John—how are we to know what God's will is so that we can agree with Him in faith? We'll discuss that in our next lesson.

LESSON ELEVEN

————————∝————————

In our last lesson, we started to go in depth into that part of the Lord's Prayer where we are taught to pray, "Your will be done on earth as it is in heaven." We saw that the greatest barrier to God's will in a person's life is that person's own will set in opposition to Him. And we studied 1st John 5:14 to15 which says:

1 John 5:14-15

14 Now this is the confidence that we have in Him, that if we ask anything according to His will, He hears us.

15 And if we know that He hears us, whatever we ask, we know that we have the petitions that we have asked of Him. (NKJV)

So we have a tremendous promise of receiving what we ask for, when we pray *according to the Lord's will*. But if we do not pray according to His will, if we are opposed to His will and are acting as though members of the kingdom of darkness, we should not expect to receive anything. James makes this clear in the letter of James Chapter 4 verses 1 through 6. Here James chastises those believers who are not living, nor praying, as subjects of the kingdom of heaven. As you read it, understand that James might be using some intense expressions to describe their sins in this passage in order to emphasize how damaging their pride and strife can be and the reality of where these attitudes can lead.

James 4:1-6

1 Where do wars and fights come from among you? Do they not come from your desires for pleasure that war in your members?

2   You lust and do not have. You murder and covet and cannot obtain. You fight and war. Yet you do not have because you do not ask.

3   You ask and do not receive, because you ask amiss, that you may spend it on your pleasures.

4   Adulterers and adulteresses! Do you not know that friendship with the world is enmity with God? Whoever therefore wants to be a friend of the world makes himself an enemy of God.

5   Or do you think that the Scripture says in vain, "The Spirit who dwells in us yearns jealously"?

6   But He gives more grace. Therefore He says:

"God resists the proud,
But gives grace to the humble." (NKJV)

Filled with pride they were acting like people in the world under Satan's control and associating with its sins and lusts. Not only that, but they were fighting among themselves and harming each other, coveting in order to satisfy their own pleasures. We see several things from these verses. In verse 2 he says, "You lust and do not have. You murder and covet and cannot obtain." So their overwhelming desires actually result in them having <u>nothing</u>. Their selfishness leads to coveting and other wrong attitudes and sins, and God just can't bless that. It is idolatry. It is spiritual adultery, because it is not putting God first nor being faithful to His ways.

Now there are obviously things that we need in this world, but our attitude and actions should always reflect the Lord's priorities. Jesus teaches us in Matthew 6:31-33:

Matthew 6:31-33
31   "Do not worry then, saying, 'What will we eat?' or 'What will we drink?' or 'What will we wear for clothing?'

32   "For the Gentiles eagerly seek all these things; for your heavenly Father knows that you need all these things.

33   "But seek first His kingdom and His righteousness, and all these things will be added to you." (NASB)

Clearly the Father knows we need things to survive and live and thrive in this life, and He desires to give them to us. But for our part, we must seek His kingdom and His righteousness first. Obviously, given the strong language James uses, the people he is addressing in his letter were not doing this. Notice how James also says to them in verse 2:

James 4:2b

2   *...Yet you do not have because you do not ask.* (NKJV) *{Emphasis added}*

Many times when believers fall back into sin, their prayer life suffers. It is just like dodging a conversation with someone that you are trying to avoid. The sins of the backsliders push them out of fellowship with God, and asking God in prayer becomes uncomfortable. Actually, while all of their coveting and lusting and evil striving has obtained nothing for them, if they turned back to God in sincerity and prayer, asking Him for what they need, they *would* begin to receive.

It is extremely important to understand, though, that this principle of not receiving because we do not ask is not confined only to those in sin. To receive we must ask of the Lord. Throughout the gospels people came to Jesus asking for healing and help, and they received it. In Luke Chapter 18 we read how, when blind Bartimaeus was brought to Jesus, the Lord said to him:

Luke 18:41-42

41   "What do you want Me to do for you?" And he said, "Lord, I want to regain my sight!"

42   And Jesus said to him, "Receive your sight; your faith has made you well." (NASB)

And in Matthew Chapter 7 verses 7 through 11 Jesus says:

Matthew 7:7-11

7   "Ask, and it will be given to you; seek, and you will find; knock, and it will be opened to you.

8   "For everyone who asks receives, and he who seeks finds, and to him who knocks it will be opened.

9   "Or what man is there among you who, when his son asks for a loaf, will give him a stone?

10   "Or if he asks for a fish, he will not give him a snake, will he?

11   "If you then, being evil, know how to give good gifts to your children, how much more will your Father who is in

heaven give what is good *to those who ask Him!*" (NASB)
{Emphasis added}

In John 16:24 Jesus tells His disciples:

John 16:24
24 "Until now you have asked nothing in My name. Ask, and
you will receive, that your joy may be full." (NKJV)

So God desires His people to ask Him for the things they truly
need to live in this world and serve Him—those things that are righteous and good for themselves and for the loved ones who are their
responsibility—that their joy may be full! But notice what else James
says in Chapter 4 verse 3. Sometimes the people he was addressing
did ask God, but he tells them:

James 4:3
3 You ask and do not receive, *because you ask amiss*, that you
may spend it on your pleasures. (NKJV) *{Emphasis added}*

They are not praying according to the heart's desire of God.
Rather, they ask "amiss." They pray with the wrong motive, seeking
to feed their lusts and pleasures. God will not hear these prayers,
because they are not praying according to His will but according to
the will of sinful flesh. As God's people, we need to discern the difference. So the question with which we ended the last lesson is an
extremely important one: *"How are we to know what God's will
is?"* For prayer to be successful, we must be able to agree with God
and stand by faith on that which we know to be His will. Now the
Bible tells us that in this world we can know only in part. Paul writes:

1 Corinthians 13:9-12
9 For we know in part, and we prophesy in part.
10 But when that which is perfect is come, then that which is in
part shall be done away.
11 When I was a child, I spoke as a child, I understood as a child,
I thought as a child: but when I became a man, I put away
childish things.

12 For now we see through a glass darkly; but then face to face: now I know in part; but then shall I know even as also I am known. (Webster)

I look forward to the resurrection, when the Lord will fully open our minds and our understanding, and we will be able to ask Him questions face to face. Then all the hidden things will be revealed. There are some things that we just will not be able to fully comprehend until that day. And yet, even though for now, in this world, we have limited knowledge, still we must recognize that the apostles and the early church as a whole seemed to know God's will more specifically and in greater depth than in any church age since. In Acts Chapter 20:27 Paul told the Ephesian elders:

Acts 20:27
27 For I have not shunned to declare unto you all the counsel of God. (KJV)

…or as the NIV translates it:

27 For I have not hesitated to proclaim to you *the whole will of God*. (NIV) *{Emphasis added}*

I believe the Lord desires His children today to know all that they need to know for this life, equipped in the same way as they were back in the initial church. In Luke 8:10, Jesus tells His disciples:

Luke 8:10
10 …"To you it has been granted to know the mysteries of the kingdom of God, but to the rest it is in parables, so that SEEING THEY MAY NOT SEE, AND HEARING THEY MAY NOT UNDERSTAND." (NASB)

He goes on to say in verses 16 to 18:

Luke 8:16-18
16 "Now no one after lighting a lamp covers it over with a container, or puts it under a bed; but he puts it on a lampstand, so that those who come in may see the light.

17 "For nothing is hidden that will not become evident, nor anything secret that will not be known and come to light.

18 "So take care how you listen; for whoever has, to him more shall be given; and whoever does not have, even what he thinks he has shall be taken away from him." (NASB)

Therefore, for those who belong to Jesus, who desire to hear His Word and know His will, the more diligent they are to listen carefully for His will, the more shall be given to them. He desires to reveal His truth to them, not to hide it.

So where do we start in knowing the will of God? Having completed ten lessons and read all of the verses I reference, I am sure you will anticipate my first answer to that question. It is of course the Bible. The Bible, also known as the written Word or the Scriptures, is God's revealed will for man via the inspiration of the Holy Spirit. In 2ⁿᵈ Timothy Chapter 3, we read in verses 16 and 17:

2 Timothy 3:16-17

16 All Scripture is <u>God-breathed</u> and is useful for teaching, rebuking, correcting and training in righteousness,

17 so that the servant of God may be thoroughly equipped for every good work. (NIV) *{Emphasis added}*

Now read from 2ⁿᵈ Peter Chapter 1 verse 19 through 21. This is the section just after Peter speaks about the transfiguration of Jesus on the mountain, which we looked at a few lessons back. He says:

2 Peter 1:19-21

19 And so we have the prophetic word confirmed, which you do well to heed as a light that shines in a dark place, until the day dawns and the morning star rises in your hearts;

20 knowing this first, that no prophecy of Scripture is of any private interpretation,

21 for prophecy never came by the will of man, but holy men of God spoke as they were moved by the Holy Spirit.   (NKJV)

So what is the true origin of Scripture prophecy? It is from God. God's breath—His Holy Spirit—moved prophets and holy men to speak. And so what we have in the Bible, though associated with different men—Moses, David, Isaiah, Daniel, etc.—is in fact the very

Word of God. No prophecy of Scripture ever came about by private interpretation; that is, no prophecy ever came about by the prophet's own disclosure or interpretation. The prophecy does not originate or spring from the prophet. Neither did the Old Testament prophets put their own construction upon the God-breathed words they spoke or wrote. It was not their message, but rather they were a vessel for God. And the same is true for the New Testament authors. Peter says that under the new covenant, he and the other apostles and writers have the words of the prophets confirmed or made more certain. Therefore what they have written is an even higher and more complete revelation from God.

Now we know that all Scripture is God-breathed, and Peter goes on to include the New Testament writings as Scripture when he says in Chapter 3 verses 15 and 16:

2 Peter 3:15-16

> 15 and regard the patience of our Lord as salvation; just as also our beloved brother Paul, according to the wisdom given him, wrote to you,
>
> 16 as also in all his letters, speaking in them of these things, in which are some things hard to understand, which the untaught and unstable distort, <u>as they do also the rest of the Scriptures</u>, to their own destruction. (NASB) *{Emphasis added}*

The light of the gospel has not been hidden under a vessel with these men. Rather these apostles are lamp stands shining out the very words of Jesus and the teachings He entrusted to them, through the Holy Spirit. And we would do well to heed it.

Up above, in Chapter 1 and verse 19, Peter mentions the morning star rising in our hearts. We will talk more about the significance of this in our next lesson. But as we close this study-time let me take this opportunity to encourage you, if you are not already in the practice of doing so, to read your Bible every day. In Isaiah 40 verse 8 it says:

Isaiah 40:8

> 8 "The grass withereth, the flower fadeth: but the word of our God shall stand forever." (Webster)

Jesus taught in Matthew 24 verse 35:

Matthew 24:35

35 "Heaven and earth shall pass away, but My words shall not pass away." (KJV)

And God assures us in Isaiah Chapter 55 verses 10 and 11:

Isaiah 55:10-11

10 "As the rain and the snow
　　come down from heaven,
　and do not return to it
　　without watering the earth
　and making it bud and flourish,
　　so that it yields seed for the sower and bread for the eater,
11 so is My word that goes out from My mouth:
　　It will not return to Me empty,
　but will accomplish what I desire
　　and achieve the purpose for which I sent it." (NIV)
　　{Capitalization for deity added}

Will you allow the Lord's Word to accomplish what He pleases to do in your life today? I pray you do.

There are wonderful promises in the very next verses associated with the activity of God's holy Word:

Isaiah 55:12-13

12 "For you will go out with joy
　And be led forth with peace;
　The mountains and the hills will break forth into shouts of joy before you,
　And all the trees of the field will clap their hands.
13 "Instead of the thorn bush the cypress will come up,
　And instead of the nettle the myrtle will come up,
　And it will be a memorial to the LORD,
　For an everlasting sign which will not be cut off." (NASB)

LESSON TWELVE

———————∝———————

W e've been looking at that part of the Lord's Prayer where Jesus teaches us to pray, "Your will be done on earth as it is in heaven." And in our last lesson we began to answer the question, "How can we know what God's perfect pleasing will is, so that we can pray and ask according to His will and be able to stand in agreement with Him in faith?" The first part of the answer to knowing the will of God is of course the Bible. The last time we saw that we could know God's will through His written Word which is totally inspired and totally true. The Bible, both the Old and New Testaments, is the only written Word of God. It is God-breathed and binding.

Furthermore, no man can add to or detract from any part of God's written Word. In the book of Revelation, the last book in the Bible and logically so, we read a warning at its close in Chapter 22 verses 18 and 19 that applies to that particular book and, by extension, really to the Bible as a whole:

Revelation 22:18-19

18 For I testify to every man that heareth the words of the prophecy of this book, if any man shall add to these things, God will add to him the plagues that are written in this book:

19 And if any man shall take away from the words of the book of this prophecy, God will take away his part out of the book of life, and out of the holy city, and from the things which are written in this book. (Webster)

Sermons can be given and books, such as the one you are reading right now, can be written to aid in understanding the Bible and to give the proper sense, interpretation and application. But only the Bible can be accepted as canon—God's pure Word. That word **canon** means *a rod with graduated marks used for measuring length*. The word originally designated a rule or ruler used in building. The tool had to be of unbendable material, dependable for its straightness and accuracy, so that the measurements were correct and structural defects were avoided. And the individual books of the Old and New Testament were judged by the early church as authoritative and divine—as the only canon or absolute standard with which to measure and know the truth of God. No other writings can claim this status.

There is another point that also should be made. Remember in our last lesson we read in 2nd Peter 1:20-21 the apostle's teaching, where he says:

2 Peter 1:20-21
> 20 knowing this first, that no prophecy of Scripture is of any private interpretation,
> 21 for prophecy never came by the will of man, but holy men of God spoke as they were moved by the Holy Spirit. (NKJV)

And we discussed how Bible prophecy did not have its origin in the will of man: it was not the prophet's own interpretation or construction, but rather these men of God were moved by the Holy Spirit. Neither then should any one Scripture verse be interpreted "privately" or on its own by the reader, but instead it should be considered in the context in which it is given and the Bible as a whole. Since the Holy Spirit inspired the entire Bible, by checking the interpretation of one verse against other verses, we can better understand what God meant by that particular Scripture.

Scripture confirms Scripture.

As it says in a number of places in the Bible:

Deuteronomy 19:15b
> 15 "...by the mouth of two or three witnesses the matter shall be established." (NKJV)

But any doctrine built on only a portion of Scripture will fall short of the full revelation of God and actually is in danger of going off on some wild tangent.

This Scripture from Deuteronomy 19:15 and elsewhere in the Bible—"by the mouth of two or three witnesses the matter shall be established"—is also important in another way toward fully answering the question, "How do we know the will of God?" For although the Bible is without error in all points, not all points reflect obviously and in an outright way the *full* revelation of God's will for us. The Levitical sacrifices listed in the Old Testament would be an example of this. These sacrifices were appointed by God with the purpose of acknowledging man's sin and pointing to the true sacrifice, Christ. And yet if we pick up the book of Leviticus, without the full revelation of the fulfillment in Jesus, we might mistakenly believe that these ceremonies apply for us today.

Not only that, but Scripture can be misapplied. Did not Satan use a quote from one of the Psalms to try and tempt Jesus into throwing Himself from the top of the temple? And Jesus countered with Scripture, this time properly applied:

Luke 4:9-12
> 9 And he brought Him to Jerusalem, and set Him on a pinnacle of the temple, and said to Him, "If Thou art the Son of God, cast Thyself down from hence.
> 10 "For it is written, 'He will give His angels charge over thee, to keep thee:
> 11 "'And in their hands they will bear thee up, lest at any time thou dash thy foot against a stone.'"
> 12 And Jesus answering, said to him, "It is said, 'Thou shalt not tempt the LORD thy God.'" (Webster)

Satan twisted the meaning of Psalm 91:11-12, and Jesus responded accurately with Deuteronomy 6:16. In like manner, it is important for us to know and study the Scriptures so that we do not fall for the false logic of the enemy. How many times do we see people who are not even believers in God's Word quoting from Scripture in debates on TV to support a position that is totally unbiblical!

There is another problem we should also consider. Jesus said in John 5 verses 39 to 40 to the religious leaders of His day who read and studied and memorized Scriptures:

John 5:39-40

> 39 "You study the Scriptures diligently because you think that in them you have eternal life. These are the very Scriptures that testify about Me,
>
> 40 yet you refuse to come to Me to have life." (NIV) *{Capitalization for deity added}*

You see, they diligently searched the Scriptures, but it was without their hearts in tune to what God wanted them to see. And so they missed the very Messiah promised for them in those same Scriptures. From those verses we learn that it is not the reading or the studying of the Bible that brings eternal life, but instead, we have eternal life by coming to the Jesus of the Bible.

Knowing God's Will: the Bible

So we have several problems we have to consider. The Bible is the only written Word of God, but we have seen that it can be read and studied with dulled eyes and a wrong heart; it can be misapplied or twisted; and even a sincere student can have difficulties if he or she is focusing on a verse that does not straightforwardly reflect God's full revelation or if they don't understand the foundational gospel message. It is as though there is all this wealth of knowledge of God's will in the Bible, but it has a lock sealing it closed. And the key to opening that lock is the Lord Jesus Himself. We spoke last time about how He desires to give to His disciples the mysteries of the kingdom of God, and He Himself is the key to that revelation. Remember what we read in 2nd Peter?

2 Peter 1:19-20

> 19 And so we have the prophetic word confirmed, which you do well to heed as a light that shines in a dark place, until the day dawns and the morning star rises in your hearts;
> 20 knowing this first, that no prophecy of Scripture is of any private interpretation, (NKJV)

In the last lesson I noted Peter's use of the expression, "until the day dawns and the morning star rises in your hearts." What does he mean by that? In the last chapter of the book of Revelation, Chapter 22, and down at verse 16, the Lord says to John:

Revelation 22:16

> 16 "I Jesus have sent My angel to testify to you these things in the churches. I am the Root and the Offspring of David, and the Bright and Morning-star." (Webster)

Jesus is the bright and morning star. We have been talking about the Bible, God's written Word, but Jesus is the living Word:

John 1:1

> 1 In the beginning was the Word, and the Word was with God, and the Word was God. (KJV)

That word for "Word" is *Logos* in the Greek. That is where we get the "logy" part of such words as biology and geology, meaning the study, knowledge, or science of a certain topic. *Logos* is the expression of thought, a word spoken which is the embodiment of a conception or an idea. And Jesus is the *Logos*—the absolute Word or thought of God—the ultimate solution for us. All answers to all topics are in Him. He is the reasoning and the motive, the computation and thought behind the entire creation. And He is the exact divine expression.

And as the living Word, He is essential to any Biblical interpretation. A morning star heralds the appearance of the sun. And the sun brings light. In Numbers 24:17 He is prophesized as the star that will come out of Jacob:

Numbers 24:17

> 17 "I see him, but not now;

I behold him, but not near;
A star shall come forth from Jacob,
A scepter shall rise from Israel,
And shall crush through the forehead of Moab,
And tear down all the sons of Sheth *(or sons of tumult).*"
(NASB) *{Clarification in parenthesis added}*

And in Malachi 4:2, speaking of Messiah, it says:

Malachi 4:2a

2 "But to you that fear My name, shall the Sun of Righteousness arise with healing in His wings;..." (Webster)

In Luke Chapter 1, Jesus is referred to as the Dayspring or literally the Dawn from on high who has visited us. Here we read about the day of the circumcision of Zacharias' newborn son, John, who would be called the Baptist:

Luke 1:67-69, 76-79

67 And his father Zacharias was filled with the Holy Spirit, and prophesied, saying,
68 "Blessed be the Lord God of Israel; for He hath visited and redeemed His people.
69 And hath raised up a horn of salvation for us, in the house of His servant David:"
76 "And thou, child, shalt be called the prophet of the Highest, for thou shalt go before the face of the Lord to prepare His ways;
77 To give knowledge of salvation to His people, by the remission of their sins,
78 Through the tender mercy of our God; by which **the Dayspring** from on high hath visited us,
79 To give light to them that sit in darkness and in the shades of death, to guide our feet into the way of peace." (Webster) *{Emphasis added}*

So Jesus, as the Bright Morning Star, as the Sun of righteousness, as the Dawn, brings God's full revelation of Himself and His will for mankind. That is what Peter meant when he said that he had the prophetic word, or the words of the prophets, confirmed or made more certain, for he knew Jesus of Nazareth. The Lord, after His resurrection, had opened Peter's mind to understand the Scriptures. And Peter had seen and been a witness to the transfiguration and glory of the Lord. So he can say without hesitation, you will do well to heed this confirmation of the prophecies which we have—this gospel of the glory of the Messiah—"as a light that shines in a dark place, until the day dawns and the morning star rises in your hearts;" that is, when Jesus Christ rises in your hearts and gives you light and revelation and understanding.

So then how do we unlock the mysteries of God's will in the Bible? First we must realize that a true understanding of Scripture can only result when based upon the ultimate solution: Jesus Christ, the Rock upon which any interpretation must be built! This is a critical point.

Knowing God's Will: the Lord Jesus

Whenever we read a passage then, we need to do so with the Lord and the gospel in mind. We need to see Jesus in the passage and remember the things He did and taught in the gospels. Then we cannot go astray to the left or to the right. If our interpretation lines up with the testimony of Jesus, then we have that added witness we mentioned before to establish the matter.

The apostle Paul said that in Christ:

Colossians 2:3
3 ...are hid all the treasures of wisdom and knowledge. (KJV)

The apostle John wrote:

John 1:18
18 No one has seen God at any time. The only begotten Son, who is in the bosom of the Father, He has declared Him. (NKJV)

And when the apostle Philip asked Jesus to show them the Father, Jesus answered in John 14:9:

John 14:9

> 9 ..."Have I been so long with you, and yet you have not come to know Me, Philip? He who has seen Me has seen the Father; how can you say, 'Show us the Father'?" (NASB)

And that brings us to the second point: To know God's will as we read the Scriptures, not only must we base any interpretation upon Jesus Christ, but we must also know Jesus personally.

As we discussed in previous lessons, we must be born again to see the kingdom of God. Just like Peter, we need the day to dawn and the bright and morning star to rise in our hearts. We need Jesus in our hearts. And through Him we can understand God's Scriptures. We can begin to see the perfect pleasing will of God, and so we can ask in faith in agreement with it, knowing God hears our prayers.

And if He hears us, whatever we ask, we know that we have the petitions that we have asked of Him.

LESSON THIRTEEN

------------∝------------

I n our study on prayer, we have been focusing on praying according to the perfect pleasing will of the Father, and we have asked the question, "How do we know God's absolute heart's desire, His positional will?" To answer that question, we first talked about God's written Word, the Bible. Then in our last lesson we discussed His living Word, His Son Jesus. We said that a true understanding of Scripture can only result when we read a Bible passage *through* the Lord Jesus, knowing that He is the Rock upon which any Biblical interpretation must be built. He is the ultimate solution and in Him are hidden all the treasures of wisdom and knowledge. And if our interpretation of any portion of the Bible is based upon the person of the Lord Jesus, we are not going to go off in error to the left or the right. As it says in Hebrews Chapter 12 verses 1 and 2:

Hebrews 12:1b-2a
1 ...let us run with endurance the race that is set before us,
2 fixing our eyes on Jesus, the author and perfecter of faith... (NASB)

We also said that to know God's will we must know His Son Jesus personally. We have read in Luke 8:10 how Jesus clearly tells those who are His disciples—those who are His students—that:

Luke 8:10
10 ..."To you it has been granted to know the mysteries of the kingdom of God, but to the rest it is in parables, so that SEEING THEY MAY NOT SEE, AND HEARING THEY MAY NOT UNDERSTAND." (NASB)

So, if someone is not born again and has not given his or her life to the Lord Jesus, the Bible can be purposely cryptic and confusing when they read it. First Corinthians 1:19 reminds us:

1 Corinthians 1:19
19 For it is written:

> "I will destroy the wisdom of the wise;
> the intelligence of the intelligent I will frustrate." (NIV)

And Jesus taught in Matthew Chapter 13 starting at verse 14:

Matthew 13:14-17
14 "In them is fulfilled the prophecy of Isaiah:

> "'You will be ever hearing but never understanding;
> you will be ever seeing but never perceiving.
15   For this people's heart has become calloused;
> they hardly hear with their ears,
> and they have closed their eyes.
> Otherwise they might see with their eyes,
> hear with their ears,
> understand with their hearts
> and turn, and I would heal them.'

16 But blessed are your eyes because they see, and your ears because they hear.
17 For truly I tell you, many prophets and righteous people longed to see what you see but did not see it, and to hear what you hear but did not hear it." (NIV)

This is truly a blessing given by God to His children in His Son Jesus: our eyes and ears are opened to see the kingdom of God and we begin to understand its mysteries. Our Heavenly Father reveals to us His heart's will as we know and give our lives to Jesus, the King and Messiah He has established!

We have spoken about the Mount of Transfiguration several times so far in this study series, and in the transfiguration episode we see this principle of the centrality of Jesus to Biblical interpretation. Look again at Matthew Chapter 17:

Matthew 17:1-8

1   And after six days, Jesus taketh Peter, James, and John his brother, and bringeth them upon a high mountain apart.

2   And He was transfigured before them: and His face shone as the sun, and His raiment was white as the light.

3   And behold, there appeared to them Moses and Elijah talking with Him.

4   Then answered Peter, and said to Jesus, "Lord, it is good for us to be here: if Thou wilt, let us make here three tabernacles; one for Thee, and one for Moses, and one for Elijah."

5   While he was yet speaking, behold, a bright cloud over-shadowed them: and behold, a voice out of the cloud, which said, "This is My beloved Son, in whom I am well pleased: hear ye Him."

6   And when the disciples heard it, they fell on their face, and were in great fear.

7   And Jesus came and touched them, and said, "Arise, and be not afraid."

8   And when they had lifted up their eyes, they saw no man, save Jesus only. (Webster)

They saw no one but Jesus only. In the corresponding account that Mark gives, he tells us that Peter offered to build the three tabernacles or dwellings because he was greatly afraid and did not know what to say. Now God had given the people of Israel the Old Testament Law through *Moses.* And *Elijah* stood as the greatest example of the Old Testament prophets. Furthermore, we have seen that both the Old Testament Law and the Prophets are God's written Word and totally true. And yet the supreme authority of the new revelation and covenant in Jesus Christ is seen by the Father's words:

Matthew 17:5b

5   ..."This is My beloved Son, in whom I am well pleased: hear ye Him." (Webster) *{Emphasis added}*

Thus the New Testament takes precedence over the Old Testament in matters of our Christian walk. The New Testament writers had, as we have studied, "the prophetic word confirmed" or "made more certain" (2 Peter 1:19), and we are not to build three equal dwellings but instead one single dwelling for Jesus who alone is God the Son. Remember, when they lifted up their eyes, the apostles saw only Jesus. And when we read Moses and the Prophets *seeing Jesus*, we begin to build a proper comprehension of Scripture.

This hermeneutical or interpretative principle is true of the New Testament as well. People can read the New Testament and still not "see Jesus." They may quote all types of Scriptures and never see the obvious; that is, that they **must** come to Him for salvation and believe in the sacrifice He made for them, that they must ask Him to come into their hearts and forgive them and renew them, that He must be their Lord, and that they need to hear Him! In fact, a church or assembly that so misses Jesus is in danger of being a cult. And have we not seen such groups who shamelessly quote from the New Testament but who follow some other person as christ or lord either explicitly or in practice. Their Biblical interpretation is dangerously in error, creating a terrible situation.

This command of God the Father to hear or listen to His Beloved Son addresses not only our understanding of the Bible but our whole relationship with God. Jesus is the only true Teacher, and we must desire to hear Him and learn from Him; we must desire to truly be His disciples. And as we know Him and are trained by Him and have this bond with Him, we will see the Father and we will know the Father's will.

Now at this point, someone might very well ask, "How does this personal relationship with the Lord, this knowledge of Jesus Christ, become real and effective in my life?" And from what we have just studied someone could also ask, "How can my mind be opened to understand and see Jesus in the Scriptures?" These are important questions. But there is another area of concern which we must address as well. What about specifics in our lives which fall outside the absolute truths of the Scriptures? An example of this would be careers. Many careers are permissible by Biblical standards, and yet one specific career may be God's will for you. Another field may be wrong, not because that field is bad or unbiblical, but because it is wrong for you. For someone else, that same career could be the perfect will of God. Likewise the plan God has for you could be wrong for someone else. How can we each know what the right path is for us as individuals?

Before we attempt to answer these three very good questions, let me pose just one more. What about when we do know the will of

God? That is, once we know His will in our mind, how can we get it into our hearts so that there is power to act upon it? Let me give an example. We may know it is God's will that we love our enemies and pray for those who persecute us, but how can we really know that love in our hearts? This is a very difficult or even an impossible thing in the human sense. But the answer to that problem and to the other questions raised is **the Holy Spirit**. Let us read a few Scriptures, starting with 1ˢᵗ Corinthians Chapter 2 verses 6 to 16:

1 Corinthians 2:6-16

6   However, we speak wisdom among them that are perfect: yet not the wisdom of this world, nor of the princes of this world, that come to naught:

7   But we speak the wisdom of God in a mystery, even the hidden wisdom which God ordained before the world to our glory:

8   Which none of the princes of this world knew: for had they known it, they would not have crucified the Lord of glory.

9   But as it is written, "Eye hath not seen, nor ear heard, neither have entered into the heart of man, the things which God hath prepared for them that love Him."

10 But God hath revealed them to us <u>by His Spirit</u>; for the Spirit searcheth all things, even the deep things of God.

11 For what man knoweth the things of a man, save the spirit of man which is in him? even so the things of God knoweth no man, but the Spirit of God.

12 Now we have received, not the spirit of the world, but the Spirit which is from God; that we may know the things that are freely given to us by God.

13 Which things also we speak, not in the words which man's wisdom teacheth, but which the Holy Spirit teacheth; comparing spiritual things with spiritual.

14 But the natural man receiveth not the things of the Spirit of God: for they are foolishness to him: neither can he know them, because they are spiritually discerned.

15 But he that is spiritual judgeth all things, yet he himself is judged by no man.

16 For who hath known the mind of the Lord, that he may instruct Him? But we have the mind of Christ. (Webster)
{Emphasis added}

It is the Holy Spirit who opens our minds to the Scriptures and shows us Jesus. Through Him we have the "mind of Christ." And He gives us spiritual wisdom that the world cannot discern. It is foolishness to them because their ears are hard of hearing and their eyes they have closed, as we studied earlier in Matthew Chapter 13. But through His Holy Spirit, God reveals to us His hidden wisdom.

Knowing God's Will: the Holy Spirit

John 14:15-26

15 "If you love Me, you will keep My commandments.

16 "I will ask the Father, and He will give you another Helper, that He may be with you forever;

17 that is the Spirit of truth, whom the world cannot receive, because it does not see Him or know Him, but you know Him because He abides with you and will be in you.

18 "I will not leave you as orphans; I will come to you.

19 "After a little while the world will no longer see Me, but you will see Me; because I live, you will live also.

20 "In that day you will know that I am in My Father, and you in Me, and I in you.

21 "He who has My commandments and keeps them is the one who loves Me; and he who loves Me will be loved by My Father, and I will love him and will disclose Myself to him."

22 Judas (not Iscariot) said to Him, "Lord, what then has happened that You are going to disclose Yourself to us and not to the world?"

23 Jesus answered and said to him, "If anyone loves Me, he will keep My word; and My Father will love him, and We will come to him and make Our abode with him.

24 "He who does not love Me does not keep My words; and the word which you hear is not Mine, but the Father's who sent Me.

25 "These things I have spoken to you while abiding with you.

26 "But the Helper, the Holy Spirit, whom the Father will send
in My name, He will teach you all things, and bring to your
remembrance all that I said to you." (NASB)

The Holy Spirit is the activating person of the Trinity—God's
manifestation to us. He is the Helper who comes to live inside of
us forever. And, through Him, the Father and Jesus dwell inside of
us making our faith alive and effective as we are changed into the
image of the Son. By the Holy Spirit we are empowered to walk
as Jesus walked, even when humanly speaking it is impossible.
Moreover, as the Helper, as the Spirit of truth, the Holy Spirit teaches
us all things. Read Jesus' elucidation to His disciples further down
in the gospel of John at Chapter 16 and verse 7:

John 16:7-15

7   "But I tell you the truth, it is to your advantage that I go away;
for if I do not go away, the Helper will not come to you; but
if I go, I will send Him to you.

8   "And He, when He comes, will convict the world concerning
sin and righteousness and judgment;

9   concerning sin, because they do not believe in Me;

10 and concerning righteousness, because I go to the Father and
you no longer see Me;

11 and concerning judgment, because the ruler of this world has
been judged.

12 "I have many more things to say to you, but you cannot
bear them now.

13 "But when He, the Spirit of truth, comes, He will guide you
into all the truth; for He will not speak on His own initiative,
but whatever He hears, He will speak; and He will disclose
to you what is to come.

14 "He will glorify Me, for He will take of Mine and will disclose it to you.

15 "All things that the Father has are Mine; therefore I said that
He takes of Mine and will disclose it to you." (NASB)

The Holy Spirit guides us into all truth. He will take the words
of the Lord in the Scriptures and make them known—understandable—to us. And He gives us real guidance for the future. He is God

speaking back to us, the other side of the communication or knowledge exchange we call prayer. The Spirit of God is our connection to the words spoken centuries ago. In addition, He is the One who makes our witness effective today. It is His anointing that convicts people of sin and of their need for salvation. What great joy is ours that we are not orphans, but instead, because of the Holy Spirit, we have real communion with our Lord and God!

It was because the early church was so filled with the Spirit that they could so clearly discern God's will. By the operation of the Holy Spirit, the morning star, Jesus, rises in our hearts, and understanding dawns.

LESSON FOURTEEN

———————∞———————

I welcome you to the fourteenth part of this series on prayer. We have been focusing now over several lessons on that section of the Lord's Prayer where Jesus teaches His disciples to pray, "Your will be done on earth as it is in heaven." Early on, we studied the Scripture in 1st John 5 verses 14 to 15 which says:

1 John 5:14-15

14 Now this is the confidence that we have in Him, that if we ask anything according to His will, He hears us.

15 And if we know that He hears us, whatever we ask, we know that we have the petitions that we have asked of Him. (NKJV)

And, most recently, we have been discussing how we can know the perfect pleasing will of God so that, when we ask Him, we can ask according to His will, praying in agreement with God and believing in faith for our petitions: *That the will of the Father would be done on earth as it is in heaven.* You know, Jesus, at the Last Supper gave His disciples a wonderful promise. He said, in John 16:23-24:

John 16:23-24

23 "…Most assuredly, I say to you, whatever you ask the Father in My name He will give you.

24 "Until now you have asked nothing in My name. Ask, and you will receive, that your joy may be full." (NKJV)

We can have great confidence when we pray and ask as a member of the kingdom of heaven—when we pray according to God's will.

So then, how can we know the perfect pleasing will of God for effective prayer? As the first part of the answer to that question we discussed the Bible, God's written Word and the only canon. In addition, we have seen that to unlock the Scriptures we must base any interpretation upon the living Word, the Lord Jesus. We must belong to Him and know Him to understand the Scriptures and the mysteries of the kingdom of God.

In the last lesson we discovered just how that knowledge of Jesus becomes real and effective in our lives. We saw how our minds could be opened to understand and see Jesus in Scriptural interpretation. We saw how we could receive specific direction from God for those individual, distinct decisions we all must make. Moreover, we learned how we could receive power to act in agreement with God's will once we do know it. The answer of course was the Holy Spirit. The Holy Spirit, as the activating person of the Trinity, makes our faith alive and real, opening our eyes and giving us revelation. As we give our lives to Jesus, the Lord pours out His Holy Spirit on us. And the Spirit changes and remakes us into the image of the Son, bringing Christ into our hearts and giving us the power to bear good fruit in agreement with God's will.

Remember, Jesus taught His disciples:

John 14:16-18

16 "I will ask the Father, and He will give you another Helper, that He may be with you forever;

17 that is the Spirit of truth, whom the world cannot receive, because it does not see Him or know Him, but you know Him because He abides with you and will be in you.

18 "I will not leave you as orphans; I will come to you." (NASB)

The presence of the Holy Spirit keeps us from being orphans and keeps us in communion and fellowship with the Lord. The world cannot accept this because the world neither sees Him nor knows Him. Yet, when the Holy Spirit has come to live within us and when we stand in the beautiful outpouring of His presence, we know our God is real. And as we said last time, He is God speaking back to us, the other side of the communication or knowledge exchange of prayer.

In Ephesians Chapter 5, verses 15 to 18, Paul cautions the church at Ephesus:

Ephesians 5:15-18

15 Be very careful, then, how you live—not as unwise but as wise,

16 making the most of every opportunity, because the days are evil.

17 Therefore do not be foolish, but understand what the Lord's will is.

18 Do not get drunk on wine, which leads to debauchery. Instead, be filled with the Spirit, (NIV)

Wisdom and an understanding of the Lord's will are associated with being filled with the Holy Spirit. So putting this altogether, what can we conclude about how we can know the perfect will of God? Man's final authority on God's will, then, is the written Word He gave us, the Bible, read through the living Word, His Son, read in and applied by the Spirit of truth, Who opens our minds to understand and Who guides us through prayer, His presence, and His special gifts. I think this is an extremely important statement to our study:

Man's final authority on God's will is the written Word He gave us, the Bible, both Old and New Testaments, read through the living Word, His Son Jesus, read in and applied by the Holy Spirit of truth, Who opens our minds to understand the Scriptures and Who guides us through prayer, His presence and His special gifts.

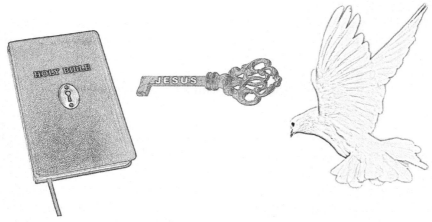

Knowing God's Will

We will speak more about receiving the Holy Spirit and His gifts later on in this series of lessons. For the time being, let me encourage you, if you are a believer in the Lord Jesus, to pray and ask the Lord to pour out His Holy Spirit upon you in abundance, that you may have the fullness of the Spirit and His power in your life. And should you be reading this study and not yet be a follower of God's Messiah, this is the perfect time to call on the Lord Jesus as your Savior and ask Him to forgive you your sins and send His Holy Spirit to change you.

John the Baptist said to the people:

Matthew 3:11

   11 "I indeed baptize you with water unto repentance, but He who is coming after me is mightier than I, whose sandals I am not worthy to carry. He will baptize you with the Holy Spirit and fire." (NKJV)

Amen. Do you remember Deuteronomy 19:15b? "By the mouth of two or three witnesses the matter shall be established." Now we have the three witnesses to establish the matter as to knowing the will of God. These three witnesses are: [1] the Bible God gave us; [2] the Lord Jesus, through whom we must interpret the Bible and to whom we must give our lives; and [3] the Holy Spirit in whom we understand the Scriptures and receive guidance from the Father.

With that foundation, let us take a few minutes to discuss what our attitude should be in desiring to know God's will. Romans Chapter 12 verses 1 and 2 is an important place to start:

Romans 12:1-2

1   I beseech you therefore, brethren, by the mercies of God, that ye present your bodies a living sacrifice, holy, acceptable unto God, which is your reasonable service.

2   And be not conformed to this world: but be ye transformed by the renewing of your mind, that ye may prove what is that good, and acceptable, and perfect, will of God. (KJV)

Notice how this Scripture says that we are to test and prove what is the good and acceptable and perfect will of God. To do so, we have to offer ourselves to God. We are to present our bodies a living sacrifice, holy and acceptable to God. Paul says that this is our reasonable or logical service. This is how we worship and serve God, by giving this life which we have in this world to Him.

This does not mean that we isolate ourselves from the world in some religious exercise. Actually it means something which can be even more difficult for some. We are called to live our regular daily lives in this world in a way that is holy and acceptable to God. Jesus prayed for His disciples in John Chapter 17 verses 15 and 16:

John 17:15-16

15   "I do not pray that You should take them out of the world, but that You should keep them from the evil one.

16   "They are not of the world, just as I am not of the world." (NKJV)

So whether it is in school or at a job or just the personal inter-actions with our families, we should not behave like the rest of the world even though we are in the world. We should not commit evil. We should not act like those who know not the Lord. Instead we should conduct ourselves according to the kingdom of righteous-ness, giving glory to the name of Jesus by the good example of our lives and by shining out the light which the gospel has produced in us. This is our reasonable service.

Such a life is a holy and living sacrifice to God. It is a selfless life dedicated to desiring the kingdom of God to go forward. And the key is in verse 2 of Romans 12:

Romans 12:2a
> 2　And be not conformed to this world: but be ye transformed by the renewing of your mind, … (KJV)

When we accept the Lord Jesus as our Savior, we have to offer all of ourselves to Him, including our minds and any preconceived notions we bring with us. There are so many personality types, and we all come to the Lord with some baggage of attitudes and ideas that are wrong and not of God. We have to present the whole of our beings as a living sacrifice. We have to lift up the entirety of ourselves to the Lord and say, "Change me Lord. Remove any wrong ideas, wrong attitudes, and wrong ways of thinking or looking at things. I don't want my way but Your way. I don't want my ideas but Your ideas. I want to see things the right way. I want to see things the way they are in truth, the way You see them."

This is a difficult thing for humans to do. It is hard **not** to be conformed to the world's way of thinking. But Proverbs 14:12 says:

Proverbs 14:12
> 12　There is a way which seems right to a man,
> But its end is the way of death. (NASB)

In John Chapter 12, we read how there were many rulers among the religious leaders in Jesus' day that believed in Him and knew He was the Messiah, yet they would not confess Him because they feared being ostracized by the rest and because they loved the praise of men more than the praise of God (verses 42-43). Therefore, if we are to know God's good and acceptable and perfect will, we must have a supreme love for His praise above all else and not be conformed to this world and the "mob" mentality it often generates.

It is amazing how effective peer pressure can be from the sandbox all the way up to the corporate board room. And it is amazing how the waves of human opinion toss to and fro and change directions like the wind. But:

Isaiah 40:8
> 8　"The grass withereth, the flower fadeth: but the word of our God shall stand forever." (Webster)

God is the same forever. And thank God His truth is not subject to the latest talk show opinion poll. If we are to know His will, we must allow Him to transform us by the <u>renewing of our minds</u>. We cannot let some cherished notion or wrong conviction keep us from the truth of God. Otherwise our prayers will be ineffective, for we will not be praying according to the kingdom of light. Jesus said:

Matthew 16:25

> 25 "For whoever wishes to save his life will lose it; but whoever loses his life for My sake will find it." (NASB)

The word in the Greek for life, *psuche*, can also be translated "soul" or "self." If we try to keep ourselves—that is, the old person we were—we will lose ourselves. But when we give up the old self—the old ways of thinking and acting—we find a new wonderful self; we become a person we could not have ever hoped to be. We have lost ourselves in Jesus and have found in Him eternal life and eternal truth and a new transformed self.

Therefore, we must offer ourselves to God. We must desire to read the Bible. We must desire to know the Son personally. We must desire to be filled with the Spirit of God. Then we can prove what God's good, perfect and acceptable will is. Then we can pray according to His will and, as we studied in 1st John 5:14-15, have <u>confidence</u> in Him "…that if we ask anything according to His will, He hears us. And if we know that He hears us, whatever we ask, we know that we have the petitions that we have asked of Him." (NKJV)

Please note that in this offering of the self to God as a living sacrifice, in this transformation and the renewing of the mind, we are demonstrating our submission to God. And submission is central to the section of the Lord's Prayer which we are studying: "Father, <u>Your</u> will be done on earth as it is in heaven." Consider the Lord Jesus in the Garden of Gethsemane. In Luke 22:42 we read His prayer:

Luke 22:42

> 42 saying, "Father, if it is Your will, take this cup away from Me; nevertheless not My will, but Yours, be done." (NKJV)

It is so important that we submit every area to God; otherwise, we will not be able to hear His voice or know His will for our situation. So we have two words that might seem contradictory to

117

the unspiritual mind. These words are *confidence* and *submission*. But to the child of God these words mean the power and anointing of our prayers. For, we pray in submission to God's will. We want God's holy desires to become our desires. On every issue and in every matter, we want to have the mind of Christ. And when we pray as such, we pray in confidence, asking in the name of Jesus and knowing that we will receive, that our joy may be full.

LESSON FIFTEEN

———————∞———————

Matthew 6:9-11

9   "In this manner, therefore, pray:
     Our Father in heaven,
     Hallowed be Your name.

10   Your kingdom come.
     Your will be done
     On earth as it is in heaven.

11   Give us this day our daily bread." (NKJV)

Today we will start the next section in our Bible study series on prayer. The focus for this section will be on Matthew 6:11 where Jesus teaches us to pray: "Give us this day our daily bread." This is the part of the Lord's Prayer where we bring our petitions before God. We recognize Him as the source of our sustenance and seek His provision. In Psalm 34 verses 8 to 10 it says:

Psalm 34:8-10

8   Oh, taste and see that the LORD is good;
    Blessed is the man who trusts in Him!

9   Oh, fear the LORD, you His saints!
    There is no want to those who fear Him.

10 The young lions lack and suffer hunger;
    But those who seek the LORD shall not lack any good thing.
    (NKJV) *{Emphasis added}*

Bread, which satisfies physical hunger and which was such a staple food in Bible times, is an excellent representative and symbol of the various needs of life. And we are to **ask** for our daily bread.

119

Now the word in the Greek which is translated "daily" is a difficult word for scholars (*epiousios* pronounced ep-ee-oo'-see-os). It is a rare word which appears in the Bible only in the Lord's Prayer given in Matthew and Luke. A kindred word used in the Book of Acts means, "the next day" or "on the following day." So the meaning of daily bread seems to be "bread for the coming day." That translation makes sense coming after the phrase, "Give us this day." We are to go before the Lord each day and ask Him to give us today the bread that suffices for this day and the next. The same Greek word was also discovered in an ancient housekeeping book, and the usage there agrees with the definition, "for the coming day."[1] Certainly a daily prayer for the needs of the next day is a prayer that every housekeeper understands. And there is a peace of mind in knowing that God is going to supply this day those things necessary for the new day we face. We are not to be anxious for tomorrow. Paul says in Philippians 4 verses 6 to 7:

Philippians 4:6-7
> 6 Be anxious for nothing; but in every thing by prayer and supplication with thanksgiving let your requests be made known to God.
> 7 And the peace of God, which passeth all understanding, will keep your hearts and minds through Christ Jesus. (Webster)

We are **supposed** to let our requests be known to God. Remember when we studied James Chapter 4 and verse 2? This is where James says:

James 4:2b
> 2 …Yet you do not have because you do not ask. (NKJV)

We must bring our needs before God, our Provider. We must remember that He is our Father, and we should not hesitate to ask of Him in the small matters as well as the big. Some people feel they should only ask of God when those really huge problems arise, as though they have only so many wishes allowed and they are saving up their requests. Usually these people speak to God in prayer with

---

[1] Archibald Thomas Robertson, *Word Pictures in the New Testament, Volume 1* (Grand Rapids, MI: Baker Book House, 1930), 53.

the same infrequency, because they lack a real relationship with Him. But we know our God as our Father! He is not some genie in a bottle. We should **never** feel as though we are bothering Him, for our God is greater than that. Really, are not all needs small compared to His incomparable might?

We learned from 1st John 5:14-15, in our previous lessons, that we should have confidence when we ask anything according to God's will. Likewise, Hebrews Chapter 4 verse 16 tells us to:

Hebrews 4:16

16 ...therefore come boldly *(or with confidence)* to the throne of grace, that we may obtain mercy, and find grace to help in time of need. (Webster) *{Clarification in parenthesis added}*

Our Father does not want us to have any reservations about coming before Him and asking for help. We should understand this just from looking at the natural parent-child relationship. A good parent desires their child to share his or her needs and concerns with them. It is when the child does not ask and does not have confidence in the parents' provision that problems begin. And I do not believe I can emphasize too much that important Scripture in Matthew Chapter 7 verses 7 to 11 which we read back in Lesson Eleven. That is where Jesus teaches:

Matthew 7:7-11

7 "Ask, and it will be given to you; seek, and you will find; knock, and it will be opened to you.

8 "For everyone who asks receives, and he who seeks finds, and to him who knocks it will be opened.

9 "Or what man is there among you who, when his son asks for a loaf, will give him a stone?

10 "Or if he asks for a fish, he will not give him a snake, will he?

11 "If you then, being evil, know how to give good gifts to your children, how much more will your Father who is in heaven give what is good to those who ask Him!" (NASB)

Or as it says in the *King James Version*, "give good things to them that ask Him." Here Jesus refers to the natural parent-child relationship and shows how the majority of parents, even though they are sinners and do evil, will not deny the necessary things to their children. What a dramatic picture Jesus paints for us. What man, if his child asks for bread, will give that child a stone? Or if the child asks for a fish, will give him a serpent? No halfway normal person would play such a horrible, unfeeling game with his child. And yet many people have this type of perverse image of God, and that wrong understanding has even touched the church. They feel God does not want, or rarely wants, to give them the things they truly need. Or they feel that He does not care. Even worse, if Satan is trying to give them a serpent, they think this is God's will and forget that it is their Father's desire to give them bread.

When a child asks a parent, it is a natural thing for the parent to want to provide the good gift requested. But let me stop there for a minute, because we have an important qualifier: the gift must be a good gift, something that truly benefits the child. Jesus gave the examples of bread and fish to eat. If what we are asking is ultimately not good for us, it is not then in the Father's will. But if a child asks for a good gift, it is a natural thing for a parent to want to give it to him. Children touch the hearts of their parents. Consider the lengths people go to in order to make their children happy on their birthdays and at Christmas.

And if we who are evil know how to give good gifts to our children, how much more... HOW MUCH MORE... **HOW MUCH MORE**... will your Father in heaven—the Holy One, the One who is all good, the One who is Love and in whom there is no evil—give what is good to those who are His children through Jesus Christ. As we come to the kingdom of heaven as little children, He is *Abba*, our heavenly Dad who has entered into a covenant of love with us. And what does it say in Matthew 7:11? He gives good things to whom? He gives to those who ask Him! So again we see the importance of asking God. And that is exactly how Jesus starts the teaching:

Matthew 7:7

7   "Ask, and it will be given to you; seek, and you will find; knock, and it will be opened to you." (NASB)

The form of the Greek words used can mean a continual action: "keep asking", "keep seeking", "keep knocking." Even the succession of the phrases—ask, seek, knock—implies determination on the part of the petitioner. And that resolve is not without reward:

Matthew 7:8

8 "For everyone who asks receives, and he who seeks finds, and to him who knocks it will be opened." (NASB)

Remember back to early on in the study when we talked about God's rewards and looked at Hebrews 11:6 which says:

Hebrews 11:6

6 But without faith it is impossible to please Him: for he that cometh to God must believe that He is, and that He is a rewarder of them that <u>diligently seek</u> Him. (KJV) *{Emphasis added}*

God wants us to come to Him and seek His help, and the fact that Jesus teaches us to pray, "Give us this day," reinforces the understanding that we are to come regularly, daily, before God with our requests. He teaches them to pray on another occasion in Luke Chapter 11 verse 3:

Luke 11:3

3 "Give us <u>day by day</u> our daily bread." (NKJV) *{Emphasis added}*

This day by day principle is an important one. Bread, even today with all the preservatives that are added, will still spoil in a relatively short period of time, and new bread always needs to be made or purchased. So too there must be a constant asking of our Father and looking to Him each and every day for our requirements. And this is not without reason. Let us take a few moments to read the account of the *manna* from Exodus Chapter 16. In the second month of their departure from Egypt and its terrible slavery, in the wilderness the Israelites complained against Moses and Aaron. Starting at verse 3 we read:

Exodus 16:3-5

3 The Israelites said to them, "If only we had died by the LORD's hand in Egypt! There we sat around pots of meat and ate all the food we wanted, but you have brought us out into this desert to starve this entire assembly to death."

4 Then the LORD said to Moses, "I will rain down bread from heaven for you. The people are to go out each day and gather

enough for that day. In this way I will test them and see whether they will follow My instructions.

5 On the sixth day they are to prepare what they bring in, and that is to be twice as much as they gather on the other days." (NIV) *{Capitalization for deity added}*

Then down at verse 14:

Exodus 16:14-21

14 When the dew was gone, thin flakes like frost on the ground appeared on the desert floor.

15 When the Israelites saw it, they said to each other, "What is it?" For they did not know what it was.
Moses said to them, "It is the bread the LORD has given you to eat.

16 This is what the LORD has commanded: 'Everyone is to gather as much as they need. Take an omer *(approximately 2 liters)* for each person you have in your tent.'"

17 The Israelites did as they were told; some gathered much, some little.

18 And when they measured it by the omer, the one who gathered much did not have too much, and the one who gathered little did not have too little. Everyone had gathered just as much as they needed.

19 Then Moses said to them, "No one is to keep any of it until morning."

20 However, some of them paid no attention to Moses; they kept part of it until morning, but it was full of maggots and began to smell. So Moses was angry with them.

21 Each morning everyone gathered as much as they needed, and when the sun grew hot, it melted away. (NIV) *{Measurement clarification in parenthesis added}*

Exodus 16:31

31 And the house of Israel called its name Manna: and it was like coriander-seed, white; and the taste of it was like wafers made with honey. (Webster)

Thus God established this daily cycle with the Israelites for their supernatural nourishment from heaven. Notice first that the bread came down from heaven. God was the source. And really, God is ultimately the source of all the things we require. He is that He is. Second, notice that they had to gather the manna each day, day by day, except the day before the Sabbath when they were to gather for that day and the next (so that they could rest on the Sabbath). Here again we have this daily dependency. Third, even if someone gathered much, they did not have more than their present need. And if they tried to keep some overnight (apart from the Sabbath exception), the manna itself would spoil and be unusable for the following day.

And so the next day God would supply bread from heaven all over again. The manna, then, was a reminder to Israel of God's providential care for them. They needed to see first that He was the source and they were dependent upon Him. Then they needed to enter into this daily relationship with Him of believing Him for His provision. And really no matter how much a person has, no matter how secure they think they are, in one minute they can find out just how dependent they are on the Lord for their very being and survival. If there is one thing we should learn from this life, it is that, on our own, we have little guarantee of even our next breath. But everything comes from God.

Just like the rain which pours down and then cycles back to the heavens to come down again, so too is prayer. It is a constant daily cycle of dependence on God. We offer up our requests to God to give us this day our daily bread, and God rains down the provision, only for us to come back tomorrow and seek Him again. The beauty is that, under the New Covenant, we are in a blessed Sabbath relationship of rest with God through Jesus, so that we can pray for Him to give us this day the bread that suffices for this day and the morrow.

And as we walk constantly in this day to day dependence, faith and a relationship based on faith develops, which we will talk about in our next lesson.

LESSON SIXTEEN

————————✄————————

Today, we continue examining Matthew 6:11 where Jesus teaches us to pray, "Give us this day our daily bread." In our last lesson, we saw how God wants us to come before Him daily and ask Him for all our needs. As our Heavenly Father, He desires to give good things to His children. Also, we spoke about our daily reliance on Him, how we are to ask Him each day for that which we need for the coming day. And as He answers those prayers, faith grows and a relationship develops based on faith, where it becomes natural to believe each day in the goodness of our God. Our walk with the Lord is, as it says in Romans 1:17, from faith to faith, and it is not enough to ask and believe for just one day; rather, we must come to Him day by day and ask Him and believe Him for our daily bread.

Romans 1:17

> 17 For therein *[in the gospel of Christ]* is the righteousness of God revealed from faith to faith: as it is written, "The just shall live by faith." (KJV) *{Clarification added from verse 16}*

In our last lesson, we studied how the Israelites complained against Moses and Aaron after they came out of Egypt. They had seen God secure their freedom from slavery by sending miraculous plagues upon the Egyptians. They had seen the Red Sea part, so that they could cross over, and then close up again over Pharaoh's pursuing chariots. Yet, they did not believe God when they were hungry in the wilderness, but grumbled and longed for Egypt. Then God sent them bread from heaven which they called *manna*, which came each morning, and which, we are told in Psalm 78:25, was angels' food. Daily, for six days of each week, God provided the manna. During each of those days the people had to gather it, for if they kept some of it over to the next day, it bred worms and stank. But on the sixth day they were permitted to gather enough for two days. On the Sabbath they could not gather, and, miraculously, the two-day supply did not spoil.

Now God established this rule of constant dependence on Him for manna to eat for a reason. In Deuteronomy 8:3, Moses tells the Israelites why God did this. He says:

Deuteronomy 8:3

3   He humbled you, causing you to hunger and then feeding you with manna, which neither you nor your ancestors had known, to teach you that man does not live on bread alone but on every word that comes from the mouth of the LORD. (NIV)

So more important than the nourishment for their bodies was the nourishment for their souls. At the first sign of difficulty, they had forgotten God's love and concern for them. They had forgotten the promises He had made to them and to their forefathers. Therefore God humbled them and, through the system of manna, reminded them that not only is He the Provider and Source, but that they live only by an *active, living relationship with Him*. And every piece of manna they collected was a reminder of this relationship—a reminder of God's faithfulness in supernaturally providing that which He had promised, not just once, but day in and day out.

Furthermore, they each needed to live by the revelation of God's holy Word to His people. They needed to hear Him, to know His ways and obey His commands. Every word, every proclamation, every point of guidance that proceeded from His mouth was essential in order to feed the scarcity that was deep inside their beings. In Matthew Chapter 4, we read how Jesus was also in the wilderness. He had fasted forty days and, afterward, He too was hungry. We read in verses 3 and 4:

Matthew 4:3-4

3   The tempter came to Him and said, "If You are the Son of God, tell these stones to become bread."

4   Jesus answered, "It is written: 'Man shall not live on bread alone, but on every word that comes from the mouth of God.'" (NIV) *{Capitalization for deity added}*

Unlike the Israelites, who after one and a half months of freedom grumbled because of their lack of food, though they had left Egypt with a great deal of livestock (Exodus 12:38), Jesus purposely fasted so as to have spiritual strength to face the enemy. And when Satan tried to get Him to perform an act out of desperation, to break the fast because of the hunger, Jesus quoted from Deuteronomy 8:3, "It is written: 'Man shall not live on bread alone, but on every word that comes from the mouth of God.'" His most important food, His most important sustenance, was not physical bread but spiritual bread— every Word from His Father's mouth. This was where He received His strength.

Understand that we are made the very same way. And we must remember this when we go before God and we ask in prayer. We are not just a body: we are each a tripartite person. You might be asking what I mean by this. It means that we have three parts to ourselves: a spirit, a soul, and a body. In 1st Thessalonians 5:23, Paul writes:

1Thessalonians 5:23

> 23 Now may the God of peace Himself sanctify you entirely; and may your spirit and soul and body be preserved complete, without blame at the coming of our Lord Jesus Christ. (NASB) *{Emphasis added}*

Because we are tripartite, when we pray we must bear in mind that we need nourishment for all three. Remember the account when Jesus fed the five thousand? With only five barley loaves and two fish He miraculously multiplied them to feed five thousand men plus women and children. And when they had all eaten and were satisfied, Jesus instructed His disciples to…

John 6:12b

> 12 …"Gather the fragments that remain, that nothing may be lost." (Webster)

They were able to pick up twelve full baskets of the broken pieces, a full basket for each of the twelve apostles, and these would be ample provisions for the next day for the Lord's close group of immediate followers. Under the New Covenant, there is excess bread; that is, there is a special Sabbath provision this day for the needs of the morrow which believer's in Jesus experience every day!

So, when the multitude saw the sign which He had performed, they intended to come and make Him king by force. But Jesus sent His disciples on ahead that evening in a boat to the other side of the Sea of Galilee and He withdrew to the mountain alone. This was the night when the disciples encountered a severe storm and were battered by the winds until Jesus came to them in the early morning hours, walking on the water. And the next day, the multitude that had been fed, when they discovered that Jesus was no longer there, got into boats and crossed over seeking Him. However, Jesus reproves them in John 6:26, saying:

John 6:26

> 26 ..."Truly, truly, I say to you, you seek Me, not because you saw signs, but because you ate of the loaves and were filled." (NASB)

The Lord knew their wrong attitude. They did not want to make Him king because the miraculous sign had demonstrated to them that they needed the truth of His way and His salvation. Rather, they enjoyed having their physical needs met. And Jesus goes on to tell them in verse 27:

John 6:27-29

> 27 "Do not work for the food which perishes, but for the food which endures to eternal life, which the Son of Man will give to you, for on Him the Father, God, has set His seal."
> 28 Therefore they said to Him, "What shall we do, so that we may work the works of God?"
> 29 Jesus answered and said to them, "This is the work of God, that you believe in Him whom He has sent." (NASB)

People sometimes ask, "What work must I do to go to heaven?" But Jesus tells us that the work required of us is to believe in Him whom God sent. Then Jesus gives us real food, spiritual food that endures to everlasting life.

It is amazing to me that, even after experiencing the great miracle of the multiplying of the loaves and fish, they answer this teaching by saying in John 6:30-31:

John 6:30-31

    30 ..."What then do You do for a sign, so that we may see, and believe You? What work do You perform?

    31 "Our fathers ate the manna in the wilderness; as it is written, 'HE GAVE THEM BREAD OUT OF HEAVEN TO EAT.'" (NASB)

Perhaps they were hoping they could get Him to supernaturally multiply bread every day so that they would never have to work again. They were locked in on their bodily needs but they did not recognize their spiritual starvation, which the Son of Man came to satisfy. And this does not mean that our physical needs are not important to God. Did not Jesus wonderfully provide for them the day before, when the hour was late and they had come to see Him in a desolate place. In addition, Matthew and Luke tell us that He had compassion on that multitude and healed their sick. But we are also told in Mark and Luke that He taught them many things about the kingdom of God. And that is the key. The Lord knows there are physical necessities required for us to live and be productive for Him in this world, and He does not want us to worry about tomorrow. We must trust that He cares about us, and all—**all!**—the things we need will be added to us, as we do what is right. But our first priority must be to seek the kingdom of God and His righteousness.

We have touched on this before, but let us take a minute to read the Scripture from Matthew Chapter 6 verses 25 to 33:

Matthew 6:25-33

    25 "For this reason I say to you, do not be worried about your life, as to what you will eat or what you will drink; nor for your body, as to what you will put on. Is not life more than food, and the body more than clothing?

    26 "Look at the birds of the air, that they do not sow, nor reap nor gather into barns, and yet your heavenly Father feeds them. Are you not worth much more than they?

    27 "And who of you by being worried can add a single hour to his life?

    28 "And why are you worried about clothing? Observe how the lilies of the field grow; they do not toil nor do they spin,

    29 yet I say to you that not even Solomon in all his glory clothed himself like one of these.

30 "But if God so clothes the grass of the field, which is alive today and tomorrow is thrown into the furnace, will He not much more clothe you? You of little faith!

31 "Do not worry then, saying, 'What will we eat?' or 'What will we drink?' or 'What will we wear for clothing?'

32 "For the Gentiles eagerly seek all these things; for your heavenly Father knows that you need all these things.

33 "But seek first His kingdom and His righteousness, and all these things will be added to you." (NASB) *{Emphasis added}*

Like most people, the multitude on the shores of Galilee that day did not understand their overriding spiritual emptiness. So when they ask for a sign and remind Him about the manna in the desert, He answers them starting in verse 32:

John 6:32-35

32 Then Jesus said to them, "Most assuredly, I say to you, Moses did not give you the bread from heaven, but My Father gives you the true bread from heaven.

33 "For the bread of God is He who comes down from heaven and gives life to the world."

34 Then they said to Him, "Lord, give us this bread always."

35 And Jesus said to them, "I am the bread of life. He who comes to Me shall never hunger, and he who believes in Me shall never thirst." (NKJV)

And down at verse 47 He tells them:

John 6:47-51

47 "Most assuredly, I say to you, he who believes in Me has everlasting life.

48 "I am the bread of life.

49 "Your fathers ate the manna in the wilderness, and are dead.

50 "This is the bread which comes down from heaven, that one may eat of it and not die.

51 "I am the living bread which came down from heaven. If anyone eats of this bread, he will live forever; and the bread that I shall give is My flesh, which I shall give for the life of the world." (NKJV)

The sacrifice that Jesus made for us on the cross would provide us with real food—new life for our spirits and souls and even our bodies, even unto the resurrection from the dead. And when we feed on Jesus, when we desire His life to be inside our hearts, we will never hunger. He is the true bread from heaven which, unlike the manna, never spoils. So then when we pray, we should desire and ask not just for the "food" that satisfies our physical needs, but we must also earnestly seek the food for our souls—that is, His Word—and the food for our spirits—that is, His Holy Spirit and His life.

We should daily pray for the Father to feed us through His Word, the Bible. We should ask Him to open and renew our minds—our souls—to understand the Scriptures and to show us what we need to know so that we are well fed and nourished and prepared for the day to come. And we should pray daily and ask for the abundance of the Holy Spirit—an outpouring of the Spirit's life and grace, gifts and guidance, into our spirits that we can be new people. We should ask this so that we would not be empty and dead but alive in fellowship with God, the bread of His Son Jesus sustaining us.

Jesus said in Matthew 5 verse 6:

Matthew 5:6

6   "Blessed are they who hunger and thirst for righteousness: for they <u>shall</u> be filled." (Webster) *{Emphasis added}*

It is certainly a sign of salvation when we yearn for every word that proceeds from the mouth of our God—when we desire His guidance and long for the inner food of His righteousness. Any less of an attitude will end in starvation. And when a man starves in his inner self, how great is the starvation!

LESSON SEVENTEEN

——————∝——————

Today we come to a very important part of the Lord's Prayer, where Jesus teaches us to pray to the Father in Matthew 6:12:

Matthew 6:12

12 "And forgive us our debts,
As we forgive our debtors." (NKJV)

And in Chapter 11 of the gospel of Luke, when Jesus' disciples asked Him to teach them to pray, Jesus again taught them the Lord's Prayer, this time saying in verse 4:

Luke 11:4a

4 "And forgive us our sins,
For we also forgive everyone who is indebted to us. ..." (NKJV)

Let us begin by discussing the first part of this petition, "forgive us our debts," or as we have it in Luke, "forgive us our sins." It is so crucial to successful prayer for us to deal with our sins. In Psalm 66 verses 18 to 20, the Scripture reads:

Psalm 66:18-20

18 If I had cherished *(or regarded)* sin in my heart,
the Lord would not have listened;
19 but God has surely listened
and has heard my prayer.
20 Praise be to God,
who has not rejected my prayer
or withheld His love from me! (NIV)
{Clarification in parenthesis and capitalization for deity added}

If we hold on to our sins in our hearts, if we do not face them and confess them to God, and if we do not seek His forgiveness and His grace and the ability to sin no more, the Lord will not hear our prayers. We are not praying as we have learned in 1st John 5:14, "according to His will," and so our prayers are in danger of being rejected.

Sadly, it is one of the great dangers of our generation that sin is often denied. The very word *"sin"* brings up images to many of some uneducated, medieval value system. And since, by modern standards, very little is considered sinful, if you speak about the reality of sin you are at risk of being criticized for creating unnecessary guilt. Yet the sinfulness of the world is as evident as ever. But society today is, to a large part, in a state of denial. And in that denial, there is a lack of concern for what God has told us in His Word is right and what is wrong. Too often on TV you will see the truth of God's Word used as the food for some comedian's derisive joke. And too often a minister or someone coming from the Christian perspective, who is attempting to deal with the moral wrongs of our culture, will be laughed away by the "you don't still believe that" posture of the other debaters.

We have become the laughing generation. But there is nothing funny about the end results of sin. In America, we see our families literally dissolving at an astounding rate. Children no longer can enjoy neither the security of childhood nor its innocence. Hardheartedness and ignorance, brutality and lust, are rampant. Hopelessness and despair have become epidemic as many cannot find any reason for life, and many do not even care. And yet our prayers as a nation are often flowery and bright, often asking for God's blessing while side stepping totally the question of sin. But Proverb 28:9 warns that:

Proverbs 28:9

9 He that turneth away his ear from hearing the law, even his prayer shall be abomination. (KJV)

And Proverb 28:13 states:

Proverbs 28:13

13 He that covereth his sins shall not prosper: but he who con-
fesseth and forsaketh them shall have mercy. (Webster)

When we are not concerned for God's ways, when we try to whitewash and deny our sins, our very prayers are an abomination to God, and we should not think that He will prosper us. Rather we find mercy when we come out of our prideful denial and we confess our sins and renounce them. Remember early in the study when we read from Solomon's temple dedication in 1st Kings? This dedication is also spoken of in the book of 2nd Chronicles. After the dedication ceremony, the Lord appeared to Solomon by night. We will read from 2nd Chronicles Chapter 7 verses 12 to 14:

2 Chronicles 7:12-14

12 And the LORD appeared to Solomon by night, and said to him, "I have heard thy prayer, and have chosen this place to Myself for a house of sacrifice.

13 "If I shut up heaven that there be no rain, or if I command the locusts to devour the land, or if I send pestilence among My people;

14 "If My people, who are called by My name, shall <u>humble themselves</u>, and <u>pray</u>, and <u>seek My face</u>, and <u>turn from their wicked ways</u>; then will I hear from heaven, and will forgive their sin, and will heal their land." (Webster) *{Emphasis added}*

It is clear from this passage that there is a terrible price to be paid for sin. However, when we humble ourselves and pray and seek our God, confessing and turning from our iniquities, then and only then can we receive His forgiveness and the healing of our land. And that is true for a nation, and it is true for an individual.

It is sinful human nature to recognize sin in others while minimizing our own sins—being in that state of denial I mentioned before. Because of our sins, we owe, as Jesus taught, a debt or a penalty to God. Our sins cause hurt and they cause pain and they cause unrighteousness to prosper, and God just cannot laugh that away, as some modern theologies would like us to believe. Our God is love, but our God is also justice, and sin breaks our fellowship with God.

A debt is incurred which demands expiation, that is, payment by way of penalty to atone or make amends for the trespass. But the good news of the gospel is that Jesus paid this price for us. He <u>redeemed</u> us. That which was owed because of our sins, that which was legally due to fulfill righteousness, He paid on the cross with His life.

In Romans Chapter 3 verses 21 to 26 we read:

Romans 3:21-26

21 But now apart from the Law the righteousness of God has been manifested, being witnessed by the Law and the Prophets,

22 even the righteousness of God through faith in Jesus Christ for all *(to all and upon all)* those who believe; for there is no distinction;

23 <u>for all have sinned and fall short of the glory of God</u>,

24 being justified as a gift by His grace through <u>the redemption</u> which is in Christ Jesus;

25 whom God displayed publicly as a <u>propitiation</u> in His blood through faith. This was to demonstrate His righteousness, because in the forbearance of God He passed over the sins previously committed;

26 for the demonstration, I say, of His righteousness at the present time, so that He would be just and the justifier of the one who has faith in Jesus. (NASB) *{Emphasis and clarification in parenthesis added}*

That word *propitiation* in verse 25 could be translated, "a sacrifice of atonement." Jesus made that sacrifice with the shedding of His blood. And this Scripture tells us that in this sacrifice God demonstrates His righteousness. He is a Just God, understanding the horror of sin and requiring a penalty for it. But He is also the Justifier, the price being paid not by us but in an act of love by God the Son. So we see His righteousness in His justice, and we see His righteousness in His love and mercy, and we see both at the cross.

We all have sinned, we all "fall short" of the glory of God. The literal meaning of the Greek word for sin is "to miss the mark," and if we are honest with ourselves we all know how we have "missed the mark" many times in our lives. But God freely gives us the gift of redemption in Christ Jesus as we believe and have faith in Him. His shed blood paid the debt we owed. It is only on the foundation of what He accomplished that we can pray, "Father, forgive us our sins." Remember what we read in Ephesians 1:7 back in Lesson Nine:

Ephesians 1:7

7   In Him we have redemption through His blood, the forgiveness of sins, according to the riches of His grace (NKJV)

Isaiah prophesied ahead seven centuries before the birth of Jesus:

Isaiah 53:5-6

5   But He was wounded for our transgressions, He was bruised for our iniquities: the chastisement of our peace was upon Him; and with His stripes we are healed.

6   All we like sheep have gone astray; we have turned every one to his own way; and the LORD hath laid on Him the iniquity of us all. (KJV)

And Hebrews 9:22 tells us:

Hebrews 9:22

22 And almost all things are by the law cleansed with blood; and without shedding of blood is no remission *(that is, there is no forgiveness)*. (Webster) *{Clarification in parenthesis added}*

I believe the price of this forgiveness is often not fully appreciated. Peter writes in 1st Peter Chapter 1 and verses 17 to 19:

1 Peter 1:17-19

17 If you address as Father the One who impartially judges according to each one's work, conduct yourselves in fear during the time of your stay on earth;

18 knowing that you were not redeemed with perishable things like silver or gold from your futile way of life inherited from your forefathers,

19 but with precious blood, as of a lamb unblemished and spotless, the blood of Christ. (NASB)

Later, in Chapter 2 starting at verse 22, he writes the following of Jesus:

1 Peter 2:22-24

22 WHO COMMITTED NO SIN, NOR WAS ANY DECEIT FOUND IN HIS MOUTH;

23 and while being reviled, He did not revile in return; while suffering, He uttered no threats, but kept entrusting Himself to Him who judges righteously;

24 and He Himself bore our sins in His body on the cross, so that we might die to sin and live to righteousness; for by His wounds you were healed. (NASB)

Because He never once sinned, He could redeem us from our sins. And we are called, in Him, to live for righteousness. Now this does not mean that once we come to the Lord Jesus we will never sin again. Remember He teaches His disciples to pray, "Forgive us our debts." The apostle John tells us in 1st John 1:8 that:

1 John 1:8

8 If we say that we have no sin, we deceive ourselves, and the truth is not in us. (KJV)

But then in verse 9 he tells us what we must do if we sin:

1 John 1:9

9 If we confess our sins, He is faithful and just to forgive us our sins, and to cleanse us from all unrighteousness. (KJV)

Again we see that we must face our sins and confess them to God and not hide them. And then we have this wonderful promise, "He is faithful and just to forgive us our sins, and to cleanse us from all unrighteousness." Now this promise does not mean that we have a free ticket to sin. For that matter, John goes on to say in Chapter 2 verse 1:

1 John 2:1a

1 My little children, I am writing these things to you so that you <u>may not sin</u>. ... (NASB) *{Emphasis added}*

But then he continues:

1 John 2:1b

1   …And if anyone sins, we have an Advocate with the Father, Jesus Christ the righteous; (NASB)

So our overwhelming desire should be not to sin. But when we do sin, we should immediately go to the Father through our Lord Jesus to seek His forgiveness and the power to sin no more. Later in this first letter of John, starting at Chapter 3 verse 4, the apostle writes:

1 John 3:4-9

4   Everyone who practices sin also practices lawlessness; and sin is lawlessness.

5   You know that He appeared in order to take away sins; and in Him there is no sin.

6   No one who abides in Him sins; no one who sins has seen Him or knows Him.

7   Little children, make sure no one deceives you; the one who practices righteousness is righteous, just as He is righteous;

8   the one who practices sin is of the devil; for the devil has sinned from the beginning. The Son of God appeared for this purpose, to destroy the works of the devil.

9   No one who is born of God practices sin, because His seed abides in him; and he cannot sin, because he is born of God. (NASB)

John is talking here about an intentional attitude of sin. When we are in Christ and His Spirit is in us, it hurts when we sin. We do not want to sin. And we are constantly confessing to the Lord in prayer so that we will not continue to sin. But we know all too well the twist on Christianity that rears its head in all different types of churches, which basically says, "I don't have to worry about what I do. I can do anything I want, and all I have to do then is confess it and God will forgive me. And then I can go out and do it all over again." But what does the Scripture say about such an attitude:

Galatians 6:7

7   Be not deceived; God is not mocked: for whatsoever a man soweth, that shall he also reap. (KJV)

And to the church at Corinth, Paul writes:

1 Corinthians 6:9-11

9   Or do you not know that the unrighteous will not inherit the kingdom of God? Do not be deceived; neither fornicators, nor idolaters, nor adulterers, nor effeminate, nor homosexuals,

10 nor thieves, nor the covetous, nor drunkards, nor revilers, nor swindlers, will inherit the kingdom of God.

11 Such were some of you; but you were washed, but you were sanctified, but you were justified in the name of the Lord Jesus Christ and in the Spirit of our God. (NASB)

Sin not faced, not brought <u>honestly</u> to the cross of Jesus, can destroy our position in the kingdom of God and impair our prayers. In 1ˢᵗ Peter 3:7 we read:

1 Peter 3:7

7   Husbands, in the same way be considerate as you live with your wives, and treat them with respect as the weaker partner and as heirs with you of the gracious gift of life, <u>so that nothing will hinder your prayers</u>. (NIV) *{Emphasis added}*

We cannot expect to receive from God the great answers to our prayers if we are secretly holding on to some sin in our hearts with no intention of letting go. But acknowledging and confessing our sin restores our relationship in the Lord and the access to all His wonderful promises. James writes starting in James 5:14:

James 5:14-16

14 Is anyone among you sick? Then he must call for the elders of the church and they are to pray over him, anointing him with oil in the name of the Lord;

15 and the prayer offered in faith will restore the one who is sick, and the Lord will raise him up, and if he has committed sins, they will be forgiven him.

16 Therefore, confess your sins to one another, and pray for one another so that you may be healed. The effective prayer of a righteous man can accomplish much. (NASB)

In the same way, Paul cautioned the Corinthian church in 1ˢᵗ Corinthians Chapter 11. There were some in the church who were coming to the Lord's Supper in an unworthy manner, without examining themselves. And Paul gave this as the reason why many in the church were weak and sick and why many had died. And then he says in verse 31:

1 Corinthians 11:31
> 31 But if we judged ourselves rightly, we would not be judged. (NASB)

What an important Scripture. We could save so much pain in our lives if we would just come before the Lord and truly confess our sins and seek His forgiveness and help.

LESSON EIGHTEEN

————⟨✕⟩————

In our last lesson we were studying that part of the Lord's Prayer in Matthew 6:12 where we are taught to pray:

Matthew 6:12

> 12 "And forgive us our debts,
> As we forgive our debtors." (NKJV)

We also looked at the corresponding teaching in Luke 11:4 where Jesus says:

Luke 11:4a

> 4 "And forgive us our sins,
> For we also forgive everyone who is indebted to
> us. ..." (NKJV)

We see how the Lord, in both versions of the Our Father, brings us to a knowledge of our sins—our debts—which we must bring before God, asking His forgiveness, if prayer is to be both successful and a true communication based on sincerity. Our transgressions separate us from the Father, and unless they are faced, unless they are dealt with, the barrier that remains disables our prayers making them of little effect. We cannot come before the Lord in pride, but rather we must come before Him humbly seeking mercy. We cannot come before Him hiding and cherishing sin in our heart, but we must draw close to Him willing to let Him crucify the sin inside of us. We studied last time from 1st John 3:5-6 that:

1 John 3:5-6

5   … He appeared in order to take away sins; and in Him there is no sin.

6   No one who abides in Him sins; no one who sins has seen Him or knows Him. (NASB)

Therefore, if we truly desire this deep walk with God, if we are really genuine in our approach to God in prayer, then when He lives in us and we abide in Him, sin has no place. Instead, it is recognized, confessed, forgiven in Jesus, and done away with.

We can see from this part of the Lord's Prayer why believers' prayers are not always effective. While part of us might long for that close relationship with the Lord, part of us might also be holding on tightly to some sin. And Satan can use that unwillingness to repent as a strong wedge to drive between us and the Lord. But the wonderful promise of God, which we studied last time in 1st John 1:9, says that:

1 John 1:9

9   If we confess our sins, He is faithful and just to forgive us our sins, and to cleanse us from all unrighteousness. (KJV)

King David is a good example of this. Do you know that in the Scriptures David is called, in 1st Samuel 13:14, *a man after God's own heart*? And in 1st Kings 15:5 we read:

1 Kings 15:5

5   …David did what was right in the sight of the LORD, and had not turned aside from anything that He commanded him all the days of his life, <u>except in the case of Uriah the Hittite</u>. (NASB) *{Emphasis added}*

That was when David committed adultery with Uriah's wife, Bathsheba. Then, when she became pregnant, he tried to cover his sin by calling Uriah from the battlefield to be with his wife. But when he refused to go to his home, David, in a final attempt to conceal his sin, gave orders to his general to put Uriah in the forefront of the fiercest battle and then abandon him to be killed by the enemy (2 Samuel Chapter 11). So even David, a man who we are told in 1st Kings 14:8 followed God with all his heart, sinned and sinned terribly.

And he increased his transgression in his attempt to cover it over. And isn't that what happens when we do not face our sins, but try to hide and deny them. Matters go from bad to worse.

But then in 2ⁿᵈ Samuel Chapter 12 we read how the prophet Nathan came to David and confronted him with his offense. David, understanding how truly evil his deeds had been, repented and confessed before the prophet. And from this recognition of his sin, David composed Psalm 51. Psalm 51 is really a prayer set to music— David's prayer of repentance after Nathan went to him. Let us read from part of this very moving Psalm, and I would ask you to listen carefully for the spirit of a man who is truly penitent.

Psalm 51:1-17

1 Have mercy upon me, O God, according to Thy lovingkindness: according unto the multitude of Thy tender mercies blot out my transgressions.
2 Wash me throughly from mine iniquity, and cleanse me from my sin.
3 For I acknowledge my transgressions: and my sin is ever before me.
4 Against Thee, Thee only, have I sinned, and done this evil in Thy sight: that Thou mightest be justified when Thou speakest, and be clear *(blameless)* when Thou judgest.
5 Behold, I was shapen in iniquity; and in sin did my mother conceive me.
6 Behold, Thou desirest truth in the inward parts: and in the hidden part Thou shalt make me to know wisdom.
7 Purge me with hyssop, and I shall be clean: wash me, and I shall be whiter than snow.
8 Make me to hear joy and gladness; that the bones which Thou hast broken may rejoice.
9 Hide Thy face from my sins, and blot out all mine iniquities.
10 Create in me a clean heart, O God; and renew a right spirit within me.
11 Cast me not away from Thy presence; and take not Thy Holy Spirit from me.
12 Restore unto me the joy of Thy salvation; and uphold me with Thy free *(generous)* Spirit.
13 Then will I teach transgressors Thy ways; and sinners shall be converted unto Thee.

14 Deliver me from bloodguiltiness, O God, Thou God of my salvation: and my tongue shall sing aloud of Thy righteousness.

15 O Lord, open Thou my lips; and my mouth shall shew forth Thy praise.

16 For Thou desirest not sacrifice; else would I give it: Thou delightest not in burnt offering.

17 The sacrifices of God are a broken spirit: a broken and a contrite heart, O God, Thou wilt not despise. (KJV) *{Clarification in parentheses added}*

David could have had sacrifices offered every day and night at the altar for his sin, but if inside his heart he was not truly broken and not truly sorry—if inside he still cherished his sin and maintained his rebellion—no outward sign or observance would have restored his relationship with God. One thing is a certainty: we might fool other people, but we cannot lie to God's Holy Spirit. David was truly a broken man and God knew it. When he prayed for the Lord to have mercy on him and cleanse him from his sins, all his heart and all his will were in that prayer. That is why he prays, "Create in me a clean heart, O God; and renew a right spirit within me."

David had had enough of sin. He wanted God to restore him and change what was wrong in him. And that is why he was forgiven and can still be called a man after God's own heart. Likewise, this should be our attitude when we pray, "Father, forgive us our debts." Psalm 51 is certainly a fine example of prayer for forgiveness.

All right, now let us consider the full verse of Matthew 6:12:

Matthew 6:12

12 "And forgive us our debts,
As we forgive our debtors." (NKJV) *{Emphasis added}*

Or:

Luke 11:4a

4 "...For we also forgive everyone who is indebted to us. ..." (NKJV)

We are asking God to forgive us our sins—the debts we owe— just as we likewise forgive those who, because of their sins, are under an obligation to us: they owe us because of their sins against

145

us. But they are no more able to pay the full price for their sins than we are. Rather, Jesus paid the price for us all. In 1st Corinthians Chapter 13 verses 4 and 5, Paul writes:

1 Corinthians 13:4-5

4   Love is patient, love is kind. It does not envy, it does not boast, it is not proud.

5   It does not dishonor others, it is not self-seeking, it is not easily angered, it keeps no record of wrongs. (NIV) *{Emphasis added}*

Some translations of the Bible will read, "thinks no evil," instead of, "it keeps no record of wrongs." But the actual Greek word used means to take an inventory, to reckon or count up or take account of, as in a ledger or tally sheet. Therefore, not only does love not plan evil, but love does not take into account—it does not reckon up or calculatingly consider—the evil done to it.

And 1st John 4:16 tells us that our God is love. That is why He does not hold our sins against us but rather puts the debt on His Son's account. This is the forgiveness and mercy of love. So if we do not forgive those that have sinned against us, who owe us a debt, we are not praying as His children nor are we praying as members of the kingdom of light. John wrote in 1st John 2 verses 9 to 11:

1 John 2:9-11

9   He that saith he is in the light, and hateth his brother, is in darkness even until now.

10 He that loveth his brother abideth in the light, and there is none occasion of stumbling in him.

11 But he that hateth his brother is in darkness, and walketh in darkness, and knoweth not whither he goeth, because that darkness hath blinded his eyes. (KJV)

Not only does unforgivingness jeopardize our communion with God because we are praying as though in the kingdom of darkness, but a persistent attitude of being unwilling to forgive actually endangers the mercy God shows to us. For God's mercy depends on our position in Christ. And how much have we accepted Jesus if we do not desire His Spirit of forgiveness? As it is written in 1st John 2:4-6:

1 John 2:4-6

4   The one who says, "I have come to know Him," and does not keep His commandments, is a liar, and the truth is not in him;

5   but whoever keeps His word, in him the love of God has truly been perfected. By this we know that we are in Him:

6   the one who says he abides in Him ought himself to walk in the same manner as He walked. (NASB)

We must walk as Jesus walked, and His life was a ministry of forgiveness. Amen! Now read on ahead in Matthew Chapter 6 to verses 14 and 15. These are the verses that immediately follow the Lord's Prayer and are actually continuous with His teaching on prayer which began back in verse 5. With these verses, it is as though Jesus is emphasizing a critical point that we need to know when we pray, which He has already touched on in the prayer itself. He says:

Matthew 6:14-15

14   "For if you forgive men their trespasses, your heavenly Father will also forgive you.

15   "But if you do not forgive men their trespasses, neither will your Father forgive your trespasses." (NKJV)

You cannot get any clearer than that. When we come before the Lord in prayer we must come with an attitude of forgiveness, desiring to see others, who have sinned against us, also forgiven and brought into the kingdom. This is foundational to effective prayer: we should want to see anyone saved who can be saved, and we should not want any harm they have brought against us to be a hindrance to that salvation.

Consider Stephen, the martyr, who we read about in Acts Chapter 7. The Council and people took him out of the city and stoned him for his testimony of Jesus. In verse 59 we read:

Acts 7:59-60

59   They went on stoning Stephen as he called on the Lord and said, "Lord Jesus, receive my spirit!"

60   Then falling on his knees, he cried out with a loud voice, "Lord, do not hold this sin against them!" Having said this, he fell asleep. (NASB)

We read up above in verse 58 that as they cast Stephen out of the city to stone him, the false witnesses against him laid down their clothes at the feet of a certain young man, as though to have him protect the garments while they performed the execution. Obviously this young man was in agreement with them, and in Chapter 8 verse 1 the Scripture plainly tells us he gave approval to Stephen's death. That certain young man was Saul, later to become the apostle Paul. And I believe that Stephen's prayer of forgiveness set things in motion in the heavenly realms which would ultimately result in the conversion of Paul and the salvation of the multitudes brought in by Paul's ministry.

Now there is a very important point we must understand when we speak about forgiveness. When we talk about praying a prayer of forgiveness, it does not mean that we are asking the Lord to condone, or excuse, or bless the sin of the person we are forgiving. While Jesus teaches us in the Sermon on the Mount to bless those that curse us and to pray for those who spitefully use us and perse-cute us (Matthew 5:44), the blessing and the prayer are obviously for their repentance and salvation. We are not to bless the sin they do, nor are we to pray for their continual success so they can keep doing it. That would not be showing true love for them nor would it be praying for the kingdom of God to come.

It would be the same as if Stephen had also prayed for the Council and its members, who were persecuting believers, to be abundantly blessed in this world in all their endeavors. That would have been a wrongful prayer because it would have been asking something that would not only hurt the going forth of the gospel, but would be opposite from God's will and what Jesus had prophesied for them because of their unbelief.

So forgiveness does not mean that we automatically pray for someone to prosper! Rather we are called as members of the kingdom to have the mind of Christ and to bind and loose in the wisdom of the Holy Spirit, seeking the Spirit's guidance for the specifics of our prayers. Our foundational attitude is, however, like Stephen's—one of true forgiveness for the person who has sinned against us, with the goal that that person is saved from his or her sins, not flourish in them.

LESSON NINETEEN

———————∝———————

I n the previous lesson in this study series on prayer, we looked at
that part of the Lord's Prayer where we are taught to pray:

Matthew 6:12
> 12 "And forgive us our debts,
>   As we forgive our debtors." (NKJV)

We saw how true forgiveness for the person who has sinned
against us is foundational to our walk as a Christian and our relationship with God. Yet while that basic Biblical teaching is clear, how we
actually implement forgiveness can sometimes be very perplexing.
It is very evident from the Scriptures that we should desire to see
anyone saved who can be saved, and we should not want their
sins against us—their "debts"—to be a hindrance to that salvation.
But just how and when we communicate that forgiveness and what
boundaries, if any, apply to the forgiveness is a more difficult topic.

When Jesus appeared to the disciples on the evening of His
resurrection, we read in the twentieth chapter of the Gospel of John
starting at verse 21:

John 20:21-23
> 21 So Jesus said to them again, "Peace be with you; as the Father
>   has sent Me, I also send you."
> 22 And when He had said this, He breathed on them and said to
>   them, "Receive the Holy Spirit.
> 23 "If you forgive the sins of any, their sins have been for-
>   given them; if you retain the sins of any, they have been
>   retained." (NASB)

So when Jesus' disciples went out in the power of the Holy Spirit, preaching the good news of repentance and forgiveness of sins in His name (Luke 24:47), they also had the authority to retain sins. Under the anointing of the Holy Spirit, they were given the authority to preach the gospel that could set men and women free from their sins. And, if the message was rejected, they had the authority to testify that the ones who refused to receive God's Word and to believe in God's Son remained in their sins.

Prior to the cross, Jesus gave instructions to the twelve apostles when He first sent them out two by two. And remember the 70 we read about in Lesson Six? He also gave instructions to these 70 other disciples when He sent them before Him into every city and place where He was about to go. Both sets of instructions were very similar. In Luke Chapter 10 verses 10 to 12, He tells the 70:

Luke 10:10-12

10 "But whatever city you enter, and they <u>do not</u> receive you, go out into its streets and say,

11 'The very dust of your city which clings to us we wipe off against you. Nevertheless know this, that the kingdom of God has come near you.'

12 "But I say to you that it will be more tolerable in that Day for Sodom than for that city." (NKJV) *{Emphasis added}*

And in Mark 6:11 He tells the twelve:

Mark 6:11

11 "And whoever shall not receive you, nor hear you, when ye depart thence shake off the dust under your feet, <u>for a testimony against them</u>. Verily I say to you, It shall be more tolerable for Sodom and Gomorrah in the day of judgment, than for that city." (Webster) *{Emphasis added}*

We see this principle in action when Paul and Barnabas shake off the dust of their feet against those who persecuted and expelled them at Antioch in Pisidia in Acts 13:51:

Acts 13:49-52

49 And the word of the Lord was published *(being spread)* throughout all the region.

50 But the Jews stirred up the devout and honorable women, and the chief men of the city, and raised persecution against Paul and Barnabas, and expelled them from their borders.
51 But they shook off the dust of their feet against them, and came to Iconium.
52 And the disciples were filled with joy and with the Holy Spirit. (Webster) *{Clarification in parenthesis added}*

And we read about Paul, in the power of the Holy Spirit, pronouncing the word of the Lord against Elymas the sorcerer who was opposing their work at Cyprus:

Acts 13:8-12
8 But Elymas the magician (for so his name is translated) was opposing them, seeking to turn the proconsul away from the faith.
9 But Saul, who was also known as Paul, filled with the Holy Spirit, fixed his gaze on him,
10 and said, "You who are full of all deceit and fraud, you son of the devil, you enemy of all righteousness, will you not cease to make crooked the straight ways of the Lord?
11 "Now, behold, the hand of the Lord is upon you, and you will be blind and not see the sun for a time." And immediately a mist and a darkness fell upon him, and he went about seeking those who would lead him by the hand.
12 Then the proconsul believed when he saw what had happened, being amazed at the teaching of the Lord. (NASB)

What I am saying is that the grace and forgiveness God gave the world in His Son Jesus was not a weak forgiveness but a strong forgiveness—a forgiveness declared in power and requiring the recipient to accept the truth that they needed to repent and turn from their sins and turn to God through Christ. This stands in sharp contrast to some modern twists on Christianity where even the mention of the word repentance places one in danger of being labeled "unforgiving."

And the strength of the gospel of forgiveness was no different for those who were already in the church. In 1st Corinthians Chapter 5, Paul writes to the church about reports of gross sexual immorality where a man was in an incestuous relationship with his father's wife. And he chastises the church for being so tolerant of sin. Paul exercises his authority to bind and loose, to forgive or retain, and tells the church that, when they are gathered together in the power of the Lord Jesus Christ, they were to...

1 Corinthians 5:5

5   ...deliver such a one to Satan for the destruction of his flesh, so that his spirit may be saved in the day of the Lord Jesus. (NASB)

By this action, they were declaring in the Spirit that the arrogant and unrepentant sinner was outside their fellowship and outside the supernatural protection God has for His children. The forgiveness of God and the forgiveness this church was to exhibit had its just and righteous boundaries. And even those boundaries displayed God's love and mercy because the intended purpose was that "his spirit may be saved in the day of the Lord Jesus." If they continued to indulge his activities, he may never come to repentance and his eternal soul would be in danger. But now, in the hands of Satan and the world and outside the tent of God's blessings, hopefully the persistent offender would come to his senses.

In the church body—in the brotherhood of believers in the Lord—the importance of the wrongdoer acknowledging his or her trespass is important as it relates to any open sign of forgiveness. In Luke 17:3-4, Jesus taught His disciples:

Luke 17:3-4

3   "Take heed to yourselves. If your brother sins against you, rebuke him; and if he repents, forgive him.

4   "And if he sins against you seven times in a day, and seven times in a day returns to you, saying, 'I repent,' you shall forgive him." (NKJV) *{Emphasis added}*

Notice: we are to rebuke, we are to admonish and express strong disapproval to a brother who sins against us. We are not to ignore the sin or stay silent. Notice also: he must repent and must come to us and tell us he repents. And notice: we are to forgive him openly when he does so. And if he trips seven times in a day and repents seven times, we are to forgive him. It is not a one chance and one chance only forgiveness because, unfortunately, we all too often sin against each other more than once.

In Matthew Chapter 18, Jesus gives even more specific instructions. He says starting at verse 15:

Matthew 18:15-20

15 "Moreover if your brother sins against you, go and tell him his fault between you and him alone. If he hears you, you have gained your brother.

16 "But if he will not hear, take with you one or two more, that *'by the mouth of two or three witnesses every word may be established.'*

17 "And if he refuses to hear them, tell it to the church. But if he refuses even to hear the church, let him be to you like a heathen and a tax collector.

18 "Assuredly, I say to you, whatever you bind on earth will be bound in heaven, and whatever you loose on earth will be loosed in heaven.

19 "Again I say to you that if two of you agree on earth concerning anything that they ask, it will be done for them by My Father in heaven.

20 "For where two or three are gathered together in My name, I am there in the midst of them." (NKJV)

Again we see the binding and loosing power of believers gathered in agreement. And the Lord desires His children to be of one mind in Him; that is, they are to agree and have the mind of Christ. That is why, when one person sins against another, it must be dealt with and not ignored. First the brother who is wronged goes quietly to the one who has done the wrong. If he does not listen, one or two other believers are brought to establish the matter, as we have previously studied, "by the mouth of two or three witnesses." Then as a last resort the church becomes involved. But notice that if the wrongdoer ignores the church, then Jesus says, "Let him be to you like a heathen and a tax collector." This sounds similar to Paul's instructions to the Corinthian church. Now some of my study partners may be saying, "That sounds awfully harsh." Just how does this teaching line up with the other instructions of the Lord to "forgive men their trespasses" and when we pray to "forgive our debtors"?

It can seem confusing. But I believe we can get a better sense of it if we think back to our discussion on the will of God. Remember how we said that there is God's positional will—His perfect pleasing will—what He wants and desires in His heart. And then there is His conditional will—what He allows for a time and for a reason so that we may display our free will. Well, there is a similarity between this and our dealings with others. In our heart we should want God's heart's will. We should desire to forgive the ones who have sinned and see them restored in a right relationship with God. But when they are hard-hearted and unremorseful, we may have to outwardly take a strong stand in our relationship with them for righteousness sake—because of the condition. And the expressing of forgiveness and even the loosing of the sin may have to wait until they come and ask for it.

We should not minimize sin, and it is not always proper to express forgiveness when it is being mocked. And yet, Stephen's verbal forgiveness of those stoning him was indeed an example of forgiveness in strength, as was our Lord's words from the cross in Luke 23:34:

Luke 23:34a

> 34 Then said Jesus, "Father, forgive them; for they know not what they do." ... (KJV)

Therefore, wisdom is needed from the Holy Spirit to know exactly how we should apply these principles. Some situations are complex, and just as there are different stages of rebellion there are different stages of our corresponding response to rebellion. In Jesus' Matthew 18 discussion of church brethren, treating someone as a "heathen and a tax collector" might mean telling them that you love them and do forgive them, but that, until they come to their senses and want your forgiveness, you cannot be in close fellowship with them.

However, we should never use the boundaries of righteousness and suitability as an excuse to harbor an unforgiving bitterness in our hearts. Never! The narrative we have just studied in Matthew 18 continues at verse 21. Peter, after hearing the three step outline Jesus gave for a sinning brother and perhaps hearing an earlier sermon similar to the one we read in Luke 17:4 about a brother sinning seven times in a day, thinks he has this forgiveness thing all worked out. Continue to read from Matthew Chapter 18 starting at verse 21:

Matthew 18:21-24

21 Then Peter came to Him and said, "Lord, how often shall my brother sin against me, and I forgive him? Up to seven times?"

22 Jesus said to him, "I do not say to you, up to seven times, but up to seventy times seven.

23 "Therefore the kingdom of heaven is like a certain king who wanted to settle accounts with his servants.

24 "And when he had begun to settle accounts, one was brought to him who owed him ten thousand talents." (NKJV)

This is a huge sum of money. A talent was the largest unit of weight and was used particularly for weighing out gold and silver. The weight equivalent varied from place to place and time to time, but it is generally agreed that each talent was roughly about 75 lbs. At the current price of silver (approximately $21/oz.), ten thousand talents would be 252 million dollars in today's currency. But the actual purchasing power was even much more than that. A talent of silver was also equal to 6,000 denarii. A denarius was a Roman coin whose value, at the time of the Lord, was equal to the ordinary daily wage of a soldier or laborer. If we use an average current wage of $120/day and the servant owes 60,000,000 denarii or 60,000,000 days wages (10,000 talents times 6,000 denarii per talent), then he would owe a staggering $7.2 billion in today's dollars! And this amount would be impossible to repay.

Matthew 18:25-28

25 "But as he was not able to pay, his master commanded that he be sold, with his wife and children and all that he had, and that payment be made.

26 "The servant therefore fell down before him, saying, 'Master, have patience with me, and I will pay you all.'

27 "Then the master of that servant was moved with compassion, released him, and forgave him the debt.

28 "But that servant went out and found one of his fellow servants who owed him a hundred denarii; and he laid hands on him and took him by the throat, saying, 'Pay me what you owe!'" (NKJV)

A hundred denarii at the $120/day daily wage would be $12,000 in buying power in today's dollars and a vastly smaller amount than in verse 24: 1/600,000th of the value in verse 24.

Matthew 18:29-35

29 "So his fellow servant fell down at his feet and begged him, saying, 'Have patience with me, and I will pay you all.'

30 "And he would not, but went and threw him into prison till he should pay the debt.

31 "So when his fellow servants saw what had been done, they were very grieved, and came and told their master all that had been done.

32 "Then his master, after he had called him, said to him, 'You wicked servant! I forgave you all that debt because you begged me.

33 'Should you not also have had compassion on your fellow servant, just as I had pity on you?'

34 "And his master was angry, and delivered him to the torturers until he should pay all that was due to him.

35 "So My heavenly Father also will do to you if each of you, from his heart, does not forgive his brother his trespasses." (NKJV) *{Emphasis added}*

And there is the key phrase: our positional will should be to forgive "from the heart." The Lord has forgiven us such a great debt, how can we not forgive from the heart those who have sinned against us. In Lesson Ten we studied that great statement of faith in Mark 11:22-24. But I would like you to read now the full teaching down to verse 26:

Mark 11:22-26

22 And Jesus answered saying to them, "Have faith in God.

23 "Truly I say to you, whoever says to this mountain, 'Be taken up and cast into the sea,' and does not doubt in his heart, but believes that what he says is going to happen, it will be granted him.

24 "Therefore I say to you, all things for which you pray and ask, believe that you have received them, and they will be granted you.

25 "Whenever you stand praying, forgive, if you have anything against anyone, so that your Father who is in heaven will also forgive you your transgressions.

26 "But if you do not forgive, neither will your Father who is in heaven forgive your transgressions." (NASB) *{Emphasis added}*

Notice the importance to effective prayer that, if we hold anything against anyone, we need to forgive. Then we are praying according to His will. Then can we approach Him forgiven and with a clean conscience. And when this attitude of real love and mercy is combined with faith in what God can accomplish, the Lord promises, "All things for which you pray and ask, believe that you have received them, and they will be granted you."

* * *

Consider: In the book of Exodus, God gives Moses the plan for the tabernacle which was to be the center of worship and the place where His presence would come down in the midst of His people Israel. In the courtyard surrounding the main building were the altar of burnt offering overlaid with bronze and the bronze laver where the priests would wash. Also in the courtyard, the various sacrifices acknowledging the sin of the people were conducted. The outer coverings of the tabernacle were badger skins. So what the Israelites viewed in the courtyard displayed harshness. But within the holy place and most holy place of the tabernacle, was fine linen of blue, scarlet and purple with cherubim portrayed. And the walls and all the items were overlaid in the brilliance and softness of pure gold. So it is with our God—a severe exterior strong against sin, yet a pure, soft interior heart of mercy and love.

LESSON TWENTY

———————∝———————

I n this lesson, we pick up our study of the Lord's Prayer in Matthew Chapter 6 verse 13 where Jesus teaches us to pray:

Matthew 6:13a

13 "And do not lead us into temptation,
　 But deliver us from the evil one. ..." (NKJV)

The Greek word that is translated "temptation" in that verse is an interesting one. It is *peirasmos* {pā-ras-mos'} and in its original meaning it is simply "a trial" or "a test" or "a putting to proof." So it indicates the test or a testing which someone is put to in either a good sense or bad sense, unlike the current meaning of the English word "temptation" which has a strong association to the evil sense and the enticement to do wrong. (Note that the related English word "attempt" is still neutral.) In different translations, peirasmos and its different forms are translated *temptation*, *trial*, or *test* depending on the Scripture. And in truth, the context of the passage must be con-sidered if we are to understand the real meaning. It is the same with the corresponding verb, *peirazo* {pā-rad'-zō}, which means "<u>to</u> test," "to try," "to attempt," "to prove," and even "to examine," and which sometimes is translated "to tempt."

An example of that word being used in a good sense is in the gospel of John Chapter 6 where Jesus feeds the five thousand. When they first saw the multitude coming toward them, the Lord said to Philip:

John 6:5b

5 ... "Where are we to buy bread, so that these may eat?" (NASB)

In verse 6 we are told:

John 6:6

> 6 This He was saying <u>to test</u> him, for He Himself knew what He was intending to do. (NASB) *{Emphasis added}*

The word there "to test" is peirazo. An example of the word being used with bad connotations is Galatians 6:1 which reads:

Galatians 6:1

> 1 Brethren, even if anyone is caught in any trespass, you who are spiritual, restore such a one in a spirit of gentleness; each one looking to yourself, so that you too will not <u>be tempted</u>. (NASB) *{Emphasis added}*

The verb translated "be tempted" is still the same *peirazo*, but clearly the inference here is that of a negative trial that can lead us to sin.

And the Bible teaches us some very specific points about our trials and temptations. The first point we must realize is that the devil "tempts" us, in the English sense of the word; that is, he tries or tests us to evil for evil purposes. He is the source of the evil which tries us **and** he tries us with the goal that we also do evil. And even when temptation is unsuccessful in getting us to sin, he will bring against us various trials in the expectation that we are harmed and our lives are destroyed.

In 1st Peter Chapter 5 verses 8 and 9 we read:

1 Peter 5:8-9

> 8 Be of sober spirit, be on the alert. Your adversary, the devil, prowls around like a roaring lion, seeking someone to devour.
>
> 9 But resist him, firm in your faith, knowing that the same experiences of suffering are being accomplished by your brethren who are in the world. (NASB)

Satan might test us, in anticipation that we will sin or do evil, by placing us in evil situations where we will suffer. In Revelation Chapter 2, the risen glorified Lord Jesus sends a message to the church at Smyrna. Down at verse 10 He tells them:

Revelation 2:10

10   "'Do not fear what you are about to suffer. Behold, the devil is about to cast some of you into prison, so that you will be <u>tested</u> *(verb: peirazo)*, and you will have tribulation for ten days. Be faithful until death, and I will give you the crown of life.'" (NASB) *{Emphasis and clarification in parenthesis added}*

A clear example of the agonizing trials the devil can bring upon us is seen in Job Chapter 2, verses 1 to 7:

Job 2:1-7

1   Again there was a day when the sons of God came to present themselves before the LORD, and Satan also came among them to present himself before the LORD.

2   The LORD said to Satan, "Where have you come from?" Then Satan answered the LORD and said, "From roaming about on the earth and walking around on it."

3   The LORD said to Satan, "Have you considered My servant Job? For there is no one like him on the earth, a blameless and upright man fearing God and turning away from evil. And he still holds fast his integrity, although you incited Me against him to ruin him without cause."

4   Satan answered the LORD and said, "Skin for skin! Yes, all that a man has he will give for his life.

5   "However, put forth Your hand now, and touch his bone and his flesh; he will curse You to Your face."

6   So the LORD said to Satan, "Behold, he is in your power, only spare his life."

7   Then Satan went out from the presence of the LORD and smote Job with sore boils from the sole of his foot to the crown of his head. (NASB)

Satan can also test us to evil by a <u>spiritual</u> battle where he plays on the weaknesses of our flesh and the thoughts of our mind. Remember how we read in Ephesians Chapter 6 verses 10 to 13:

Ephesians 6:10-13

10   Finally, my brethren, be strong in the Lord and in the power of His might.

11 Put on the whole armor of God, that you may be able to stand against the wiles of the devil.

12 For we do not wrestle against flesh and blood, but against principalities, against powers, against the rulers of the darkness of this age, against spiritual hosts of wickedness in the heavenly places.

13 Therefore take up the whole armor of God, that you may be able to withstand in the evil day, and having done all, to stand. (NKJV)

Satan has a whole host and hierarchy of demons and unclean spirits that can not only bring evil circumstances upon us, but who can tempt us in our spirits and our minds and our bodies. The account of when Jesus was tempted by Satan in the wilderness illustrates how the enemy attacks us on all three of these levels. And we can learn from Jesus' example how to resist and overcome temptation. First, Jesus was filled with the Holy Spirit. Second, He had fasted for spiritual strength. And third, as we mentioned in Lesson Sixteen, He used the Scriptures, the Word of God, effectively and in truth, to repel Satan. Read now the chronicle in Matthew 4 verses 1 to 11, and as you do, notice the appeal of the temptations first to the body, then to the soul, and then to the spirit.

Matthew 4:1-11

1 Then Jesus was led by the Spirit into the wilderness to be tempted by the devil.

2 After fasting forty days and forty nights, He was hungry.

3 The tempter came to Him and said, "If You are the Son of God, tell these stones to become bread."

4 Jesus answered, "It is written: 'Man shall not live on bread alone, but on every word that comes from the mouth of God.'"

5 Then the devil took Him to the holy city and had Him stand on the highest point of the temple.

6 "If You are the Son of God," he said, "throw Yourself down. For it is written:

    "'He will command His angels concerning you,
      and they will lift you up in their hands,
      so that you will not strike your foot against a stone.'"

7 Jesus answered him, "It is also written: 'Do not put the Lord your God to the test.'"

8   Again, the devil took Him to a very high mountain and showed Him all the kingdoms of the world and their splendor.

9   "All this I will give You," he said, "if You will bow down and worship me."

10 Jesus said to him, "Away from Me, Satan! For it is written: 'Worship the Lord your God, and serve Him only.'"

11 Then the devil left Him, and angels came and attended Him. (NIV) *{Capitalization for deity added}*

Besides Satan and his demons, other sources of temptation to do evil are *the world* (which we have already seen is Satan's kingdom) and *our own flesh and desires*. In 1st Timothy Chapter 6 verses 6 to 10 we read:

1 Timothy 6:6-10

6   But godliness with contentment is great gain.

7   For we brought nothing into the world, and we can take nothing out of it.

8   But if we have food and clothing, we will be content with that.

9   Those who want to get rich fall into temptation *(peirasmos)* and a trap and into many foolish and harmful desires that plunge people into ruin and destruction.

10 For the love of money is a root of all kinds of evil. Some people, eager for money, have wandered from the faith and pierced themselves with many griefs. (NIV) *{Emphasis and clarification in parenthesis added}*

And when Jesus was in the Garden of Gethsemane, He asked Peter, James and John to stay and watch as He went on a little further to pray. But when He returned He found them sleeping:

Mark 14:37-38

37 ..."Simon," He said to Peter, "are you asleep? Couldn't you keep watch for one hour?

38 Watch and pray so that you will not fall into temptation *(peirasmos)*. The spirit is willing, but the flesh is weak." (NIV) *{Emphasis, capitalization for deity, and clarification in parenthesis added}*

Too often, we may want to do what is right and good in our spirits, but the weakness of our flesh prevails. It would be so in the case of Simon Peter who had told the Lord earlier at supper, "Lord, with You I am ready to go both to prison and to death!" (Luke 22:33) (NASB), yet he would deny even knowing Jesus three times before the night was over. We will discuss this in more detail in Lesson Twenty-three, but for now, notice the Lord's admonition to the apostles: "Watch and pray so that you will not fall into temptation." Effective prayer is crucial to overcoming temptation and having our flesh submissive to our spirit and to the Holy Spirit of God.

Returning to our focus of understanding the Greek word used for *temptation*, let us take a few moments to read carefully from the first chapter of the letter of James. In James 1 verses 2 to 4 we read:

James 1:2-4

2   My brethren, count it all joy when you fall into various <u>trials</u>,
3   knowing that the testing of your faith produces patience.
4   But let patience have its perfect work, that you may be perfect and complete, lacking nothing. (NKJV) *{Emphasis added}*

The *King James* will render verse 2:

James 1:2

2   My brethren, count it all joy when ye fall into divers <u>temptations</u>; (KJV) *{Emphasis added}*

The actual Greek word again used is *peirasmos*. The *King James* translates this word as *temptations* because, back in the English of the King James' time, the word *temptation*, coming from the Latin, had more of the neutral meaning of "a testing" or "trials whether good or bad," similar to the Greek word *peirasmos*. But the evil sense of the word *temptation* has come to dominate in modern English, making it no longer an adequate translation in certain passages. It is apparent from the context in the verse above that the Greek word *peirasmos* is used simply in the sense of trials. James is not saying that it is good to have inducements to sin but rather that the "trials" we go through confirm our faith and perfect us in the Lord.

James goes on to say down in verse 12:

James 1:12-17

12 Blessed is the man who endures temptation; for when he has been approved, he will receive the crown of life which the Lord has promised to those who love Him.

13 Let no one say when he is tempted, "I am tempted by God"; for God cannot be tempted by evil, nor does He Himself tempt anyone.

14 But each one is tempted when he is drawn away by his own desires and enticed.

15 Then, when desire has conceived, it gives birth to sin; and sin, when it is full-grown, brings forth death.

16 Do not be deceived, my beloved brethren.

17 Every good gift and every perfect gift is from above, and comes down from the Father of lights, with whom there is no variation or shadow of turning. (NKJV)

Observe from the context of verse 14, that the Greek word to try or to test, *peirazo*, is indeed being used in the sense of "to tempt":

James 1:14

14 But each one is tempted when he is drawn away by his own desires and enticed. (NKJV)

Here the word takes on the clear inference of inviting or persuading someone by enticement to sin. And notice, given that usage, we read in verse 13 that God **never** tempts anyone. That is, He is never the source of the evil we are tried with, nor does He try people in hope that they do evil. And that is why we are to pray, "Our Father, deliver us from the evil one." It is Satan who tempts.

In 1st Thessalonians 3:5, Paul tells the church:

1Thessalonians 3:5

5 For this reason, when I could stand it no longer, I sent to find out about your faith. I was afraid that in some way the tempter had tempted you and that our labors might have been in vain. (NIV) {*Emphasis added*}

Satan is the tempter (clearly here the evil sense of *peirazo*) that seeks to destroy the good work of the gospel by getting us to sin. And James is basically explaining in his letter that it is a shallow excuse to say when we are finding it difficult to withstand a trial of enticement, "I am tempted by God."

You can easily see how such a wrong attitude develops if we forget that there **is** an evil one and if we forget that human nature is basically corrupt—two denials which are prominent in today's culture. In addition, there are others who confuse the nature of God with the nature of Satan. They forget that God is the Holy and Good One. He is the Father of lights and He does not change like shifting shadows. It is Satan who brings the darkness and brings the evil, but every good and perfect gift is from God.

God the Father is the Majestic Holiness. Sin cannot dwell in Him and He cannot be in any way tempted by evil. So neither then can He deny Himself and be the source of that which allures people to evil. Even if He was found to be in the form of sinful man, even if the frail clay in which He dwelt was tempted in every way just as we are tempted and He was placed under the most severe of Satan's attacks, still—even in such weakness—still, He would not sin. And we saw that earlier when we read about the tempting of our Lord Jesus. We will speak more about this in our next lesson. But notice what James says does tempt us:

James 1:14

> 14 But each one is tempted when he is drawn away by his own desires and enticed. (NKJV)

Such is the danger of not dealing with our strong desires and cravings. It is a very small step from longing to actually sinning. What the eye considers today might easily give birth to tomorrow's sin. And sin, James tells us, when it is full-grown, brings forth death.

LESSON TWENTY-ONE

———————————∝———————————

I n this lesson, we continue our focus on that part of the Lord's Prayer where Jesus tells us to pray:

Matthew 6:13a

> 13 "And do not lead us into temptation,
> But deliver us from the evil one. ..." (NKJV)

In our last lesson we saw that the Greek word which is translated "temptation" had the original meaning of a trial or a test, and it depended on the context of the passage whether the word simply meant a test, in a neutral or even a good sense, or whether it indeed suggested a temptation—an enticement to do evil.

The first point we developed was identifying that it is the devil who "tempts" us. He is the source of the evil which tries us, and he tries us with the goal of making us do evil or destroying us even if we resist. Aided by his hierarchy of fallen angels as well as the world system which surrounds us, he can play at the weaknesses of our flesh and our own wrong ideas and sinful desires. He can attack the thoughts of our mind, and, as we saw in the case of Job, he can also bring about agonizing situations.

In contrast, at the end of the last lesson we saw how God never tempts anyone, but rather He is the source of every good and perfect gift. He is never the originator of evil, nor does He try people in hope that they do evil. It is Satan who is the tempter.

But God does test us, in the good sense of the word. This is the second point I would like to make in this section of our study. God will test us, allowing us to be tried and even leading us into such trials. Let us look back again at the section we studied last time in

166

Job Chapter 2 verses 1 to 7. We see that it is Satan who tempts and persecutes Job, but who allows it? In verse 6 the Scripture tells us:

Job 2:6

6   So the LORD said to Satan, "Behold, he is in your power, only spare his life." (NASB) *{Emphasis added}*

And in the account of the temptation of Jesus, which we also looked at last time, it tells us in Matthew 4 verse 1:

Matthew 4:1

1   Then Jesus was <u>led by the Spirit</u> into the wilderness to be tempted by the devil. (NIV) *{Emphasis added}*

So the Holy Spirit led Jesus into the wilderness to be tempted, and God permitted Satan's attack upon Job. For that matter, it seems from the dialogue in Job that it is God who brings up and reminds Satan about Job, apparently for some reason or plan. Twice we read in Job (Job 1:8 and Job 2:3):

Job 1:8

8   The LORD said to Satan, "Have you considered My servant Job? For there is no one like him on the earth, a blameless and upright man, fearing God and turning away from evil." (NASB)

All along God has been protecting not just Job, but his whole family for Job's sake (and there is clear indication in Chapter 1 verses 4 and 5 that Job's children did not share Job's character, but would feast, eating and drinking for days, which caused Job to be concerned that they might have sinned). Satan says to the Lord concerning Job in Chapter 1 verse 10:

Job 1:10

10 "Have You not made a hedge about him and his house and all that he has, on every side? You have blessed the work of his hands, and his possessions have increased in the land." (NASB)

God is Job's protector. But for a time and for a reason He lets down the hedge around Job and allows Satan's attack. And I think that it is important to know that, when God <u>allows</u> a test, it *is* for a purpose.

Moreover, when God Himself tests us it is not to do us evil or bring us down, but rather to do us good—to teach us and establish us. We see this in the famous account of God commanding Abraham to offer Isaac. In Genesis 22:1 it says:

Genesis 22:1a

1 Now it came about after these things, that God <u>tested</u> Abraham... (NASB) *{Emphasis added}*

The Hebrew word in this passage is *nasah* {naw-saw'} and means "to test, to try" (but which the *King James*, in the English of its day, again translates "tempt"). As a result of that well-known test, Abraham's fear of God and the faith he had in the promises of God was displayed and declared for all generations even to today. Afterward, God confirmed by oath all His promises to Abraham for his descendants through Isaac as well as the promise of the Messiah coming through his seed, as He tells Abraham in verse 18:

Genesis 22:18b

18 "...because you have obeyed My voice." (NASB)

Though we cannot imagine how terrible the test must have seemed to father Abraham, it would establish for all time the most vivid illustration and prophecy of what God would, and only God could, provide through His Son Jesus' death at that very same location many hundreds of years later.

And notice that God's test for Abraham was not meant to induce him to sin but, rather, that Abraham's faith would be confirmed. Throughout the Old Testament we see that when the Lord tests His people it is to prove the true character and degree of their faithfulness. Remember when we discussed the request for our daily bread in Lesson Sixteen, how we read in Deuteronomy Chapter 8 verse 3 about the reason for God sending the manna? Let me back up and read now from verse 2. Moses reminds the people:

Deuteronomy 8:2-6

2   Remember how the LORD your God led you all the way in the wilderness these forty years, to humble and <u>test you</u> in order to know what was in your heart, whether or not you would keep His commands.

3   He humbled you, causing you to hunger and then feeding you with manna, which neither you nor your ancestors had known, to teach you that man does not live on bread alone but on every word that comes from the mouth of the LORD.

4   Your clothes did not wear out and your feet did not swell during these forty years.

5   Know then in your heart that as a man disciplines his son, so the LORD your God disciplines you.

6   Observe the commands of the LORD your God, walking in obedience to Him and revering Him. (NIV) *{Emphasis and capitalization for deity added}*

When Moses says in verse 2 that God led them in the wilderness forty years to humble and test them, to know what was in their hearts, whether they would keep His commandments or not, I do not believe that he means that God has to test us to really know what we are like. God told the prophet Jeremiah in Jeremiah Chapter 1 and verse 5:

Jeremiah 1:5

5   "Before I formed you in the womb I knew you,
before you were born I set you apart;
I appointed you as a prophet to the nations." (NIV)

The test is not for Him to know what we are like, **but rather that we might know ourselves**. Keep in mind that the Israelites had grumbled against God even after all the miraculous signs He had performed before them. And their sin was responsible for them having to wander in the desert for the forty years. Now Moses reminds their children, who would enter the Promised Land, how God made them to count on His supernatural provision of manna—how He humbled and tested them these forty years. Why? The answer starts in verses 5 and 6:

Deuteronomy 8:5-6

5 <u>Know then in your heart</u> that as a man disciplines his son, so the Lord your God disciplines you.

6 Observe the commands of the Lord your God, walking in obedience to Him and revering Him. (NIV) *{Emphasis and capitalization for deity added}*

Through the test, as a loving Father, God is letting the Israelites really come to the knowledge of themselves and their dependence on Him—that they should no longer rebel but keep His commandments and His ways.

Moses goes on to tell them, starting in Deuteronomy 8:7, how the Lord God is now going to bring them into a good land and a prosperous land where they will lack nothing. He warns them that, when they have eaten and are full, they must beware that they do not forget the Lord their God by not keeping His commandments:

Deuteronomy 8:12-17

12 "otherwise, when you have eaten and are satisfied, and have built good houses and lived in them,

13 and when your herds and your flocks multiply, and your silver and gold multiply, and all that you have multiplies,

14 then <u>your heart will become proud</u> *(lifted up)* and you will forget the Lord your God who brought you out from the land of Egypt, out of the house of slavery.

15 "He led you through the great and terrible wilderness, with its fiery serpents and scorpions and thirsty ground where there was no water; He brought water for you out of the rock of flint.

16 "In the wilderness He fed you manna which your fathers did not know, that He might humble you and that He might test you *(nasah)*, to do good for you in the end.

17 "Otherwise, you may say in your heart, 'My power and the strength of my hand made me this wealth.'" (NASB) *{Emphasis and clarification in parentheses added}*

You should make note of the reason for the test which we just read in verse 16: "...that He might humble you and that He might test you, <u>to do good for you in the end</u>"!

God needed to deal with their pride—literally, the lifting up of the heart. Pride was responsible for their initial grumbling against Him. And since in His plan He would bless them mightily in the Promised Land, they were in danger of saying, after they had eaten and were full and had greatly prospered, "My power and the strength of my hand made me this wealth."

So the test in the wilderness was meant to do them good in the end. It was to teach them humility and their dependence on the Lord, that they would learn from what went before and avoid "lifting up the heart" in the Promised Land. Pride unchecked will lead an individual to ultimately become like Satan himself. And God often will use a trial to hold up a mirror before us to see ourselves and our rebellion so that that horrible end will not come about. As it says in Deuteronomy 8:2, the test was to "know what was in your heart." In the history that follows in the Bible, every time the people of Israel forgot the lesson of the wilderness, they got into trouble.

How many people today have this very same attitude (which Moses is cautioning against here) of forgetting the Lord and saying, "My power and the strength of my hands have produced this wealth for me"? They are secure in themselves and their own abilities and sometimes even in their own righteousness. I believe that, in order to humble us, our society might very well be facing a time of trials ahead.

OK. So we have seen that while God never tempts us, He will test us, allowing us to be tried and even leading us into such trials. Furthermore, when He allows a test it is always for a purpose, one primary purpose being that we come to know ourselves, to confirm either our faithfulness or our sinfulness.

And everyone has sinned, even Abraham. Only Jesus could live His whole life in a world of trials and temptations and never once sin, as it is written in James 1:13:

James 1:13b

13 ...for God cannot be tempted by evil... (NKJV)

God cannot be tempted to actual sin. Yet we must realize that Jesus the Messiah took on the very nature of a human being. In Romans 8:3 we read:

Romans 8:3

3 For what the Law could not do, weak as it was through the flesh, God did: sending His own Son in the likeness of sinful flesh and as an offering for sin, He condemned sin in the flesh, (NASB)

And the writer of Hebrews tells us in Chapter 2 starting at verse 14:

Hebrews 2:14-18

14 Therefore, since the children share in flesh and blood, He Himself likewise also partook of the same, that through death He might render powerless him who had the power of death, that is, the devil,

15 and might free those who through fear of death were subject to slavery all their lives.

16 For assuredly He does not give help to angels, but He gives help to the descendant *(seed)* of Abraham.

17 Therefore, He had to be made like His brethren in all things, so that He might become a merciful and faithful high priest in things pertaining to God, to make propitiation for the sins of the people.

18 For since He Himself was tempted in that which He has suffered, He is able to come to the aid of those who are tempted. (NASB) *{Clarification in parenthesis}*

As a man, Jesus suffered when He was tried and tempted. In Chapter 5 verse 7, the writer of Hebrews tells us that in the days of His flesh, Jesus offered up prayers and supplications with vehement cries and tears to the Father. He also says in Chapter 4 starting at verse 14:

Hebrews 4:14-16

14 Therefore, since we have a great high priest who has passed through the heavens, Jesus the Son of God, let us hold fast our confession.

15 For we do not have a high priest who cannot sympathize with our weaknesses, but One who has been tempted in all things as we are, yet without sin.

16 Therefore let us draw near with confidence to the throne of grace, so that we may receive mercy and find grace to help in time of need. (NASB)

As a man, the Lord Jesus was tempted in every way as we are, yet was without sin. Even in all the weakness and frailty of this human flesh, the purity and holiness of the heart of God would not sin. Now as the conqueror over Satan and sin, Jesus sits at the right hand of the Father as our High Priest—One who sympathizes with our weaknesses and who can help us in time of need.

Our trials should cause us to realize our own lack and the need for the Lord's life inside of us. And when that life is inside, our trials and the devil's failed temptations should show us the victory we now have in Christ.

LESSON TWENTY-TWO

———————◇———————

I n the last two lessons, we have been looking at the petition in the Lord's Prayer in Matthew 6:13 which reads:

Matthew 6:13a
> 13 "And do not lead us into temptation,
> But deliver us from the evil one. ..." (NKJV)

Just to review, the Greek word translated "temptation" in that verse is *peirasmos* {pā-ras-mos'} and means a trial or a test or a putting to the proof. The connotation of this word can be good, neutral or bad depending on the context of the passage. In the evil sense (which is how we normally use the word "temptation" in English—that is, a trial, the purpose of which is to entice us to sin), it is the devil who tempts us. He is the evil one.

God never tempts anyone. But as we saw in our last lesson, God will test us, allowing us to be tried and even leading us into such trials. He tests us only for a purpose. Often that purpose is to reveal to us our faithfulness or our sinfulness. He tests us, as we studied in Deuteronomy 8:16, to do us good in the end. He tests us so that we may know ourselves—that we might know what is in our hearts. And our trials in this world should cause us to recognize our lack and our need for help so that we turn to God and accept the life of Jesus inside of us. As we believe in Him, His victory over Satan and over sin can make us more than conquerors in any trial and over any temptation the devil might bring.

We read about Paul's trials in 2nd Corinthians Chapter 1 verses 8 to 10:

2 Corinthians 1:8-10

8   For we do not want you to be ignorant, brethren, of our trouble which came to us in Asia: that we were burdened beyond measure, above strength, so that we despaired even of life.

9   Yes, we had the sentence of death in ourselves, that we should not trust in ourselves but in God who raises the dead,

10 who delivered us from so great a death, and does deliver us; in whom we trust that He will still deliver us, (NKJV)

And here we come to a tremendously important point: God is a delivering God!

The trials that Paul encountered were beyond him. He despaired of life and could feel the sentence of death on himself. I am sure that many of you who read this lesson can sympathize with Paul, having come to the same point at some time in your life. Yet notice the purpose of the trial in verse 9:

2 Corinthians 1:9b

9   ...that we should <u>not</u> trust in ourselves but in God who raises the dead, (NKJV) *{Emphasis added}*

When we feel dead and dying, we must remember that God raises the dead, and hard trials, rather than destroying us, should lead us not to trust in ourselves but to trust in God. And here is the wonderful foundation for our trust: we are trusting in a God...

2 Corinthians 1:10

10 who <u>delivered us</u> from so great a death, and <u>does deliver us</u>; in whom we trust that He <u>will still deliver us</u>, (NKJV) *{Emphasis added}*

From Genesis to Revelation the Bible shouts out that our God is a delivering God, bringing His people out safely on the other side of the trial. Remember, God is not glorified by our failures but rather by His deliverance of us! He did not let Noah and his family drown in the flood with the rest of mankind, but rather He delivered them out of it and set them down safely on dry ground. He did not let the descendants of Abraham perish down in Egypt, but rather He brought them out and delivered them from Pharaoh's power with a mighty hand

and an outstretched arm. He delivered David from Goliath and from all his enemies and He delivered Daniel from the lions' den. In Acts Chapter 16, He delivered Paul and Silas from imprisonment. Let us read starting at verse 22:

Acts 16:22-33

22 The crowd rose up together against them, and the chief magistrates tore their robes off them and proceeded to order them to be beaten with rods.

23 When they had struck them with many blows, they threw them into prison, commanding the jailer to guard them securely;

24 and he, having received such a command, threw them into the inner prison and fastened their feet in the stocks.

25 But about midnight Paul and Silas were praying and singing hymns of praise to God, and the prisoners were listening to them;

26 and suddenly there came a great earthquake, so that the foundations of the prison house were shaken; and immediately all the doors were opened and everyone's chains were unfastened.

27 When the jailer awoke and saw the prison doors opened, he drew his sword and was about to kill himself, supposing that the prisoners had escaped.

28 But Paul cried out with a loud voice, saying, "Do not harm yourself, for we are all here!"

29 And he called for lights and rushed in, and trembling with fear he fell down before Paul and Silas,

30 and after he brought them out, he said, "Sirs, what must I do to be saved?"

31 They said, "Believe in the Lord Jesus, and you will be saved, you and your household."

32 And they spoke the word of the Lord to him together with all who were in his house.

33 And he took them that very hour of the night and washed their wounds, and immediately he was baptized, he and all his household. (NASB)

In our walk as Christians, we go through many trials which mature us and build our hope in God. Romans 5:3-5 reads:

Romans 5:3-5

3 And not only this, but we also exult in our tribulations, knowing that tribulation brings about perseverance;

4 and perseverance, proven character; and proven character, hope;

5 and hope does not disappoint, because the love of God has been poured out within our hearts through the Holy Spirit who was given to us. (NASB)

And we have already studied James 1:2-4 which says:

James 1:2-4

2 My brethren, count it all joy when you fall into various trials,

3 knowing that the testing of your faith produces patience.

4 But let patience have its perfect work, that you may be perfect and complete, lacking nothing. (NKJV)

Through the trials we face, we learn in Jesus to persevere and be patient. Our character is built up and our faith is confirmed. But for those who are faithless we might say that tribulations produce selfish panic, and selfish panic produces dissipation and debilitation, and debilitation despair. But notice that the end result of our trials is not despair but rather hope—hope in God, a hope that is <u>not</u> disappointed.

Peter, speaking of the living hope which we have in Jesus, tells believers in 1ˢᵗ Peter 1:6-7:

1 Peter 1:6-7

6 In all this you greatly rejoice, though now for a little while you may have had to suffer grief in all kinds of trials *(peirasmos)*.

7 These have come so that the proven genuineness of your faith—of greater worth than gold, which perishes even though refined by fire—may result in praise, glory and honor when Jesus Christ is revealed. (NIV) *{Clarification in parenthesis added}*

And it is clear from the account of Paul and Silas that there are times when we will suffer for our faith. Peter again writes in 1ˢᵗ Peter 4:12-13:

1 Peter 4:12-13

    12 Beloved, think it not strange concerning the fiery trial which is to try *(peirasmos)* you, as though some strange thing happened unto you:

    13 But rejoice, inasmuch as ye are partakers of Christ's sufferings; that, when His glory shall be revealed, ye may be glad also with exceeding joy. (KJV) *{Clarification in parenthesis added}*

Dear friends, we pray for the Spirit of joy and faith which Paul and Silas demonstrated when they sang hymns in prison. Such trials which we go through as Christians are for a purpose and for a season or a time. Often lives are touched by our witness, as in the case of the keeper of the prison and his family. Ultimately our hope is not disappointed, but God delivers us. And He delivers miraculously and in power, even as He did Paul and Silas. And should there be some reason that we cannot be delivered from without, God delivers us from within. But still God's joy and power are there, even as Paul's final imprisonment and death brought the gospel of salvation to many.

But also understand that there is a counterfeit spirit which twists this true teaching that we are matured by trials and the testing of our faith. The counterfeit embraces the trial and the misery to the exclusion of the good and delivering hand of God. This is a spirit which feeds on many Christians today trying to keep them trapped and stagnated in evil situations. Those who are victims of this spirit may speak about inner growth, but in reality they deny the power of God. While the devil furiously ravages these believers from <u>within and without</u>, they glory both in their afflictions and their sinful failings. Not that they are glorying in what God is doing in the trial and <u>will do</u> to deliver them and build their trust in Him, but as if to wear a badge of self-pity and pride—a badge which says, "Such is the cross I must bear. Woe is me."

Paralyzing circumstances are "cherished." Defeat is accepted. And suffering is purpose*less*. There is no hope in God's ability to work the miraculous—to bring true deliverance. But Jesus said to pray, "Father, lead us not into temptation, but deliver us from the evil one." Our attitude should be, "Father, do not let me be tempted to do evil against You, neither let me undergo hard trials, for **_on my own_** I'll fail and the devil will devour me. Instead Father, protect me and deliver me. Deliver me now from the enemy's grasp. And if trials must come, deliver me *__in Christ__*, to Your glory." As it says in Colossians 1:13:

Colossians 1:13

13 He has <u>delivered us</u> from the power of darkness and conveyed us into the kingdom of the Son of His love, (NKJV) *{Emphasis added}*

And Paul tells us in 1st Corinthians 4:20 that:

1 Corinthians 4:20

20 ...the kingdom of God is not in word, but in power. (KJV)

Our God is a powerful God and His deliverance of us from Satan's temptations and trials is a powerful deliverance. It is so important for those of you taking this study to realize that God does not delight in our evil circumstances. First Corinthians 13:6 tells us that love does not delight in unrighteousness or evil.

So when we pray, we should ask the Father to keep us from and not lead us into such circumstances and trials and temptations. We have learned the lesson. We have looked into the mirror; we have seen ourselves. We know there is no victory apart from the Lord, and so we do not delight or long for difficulties. There are some who long for the excitement and attention which trouble brings, but we are not to be as such. Rather we are to pray and ask the Father to keep us from Satan's schemes. And then, should the Lord allow a trial for a purpose and for a season as in the case of Job, we can believe that that which the devil means for evil, God means for good and will bring about good, as long as we learn to trust Him to deliver us.

It is significant that, in Job's case, one of the reasons God allowed the trial was for Job to recognize that it was the enemy— the Leviathan, the twisted sea dragon serpent—that was against him and that it was God who was for him. God's final questioning of Job involves this Leviathan:

Job 41:1-2

1 "Can you draw out Leviathan with a fishhook?
Or press down his tongue with a cord?
2 "Can you put a rope in his nose
Or pierce his jaw with a hook?" (NASB)

Job 41:7-9

7   "Can you fill his skin with harpoons,
Or his head with fishing spears?

8   Lay your hand on him;
Remember the battle —
Never do it again!

9   Indeed, any hope of overcoming him is false;
Shall one not be overwhelmed at the sight of him?" (NKJV)

Job 41:12-24

12 "I will not keep silence concerning his limbs,
Or his mighty strength, or his orderly frame.

13 "Who can strip off his outer armor?
Who can come within his double mail?

14 "Who can open the doors of his face?
Around his teeth there is terror.

15 "His strong scales are his pride,
Shut up as with a tight seal.

16 "One is so near to another
That no air can come between them.

17 "They are joined one to another;
They clasp each other and cannot be separated.

18 "His sneezes flash forth light,
And his eyes are like the eyelids of the morning.

19 "Out of his mouth go burning torches;
Sparks of fire leap forth.

20 "Out of his nostrils smoke goes forth
As from a boiling pot and burning rushes.

21 "His breath kindles coals,
And a flame goes forth from his mouth.

22 "In his neck lodges strength,
And dismay leaps before him.

23 "The folds of his flesh are joined together,
Firm on him and immovable.

24 "His heart is as hard as a stone,
Even as hard as a lower millstone. (NASB) *{Emphasis added}*

Job 41:31-34

31 "He makes the depths boil like a pot;
He makes the sea like a jar of ointment.

32 "Behind him he makes a wake to shine;
   One would think the deep to be gray-haired.
33 "Nothing on earth is like him,
   One made without fear.
34 "He looks on everything that is high;
   <u>He is king over all the sons of pride</u>." (NASB) *{Emphasis added}*

So the devil, who is explicitly featured in the beginning of the book of Job, is implicitly symbolized by this giant dinosaur-dragon creature at the end. He is the one against Job. He is the reason for Job's problems. And once Job comes to this recognition of his fearsome opponent and he sees the true nature of God as his protector, Job is delivered and restored and doubly blessed; however, that is a subject for a whole other study. Suffice it to say for now that Job and all God's people are in a battle with a dangerous enemy. But as we saw in Lesson Six, God is so much greater than any power the devil or his demons may have. The Scriptures rejoice in anticipation of the day of God's judgment on Satan:

Isaiah 26:20-27:1

20 Come, my people, enter into your rooms
   And close your doors behind you;
   Hide for a little while
   Until indignation runs its course.
21 For behold, the LORD is about to come out from His place
   To punish the inhabitants of the earth for their iniquity;
   And the earth will reveal her bloodshed
   And will no longer cover her slain.

CHAPTER 27
1 In that day the LORD will punish Leviathan the fleeing serpent,
   With His fierce and great and mighty sword,
   Even Leviathan the twisted serpent;
   And He will kill the dragon who lives in the sea. (NASB)

Revelation 12:9-11

9 And the great dragon was thrown down, the serpent of old who is called the devil and Satan, who deceives the whole world; he was thrown down to the earth, and his angels were thrown down with him.
10 Then I heard a loud voice in heaven, saying,

"Now the salvation, and the power, and the kingdom of our God and the authority of His Christ have come, for the accuser of our brethren has been thrown down, he who accuses them before our God day and night.

11 "And they overcame him because of the blood of the Lamb and because of the word of their testimony, and they did not love their life even when faced with death." (NASB)

Revelation 20:1-2

1 And I saw an angel coming down out of heaven, having the key to the Abyss and holding in his hand a great chain.

2 He seized the dragon, that ancient serpent, who is the devil, or Satan, and bound him for a thousand years. (NIV)

And then:

Revelation 20:10

10 And the devil who deceived them was thrown into the lake of fire and brimstone, where the beast and the false prophet are also; and they will be tormented day and night forever and ever. (NASB)

Returning to our discussion of trials, Joseph, the son of Jacob, was sold into slavery by his brothers. He was wrongly accused by Potiphar's wife and he seemed abandoned in prison. But later he would tell his brothers in Genesis 50:20:

Genesis 50:20

20 "But as for you, you meant evil against me; but God meant it for good, in order to bring it about as it is this day, to save many people alive." (NKJV)

Joseph did not give up his faith or trust in God. And God delivered Joseph in a mighty way, making him in reality the most powerful man in Egypt. Moreover, God used the evil motives of Joseph's brothers and the trials that Joseph then went through to bring salvation from the famine to many people, including Jacob's house. And we have some extraordinary promises in the Scriptures concerning our trials and temptations. In 1st Corinthians 10:13 Paul tells that church:

1 Corinthians 10:13

13 No temptation has overtaken you but such as is common to man; and God is faithful, who will not allow you to be tempted beyond what you are able, but with the temptation will provide the way of escape also, so that you will be able to endure it. (NASB)

And in 2nd Peter 2:9 we read:

2 Peter 2:9

9 ...the Lord knows how to deliver the godly out of temptations and to reserve the unjust under punishment for the day of judgment, (NKJV)

And the Greek word for "temptation" in those two Scriptures is again *peirasmos.* So God will not let us be tried or tempted beyond what we are able to endure, but will make a way of escape. However, we must believe in His faithfulness. We must believe that He knows how to deliver the godly from the evil one. And we must make sure that we have dealt with sin and any unwillingness to forgive so as not to give Satan the key to imprison us. James gives us an assurance in his letter:

James 4:7-8

7 Submit therefore to God. <u>Resist the devil and he will flee from you</u>.

8 Draw near to God and He will draw near to you. Cleanse your hands, you sinners; and purify your hearts, you double-minded. (NASB) *{Emphasis added}*

As we are in Christ and His Spirit is in us, we have power against the enemy and the trials he brings to cause evil. In prayer we can come boldly to the throne of our High Priest, Jesus, who sympathizes with our weaknesses and who can provide us with grace to help in time of need. Romans 8:37 promises that:

Romans 8:37

37 ...in all these things we are more than conquerors through Him that loved us. (KJV)

LESSON TWENTY-THREE

--------------------∞--------------------

For the last few lessons, we have been discussing Matthew 6:13 where the Lord tells us to pray:

Matthew 6:13a

13 "And do not lead us into temptation,
But deliver us from the evil one. ...." (NKJV)

In our last lesson, we saw that our God is a delivering God who, as we read in 2ⁿᵈ Peter 2:9:

2 Peter 2:9a

9 ...knows how to deliver the godly out of temptations... (NKJV)

And we also read the great promise that we have in 1ˢᵗ Corinthians 10:13. That is where Paul writes:

1 Corinthians 10:13

13 No temptation has overtaken you but such as is common to man; <u>and God is faithful</u>, who will not allow you to be tempted beyond what you are able, but with the temptation will provide the way of escape also, so that you will be able to endure it. (NASB) *{Emphasis added}*

From Genesis to Revelation we see that God delivers His people from the evil one. He delivers us victoriously through His Son Jesus from all the hard trials and tests that come upon us, and from Satan's attacks both without and within.

But even though we have this promise, we are not to be like those who long for trials, nor should we want the sifting that the devil brings through diverse temptations. Rather, we pray, "Father, do not lead us into temptation." First Corinthians 10:13 promises us that God will provide a way out, but the temptation has placed us at a terrible risk, not to mention the cost of precious time and spiritual effort. So obviously we should never desire to be tempted. Instead, we should pray not to be exposed to temptation, and, if exposed, to be delivered from surrendering to it. And we should also ask our Father to keep us from trials and difficulties—to keep us from the enemy's grasp. We are not to long for problems. Then, if for a reason and a purpose, God ordains that we must go through trials, we have the confidence and joy of knowing that the testing of our faith will produce in us perseverance and character and true hope in God's delivering power. We know that God does not delight in our evil circumstances but is on the side of His people and desires to rescue them. And we are confident that, as we are in Jesus, we will have the victory and deliverance from any trial and from any of the devil's temptations, not to our glory but to God's glory.

Thus we pray, "Father, deliver us from the evil one." And prayer is ***extremely*** important to that deliverance. We have studied that there are tests which the Lord wants us to go through and which He will lead us into to do us good in the end—to prove our faithfulness or our sinfulness—to teach us, so that we may come to know ourselves and learn our dependence on Him. And there are adversities we face simply as His servants for the sake of the going forth of the gospel of Christ. But I am convinced that many of the trials we go through are self-inflicted and not the perfect heart's will of God. Or if they are His will, they last far longer than He desires. However, if we adopt a right attitude in our prayers, I believe there is much heartache we can avoid.

What are the wrong attitudes we should avoid? There are many, but three stand out: sinfulness, hopelessness, and faithlessness. Let us look first at sinfulness. Our sins give Satan a foothold in our lives to play havoc. And when difficulties result, we often spend too much time questioning God about why He has allowed this trial to happen, rather than looking at ourselves and bringing our sins to Him in prayer. Our focus should be to ask for His forgiveness and His life changing power, and to seek Him for deliverance from the situation which was sown by our unrighteousness. Therefore a right attitude in prayer would be to deal with sin quickly and, each and every day, ask the Lord to show us those areas that we need to change and bring to the cross of Jesus—so that we will not fall under temptation or trials.

The second wrong attitude, hopelessness, says to the targeted person that he or she was just born to suffer—to go through trials and be beaten about by the enemy. And this attitude of course is itself a lie of the devil. Those stricken by hopelessness are so devoured by the enemy that the true trials and sacrifices God might have for them, for the sake of the gospel, are never known. The right attitude we should have in prayer, then, is what we studied: "Father, lead us not into temptation, neither lead us into tests or hard trials." We should appreciate and desire the hedge of protection God promises to place around us and each day pray for this barrier to Satan's assault. We should hope in the goodness of our God, and our prayer requests ought to reflect this.

The third wrong attitude, faithlessness, shows itself when a trial does occur, and it can be often linked to hopelessness. God is looking for us to persevere and be patient and trust in Him to deliver us. But patience does not mean despondent acceptance, but rather joyful belief in what God will accomplish. Those who suffer from faithlessness cannot see God ever manifesting a solution to the problem. They are like a person stuck in the mud who has given up trying to get their vehicle out. Even if a tow truck passed in front of them, their despair or unbelief or resignation (or all three) would keep them from seeing it. But a right attitude in prayer is to believe in who God is and what He can do and then to come calmly but faithfully before His throne. We are to bring each of our trials and situations before God and, with all our heart, we are to pray in the power of the Holy Spirit, "Father, deliver us from the evil one." And Jesus gives us a reason for our faith in His deliverance:

Matthew 6:13b

13 "…For Yours is the kingdom and the power and the glory forever. Amen." (NKJV)

We are brought full circle back to our discussion of the mighty power and glory of the kingdom of heaven—a kingdom permeated with the miraculous working of God.

In this series on prayer, we have spoken several times about Simon Peter. In Luke Chapter 22 we have the account of the Last Supper. In verse 28 Jesus tells the apostles:

Luke 22:28

> 28 "You are those who have stood by Me in My trials *(peirasmos)*;" (NASB) *{Clarification in parenthesis added}*

And then in verse 31 we read that the Lord says:

Luke 22:31-34

> 31 "Simon, Simon, Satan has asked to sift all of you as wheat.
> 32 But I have prayed for you, Simon, that your faith may not fail. And when you have turned back, strengthen your brothers."
> 33 But he replied, "Lord, I am ready to go with You to prison and to death."
> 34 Jesus answered, "I tell you, Peter, before the rooster crows today, you will deny three times that you know Me." (NIV) *{Capitalization for deity added}*

And in Matthew Chapter 26, Peter tells the Lord:

Matthew 26:33

> 33 ..."Even though all may fall away because of You, I will never fall away." (NASB)

Peter had been with the Lord throughout His trials. Now in the last trial, Satan will use it as a time of great temptation for Peter. Notice how Jesus says, "Satan has asked to sift all of you as wheat." Satan is the source of the evil and the "sifting", but he has to ask for the authority to do so, even as we saw in the case of Job. And God allows it for a purpose. But the Lord does <u>not</u> want Peter to fall. He prays that Peter's faith will not fail. And even though He knows Peter's weaknesses will be played on by Satan and He prophesizes that Peter will deny Him, yet Jesus knows His prayers for Peter have not gone unanswered, for He says:

Luke 22:32b

> 32 ..."And when you have turned back, strengthen your brothers." (NIV)

Earlier in Chapter 22 of Luke, up in verse 24, we read the occasion that prompted this conversation:

Luke 22:24

24 A dispute also arose among them as to which of them was considered to be greatest. (NIV)

This is not the first time that the disciples have debated this question, necessitating that the Lord teach them about humility, which He proceeds to do in verses 25 to 27. Again we see how our cherished sins can give the enemy a foothold against us. You can almost hear Satan coming before God the Father saying, "See this one who thinks he is great and will stand with Your Son. But threaten his life and he will flee and will deny Him like all the rest."

We also see how Jesus interceded for His friend in prayer. And we should likewise, in our prayer time, bring others before the Lord and ask that their faith may not fail in times of trial.

As we continue in Luke 22, Jesus and His disciples leave the upper room where they ate the Passover and go out to the Mount of Olives. In verse 40 we read:

Luke 22:40

40 When He arrived at the place, He said to them, "Pray that you may not enter into temptation." (NASB)

Peirasmos is used again, but the context here is real temptation and not just trial. How important prayer is to strengthen us so that we do not <u>enter</u> the temptation—that we are not engulfed in the sin of the situation and seduced by a trial to sin. When we pray, "lead us" or "bring us not into temptation," we are not only asking the Father not to allow us to be led into temptation, but also to give us the strength to resist temptation. The trial that was about to happen in the Garden of Gethsemane, when Judas would lead those who would arrest Jesus to that location, was ordained to happen. But the disciples were to pray for spiritual strength that they would not "enter into temptation"; that is, that they would avoid being enticed to do evil themselves. It is from the close relationship with God that develops from prayer that we find the supernatural strength of the kingdom to resist.

188

We must pray to build up spiritual strength to resist the enemy, and we must pray in order to bring this important petition before God. Remember how we studied previously that we must ask the Lord in order to receive? If we count it as of utmost importance not to enter into temptation, we will daily ask the Father for His grace. And I am sure you probably already know how hard it can sometimes be to actually spend that time in deep prayer with God. The flesh—that is, the sinful human nature we all have in these bodies—many times will fight against us when, in our hearts, we truly desire to pray.

It is amazing how many ways the flesh can become distracted when we begin to pray to God. Paul writes in Romans 7:18:

Romans 7:18

18 For I know that in me (that is, in my flesh,) dwelleth no good thing: for to will is present with me; but how to perform that which is good, I find not. (Webster)

Satan takes advantage of the weaknesses of our flesh to cause us to enter into temptation. At Gethsemane, he will use the fears in their flesh to cause Peter and the other disciples to abandon the Lord. And their weaknesses caused them earlier to ignore Jesus' admonition to pray. In Matthew 26:39-45 we read:

Matthew 26:39-45

39 And He went a little beyond them, and fell on His face and prayed, saying, "My Father, if it is possible, let this cup pass from Me; yet not as I will, but as You will."

40 And He came to the disciples and found them sleeping, and said to Peter, "So, you men could not keep watch with Me for one hour?

41 "Keep watching and praying that you may not enter into temptation; the spirit is willing, but the flesh is weak."

42 He went away again a second time and prayed, saying, "My Father, if this cannot pass away unless I drink it, Your will be done."

43 Again He came and found them sleeping, for their eyes were heavy.

44 And He left them again, and went away and prayed a third time, saying the same thing once more.

189

45 Then He came to the disciples and said to them, "Are you still sleeping and resting? Behold, the hour is at hand and the Son of Man is being betrayed into the hands of sinners." (NASB)

In verse 41, Jesus again told them to watch and pray lest they enter into temptation. Prayer is crucial to defend against temptation. But notice that their eyes were heavy. They wanted to rest and sleep. So while Peter in his heart desired to stand by the Lord, his flesh would win when the trial came. As Jesus said, the spirit is willing but the flesh is weak. And we likewise can have a battle with our flesh when we try to pray. But we must keep awake and keep asking the Father to give us strength over our human nature. By the Lord's own words, prayer is important if we are to stand firm and shun temptation—if we are to avoid falling into sin and being sifted by the enemy. We are not to be found asleep, but we are to be watchful. And our prayer life keeps us watchful as we place all our cares before God and as we ask Him to change us into the image of His Son.

Peter, who truly learned humility, would write years later in 1st Peter 5:6-10:

1 Peter 5:6-10

6 Therefore humble yourselves under the mighty hand of God, that He may exalt you at the proper time,

7 casting all your anxiety on Him, because He cares for you.

8 Be of sober spirit, be on the alert. Your adversary, the devil, prowls around like a roaring lion, seeking someone to devour.

9 But resist him, firm in your faith, knowing that the same experiences of suffering are being accomplished by your brethren who are in the world.

10 After you have suffered for a little while, the God of all grace, who called you to His eternal glory in Christ, will Himself perfect, confirm, strengthen and establish you. (NASB) *{Emphasis added}*

LESSON TWENTY-FOUR

———————✕———————

I n today's lesson, we will be closing up this section of our study where we have been focusing on the Lord's Prayer as given in Matthew Chapter 6. We have been examining the last verse, verse 13, where Jesus teaches us to pray to the Father:

Matthew 6:13

    13 "And do not lead us into temptation,
         But deliver us from the evil one.
         For Yours is the kingdom and the power and the glory forever.
            Amen." (NKJV)

Now there are two questions that often come up about this verse and it is a good idea to discuss them at this point in our study. While we have been reading this Scripture from the *New King James Version*, some liturgical renderings of the Our Father will often say, "but deliver us from evil" rather than "but deliver us from the evil one." And this is the way the old *King James* also translates this section.

Matthew 6:13

    13 "And lead us not into temptation, but deliver us from evil: For
         thine is the kingdom, and the power, and the glory, for ever.
         Amen." (KJV)

So the first question is, "Why is there this difference, and should the Scripture be rendered *evil* or *evil one*?" In the Greek, the adjective meaning evil *(ponēros)* comes after the Greek article for "the," making the expression literally "the evil." But it is used here in a grammatical case *(tou ponērou)* which makes it difficult to know whether the meaning is "the evil thing" or "the evil one." The *King James* then translated it simply "evil," but many scholars feel it is more accurately translated "the evil one," speaking clearly about Satan.

Besides the *New King James Version*, many other translations render it "the evil one" including the *New International Version*. And there is solid internal evidence in the Scriptures to do so. In Matthew 13:19, the grammatical case *(ho ponēros)* is much clearer, and this same word with its article is always translated the evil one or the wicked one (including in the *King James Version*):

Matthew 13:19

19 "When anyone hears the word of the kingdom, and does not understand it, then the wicked one comes and snatches away what was sown in his heart. This is he who received seed by the wayside." (NKJV) *{Emphasis added}*

In the sister passage to Matthew 13:19, Mark 4:15, this wicked one is called "Satan":

Mark 4:15

15 "And these are the ones by the wayside where the word is sown. When they hear, Satan comes immediately and takes away the word that was sown in their hearts." (NKJV)

In a related parable which Jesus tells a few verses down in Matthew Chapter 13, He also makes it clear that this enemy is the devil. In Matthew 13:38 to 39, we read in the NIV:

Matthew 13:38-39a

38 "The field is the world, and the good seed stands for the people of the kingdom. The weeds are the people of the evil one,
39 and the enemy who sows them is the devil. ..." (NIV) *{Emphasis added}*

It is important to note that the phrase translated "the evil one" in verse 38 is the same as the one we are studying in the Lord's Prayer in Matthew 6:13, even in its grammatical form: *tou ponērou.*

And there is no debate about 1st John 2:13 or 1st John 5:18, where this Greek phrase "the evil," because of the masculine gender used, clearly must be translated "the evil one" or "the wicked one":

1 John 2:13

13 I am writing to you, fathers,
   because you know Him who is from the beginning.
I am writing to you, young men,
   because you have overcome the evil one. (NIV)
   {Emphasis and capitalization for deity added}

1 John 5:18

18 We know that whoever is born of God does not sin; but he
who has been born of God keeps himself, and the wicked one
does not touch him. (NKJV) *{Emphasis added}*

In the *King James*, the phrase used in all of these Scriptures—
Matthew 13:19, Matthew 13:38, 1st John 2:13 and 1st John 5:18—is
likewise translated "the wicked one." Now the *King James* does
translate the Lord's words in John 17:15 as simply "the evil." We
again have the more uncertain ablative or genitive case, *tou ponērou,*
as in the Lord's Prayer:

John 17:15

15 "I pray not that Thou shouldest take them out of the world,
but that Thou shouldest keep them from the evil." (KJV)

But given John's teaching in 1st John 2:13 and 1st John 5:18, the
uncertainty of whether the Lord is saying "the evil one" or "the evil
thing" disappears and the renderings of the *New King James Version*
and *New International Version* become more accurate to the intent:

John 17:15

15 "I do not pray that You should take them out of the world, but
that You should keep them from the evil one." (NKJV)

John 17:15

15 "My prayer is not that You take them out of the world but that
You protect them from the evil one." (NIV) *{Capitalization for
deity added}*

Finally, Paul's instruction to the church at Ephesus, which we have looked at and discussed twice before, makes it scripturally apparent how we should translate *the evil*:

Ephesians 6:10-13

10 Finally, my brethren, be strong in the Lord and in the power of His might.

11 Put on the whole armor of God, that you may be able to stand against the wiles of the devil.

12 For we do not wrestle against flesh and blood, but against principalities, against powers, against the rulers of the darkness of this age, against spiritual hosts of wickedness in the heavenly places.

13 Therefore take up the whole armor of God, that you may be able to withstand in the evil day, and having done all, to stand. (NKJV)

So we have confidence in rendering the prayer in Matthew 6:13, "deliver us from the evil one" or "deliver us from the wicked one," rather than just "deliver us from evil."

OK, let us try and answer the second common question. It has to do with the last half of Matthew 6:13:

Matthew 6:13b

13 "...For Yours is the kingdom and the power and the glory forever. Amen." (NKJV)

In some churches, this part of the Lord's Prayer is not included when they say the Our Father. Also, in some modern translations, this part of the verse will be taken out of the body of the text and placed down in the footnotes. Because this part of verse 13 is missing from a few of the oldest Greek manuscripts, some believe this doxology was not an original part of the prayer but was added when the prayer was later used in public worship. That is why it is sometimes removed. But these few older manuscripts are not necessarily the most accurate representation of the original writings. And both the Textus Receptus, which is the accepted and Traditional Text and which was used for the *King James* translation, as well as the Majority Text, which is based on the consensus of the majority of existing Greek manuscripts, include this second part of verse 13.

And I believe these are indeed the accurately recorded words of our Lord Jesus. The prayer does not seem finished without them.

When Jesus prays, "For Yours is the kingdom and the power and the glory forever. Amen," He is bringing us full circle in acknowledging God as our source of all things. It is a beautiful statement of praise which sums up the confidence we have in prayer. It is because of His kingdom and His power and His glory that we know that He can and He will deliver us from temptations and from the evil one. It is because of Him that we know that we have forgiveness of sin and the answer to our daily petition. These words of praise are a wonderful summary of the power of the kingdom of heaven which comes to earth and of God's ability to bring forth His perfect pleasing will, which we have studied over these many lessons.

And just as we started our prayer with praise:

Matthew 6:9b
9   "...Our Father in heaven,
     Hallowed be Your name." (NKJV)

Now we end our prayer with praise:

Matthew 6:13b
13   "...For Yours is the kingdom and the power and the glory
     forever. Amen." (NKJV)

It is always good to end our time of prayer with the Lord with praise. When we praise God and lift Him up in worship, we are lifting up the source of our hope. We know we have a sure foundation for our hope: His kingdom, His power, and His glory. And the praising lifts our spirits.

And as we praise Him in the Holy Spirit, as our spirits are lifted in His glory, something wonderful happens: our faith in Him is established—an active living faith. We touch the throne of heaven through our praise and we receive glimpses into heavenly things. If even for a moment, we begin to see things as God sees them. We can begin to believe the way He wants us to believe. His IS the kingdom! His IS the power! His IS the glory! He is that He is. And that kingdom, power, and glory are forever—everlasting. So while we might be in a real battle right now in this life with the flesh and Satan and his demons and all the evil around us, it is a battle already won. We know the outcome. It is the Lord's battle, to be conducted in the Lord's power, and when we so believe and so submit and so pray, the victory is firm and secure in Jesus. Hallelujah! Amen.

And that is exactly how Jesus ends the prayer, with an Amen. But some people say *Amen* but they do not really understand what it means. *Amen* comes from the Hebrew into both the New Testament Greek and into English. Its definition is centered on the concept of truth and it is filled with far more meaning than simply as a period or a signing off word to end a prayer. It is a solemn word, always used with discretion and purpose. It means "truly" or "it is true, it is trustworthy," "so it is, so be it," "may it be fulfilled," and "thus it shall be." It comes off the Hebrew meaning "to make firm, to build up, to support" and thus figuratively to be firm or faithful, to be permanent and enduring, to be true and certain, to be trustworthy.

Maybe we can better understand its meaning if we see how it is used as a divine title or attribute of God. In Deuteronomy 7:9 we read:

Deuteronomy 7:9

9 "Know therefore that the LORD thy God, He is God, the faithful God, who keepeth covenant and mercy with them that love Him and keep His commandments to a thousand generations:" (Webster) *{Emphasis added}*

And the word there for *faithful* in the expression "the faithful God" is in Hebrew *'aman* (pronounced we believe as *aw-man'*) or Amen. God is the faithful God or the Amen God.

Isaiah 65:16 reads:

Isaiah 65:16a

16 "That he who blesseth himself in the earth shall bless himself in the God of truth; and he that sweareth in the earth shall swear by the God of truth; ..." (KJV) *{Emphasis added}*

The Hebrew word translated both times as "truth" is *'amen* (pronounced we believe as *aw-mane'* and coming from *'aman*). God is the God of truth. God is the God of Amen. The Lord is the One who stays eternally true. He is the One who can always be trusted. And just as God is true and faithful, so His Word and testimony are sure, as are His promises. In Psalm 19:7 we read:

Psalm 19:7

7   The law of the LORD is perfect, converting the soul: the testimony of the LORD is sure, making wise the simple. (KJV)

The word translated here as "sure" is again *'aman*. The testimony of the Lord is <u>Amen</u>. And in speaking about the salvation in Jesus, Isaiah the prophet writes in Isaiah 55:3:

Isaiah 55:3

3   "Incline your ear, and come unto Me: hear, and your soul shall live; and I will make an everlasting covenant with you, even the <u>sure</u> *('aman)* mercies of David." (KJV) *{Emphasis and clarification in parenthesis added}*

The everlasting covenant is based on the sure mercies, or literally in Hebrew, the Amen mercies of David. Also take notice that, in the New Testament, *Amen* is used as a title of the Lord Jesus Christ. In Revelation 3:14, the glorified Lord says:

Revelation 3:14

14 "And to the angel of the church of the Laodiceans write; These things saith the Amen, the <u>Faithful</u> and <u>True</u> Witness, the Beginning *(that is, the Originating Source)* of the creation of God;" (Webster) *{Emphasis and clarification in parenthesis added)*

Jesus, just like His Father, is eternally true and reliable, and through Him all the purposes and plans of God are accomplished and established. Second Corinthians declares of Christ:

2 Corinthians 1:20

20 For all the promises of God in Him are Yes, and in Him Amen, to the glory of God through us. (NKJV)

Jesus is the living Amen—the living truth and confirmation of the revelation and power of God.

The people of Israel also used *Amen* as a solemn word to associate themselves audibly with the prayer being offered. It served as an exclamation of response. The word carried the weight of support and confirmation and approval for the statement or prayer or song.

We see such usage of *'amen* in the instructions Moses gave to the people for when they would cross the Jordan into the Promised Land. In Deuteronomy Chapter 27, Moses gives directions for pronouncing blessings from Mount Gerizim and curses from Mount Ebal. And he says, starting in verse 14:

Deuteronomy 27:14-16

14 "The Levites shall then answer and say to all the men of Israel with a loud voice,

15 'Cursed is the man who makes an idol or a molten image, an abomination to the LORD, the work of the hands of the craftsman, and sets it up in secret.' And all the people shall answer and say, 'Amen.'

16 'Cursed is he who dishonors his father or mother.' And all the people shall say, 'Amen.'" (NASB)

And it continues this way up to verse 26 where it ends:

Deuteronomy 27:26

26 "'Cursed is he who does not confirm the words of this law by doing them.' And all the people shall say, 'Amen.'" (NASB)

In 1st Chronicles Chapter 16 we have David's wonderful song of thanksgiving to God. It ends in verse 36:

1 Chronicles 16:36

36 Blessed be the LORD, the God of Israel,
From everlasting even to everlasting.
Then all the people said, "Amen," and praised the LORD. (NASB)

Likewise, the early Christians followed the same example in using *Amen* as a response of affirmation and support. Paul cautions in 1st Corinthians 14:16:

1 Corinthians 14:16

16 Otherwise, if you bless with the spirit, how will he who occupies the place of the uninformed say "Amen" at your giving of thanks, since he does not understand what you say? (NKJV)

And Paul and the other epistle writers chose *Amen* as a wonderful exclamation of "SO BE IT" to end their prayers and doxologies, at the close of their letters, and when speaking about the wonders of God. Jude concludes his letter:

Jude 1:25
> 25 To God the only wise, our Savior, be glory and majesty, dominion and power, both now and ever. Amen. (Webster)

Many times Jesus would introduce His own sayings with either *Amen* or a double *Amen (Amen, Amen)* to stress the importance of His words. These are usually translated, "Verily," "Assuredly" or "I tell you the truth" and, in the case of the double *Amen*, "Verily, verily" and "Most assuredly."

In the Lord's Prayer, Jesus is using *Amen* to emphasize the truth of the preceding statement of praise to the Father—"For Yours is the kingdom and the power and the glory forever"—and as a holy declaration for the prayer as a whole. So when we close our prayers with *Amen*, we are, first, confirming our belief in the truth of what was spoken, what went before in the prayer. Second, we are petitioning and looking forward to the full manifestation of that truth. And third, we are pronouncing our faith that this truth will come about because it is based on the permanent trustworthiness of Him Who Is. It is so. May it be fulfilled. Thus it shall be. SO BE IT!

Appropriately the Bible ends:

Revelation 22:20-21
> 20 He who testifies to these things says, "Surely I am coming quickly." Amen. Even so, come, Lord Jesus!
> 21 The grace of our Lord Jesus Christ be with you all. Amen. (NKJV)

LESSON TWENTY-FIVE

———————∞———————

T oday we would like to move along in our study on prayer and consider the importance of persistence to an effective prayer life. In our last lesson, we concluded our study of the Lord's Prayer as recorded in Matthew Chapter 6, where it was part of the teaching Jesus presented to His disciples and the multitudes in His comprehensive Sermon on the Mount. In Luke Chapter 11, we read how, on another occasion, Jesus again taught His disciples to pray. And the Lord uses a similar wording to that which He gave at the Sermon on the Mount, with the exception that a closing praise is not recorded (and this is probably another reason why some churches elect to eliminate that last line when reciting the Our Father, as we discussed in our last lesson). Let us read from Luke Chapter 11 verses 1 to 4:

Luke 11:1-4

1   Now it came to pass, as He was praying in a certain place, when He ceased, that one of His disciples said to Him, "Lord, teach us to pray, as John also taught his disciples."

2   So He said to them, "When you pray, say:

Our Father in heaven,
Hallowed be Your name.
Your kingdom come.
Your will be done
On earth as it is in heaven.

3   Give us day by day our daily bread.

4   And forgive us our sins,
For we also forgive everyone who is indebted to us.
And do not lead us into temptation,

But deliver us from the evil one." (NKJV)

We notice in verse 1 that one of His disciples came to Him and asked Him to teach them how to pray after Jesus Himself finished praying. Likewise, the diligence which we give to our own time of prayer with God can serve as an example to inspire others to want to pray. The Lord Jesus is not praying here to be seen by men; rather, His concern is to spend time with His Father. But obviously, when prayer is a real part of our lives and we are dedicated to spending time with God, others will know it and will be encouraged to do likewise, especially those who are close to us.

And who is more important to set an example for than our children? Not only should we as parents teach them to say grace and to pray at bedtime, but we should teach them by the example of our lives to always seek the Lord, even as Jesus' disciples were motivated by His example. They should know from the beginning that mommy and daddy love God and talk to Him regularly. It is amazing how much little children watch and absorb. If something is real in our lives they will know it. If something is just a show or a ritual or words without substance, they will know that too. Amen.

OK. So the occasion for this teaching of the Lord's Prayer was prompted by a request from Jesus' disciples to teach them to pray, as John the Baptist also taught his disciples. And the interesting thing here is that Jesus does not stop the teaching with the Our Father, but rather, starting at verse 5 after the body of the prayer, Jesus continues to answer their request with the parable of the man who needs loaves of bread for a visiting friend. We will pick up the reading at verse 5 and read to verse 8.

Luke 11:5-8

    5   Then He said to them, "Suppose one of you has a friend, and goes to him at midnight and says to him, 'Friend, lend me three loaves;

    6   for a friend of mine has come to me from a journey, and I have nothing to set before him';

    7   and from inside he answers and says, 'Do not bother me; the door has already been shut and my children and I are in bed; I cannot get up and give you anything.'

8 "I tell you, even though he will not get up and give him anything because he is his friend, yet because of his persistence
he will get up and give him as much as he needs." (NASB)

In this story, Jesus illustrates the importance of **persistence in
prayer**. As He says in verse 8, "because of his persistence he will
get up and give him as much as he needs." The point is clear. If a
mere man will give food out of annoyance in response to continued
requests, how much more will God, who desires to give, respond
to an ardent soul who continuously seeks Him and His help. And if
a lukewarm and half-asleep friend would respond to our perseverance, how much more our one true friend who gave His life for us.
Jesus is this friend of true believers, as He says in John Chapter 15
verses 13-14:

John 15:13-14
13 "Greater love has no one than this, that one lay down his life
for his friends.
14 "You are My friends if you do what I command you." (NASB)

When we speak about determination and stick-to-itiveness in
bringing our petitions before God, we should note that this is not the
babbling of the heathens or meaningless repetitions. Instead, we
have here the constant seeking of God's face on an issue of **much**
meaning. Just as the friend in the parable knows from the man's
heartfelt requests that this is something that he really desires and
is important to him, so our concerns are revealed by our earnest-
ness in prayer.

Now this is not to say that God needs our perseverance to know
our hearts. But often we do. And not only that, but I believe that
when we persist in our requests, we set things in motion in heavenly realms. In the Old Testament book of Daniel, we read how
Daniel would pray and fast for his people and Jerusalem and to
receive understanding. On one such occasion, Daniel was praying
and fasting three full weeks. Finally he received a vision of a glorious
man whose face had the appearance of lightning and the sound of
whose words were like the voice of a multitude. This man was probably a holy angel standing in the place of—that is, giving a vision of—
the pre-incarnate Jesus. In Chapter 10 of Daniel, we read starting
at verse 10:

Daniel 10:10-14

10 Then behold, a hand touched me and set me trembling on my hands and knees.

11 He said to me, "O Daniel, man of high esteem, understand the words that I am about to tell you and stand upright, for I have now been sent to you." And when he had spoken this word to me, I stood up trembling.

12 Then he said to me, "Do not be afraid, Daniel, for from the first day that you set your heart on understanding this and on humbling yourself before your God, your words were heard, and I have come in response to your words.

13 "But the prince of the kingdom of Persia was withstanding me for twenty-one days; then behold, Michael, one of the chief princes, came to help me, for I had been left there with the kings of Persia.

14 "Now I have come to give you an understanding of what will happen to your people in the latter days, for the vision pertains to the days yet future." (NASB)

This supernatural messenger then goes on to give revelation to Daniel in great detail about future events. So Daniel's prayer for understanding was heard the first day he made his petition and the messenger was sent. But the manifestation of the answer took 21 days, because there was a battle going on in the heavenly realms. The prince of the kingdom of Persia was a demonic spirit who ruled over Persia and did not want his territory intruded on by the angel sent to Daniel. Michael, as we are told down in verse 21, is the prince or angel of the Jewish people and he comes and aids the messenger. Note that the battle between these spiritual forces delayed the answer to Daniel's prayer.

It reminds us of the Scripture we saw in our last lesson and have studied several times now in Ephesians 6:12:

Ephesians 6:12

12 For we do not wrestle against flesh and blood, but against principalities, against powers, against the rulers of the darkness of this age, against spiritual hosts of wickedness in the heavenly places. (NKJV)

203

And though we know that Daniel was heard the very first day, would the battle have been won and the prayer been answered if he had given up praying the second day or the third day or even the twentieth day? What would have happened in the heavenly realms if he had vacillated or become discouraged and said, "I guess God doesn't want to help me."?

Our persistence in prayer is a demonstration of our hope in the goodness of God's nature and of our faith. We are putting to proof our belief that He is, and that He is a rewarder of those who diligently seek Him. And our faith in God is powerful. As Jesus said in Matthew 9:29:

Matthew 9:29

29 ..."According to your faith let it be done to you"; (NIV)

We should make a distinction here. When we speak about persistence in prayer, we are not talking about persisting in whining or prayers of doubt, but rather coming calmly but fervently before the Lord in faith, believing. And we are promised that such prayers of faith produce much.

In our first lesson we studied the straightforward prayer which Elijah offered on Mount Carmel and which stood out in sharp contrast to the meaningless repetitions and antics of the heathen. Now there was at that time a drought and a severe famine which the Lord had brought on the land through Elijah's ministry. Elijah knew that it was now the Lord's will to end the drought. In faith, he tells Israel's king, Ahab, to "go up, eat and drink; for there is the sound of abundance of rain." Then in 1st Kings 18:42 we read:

1 Kings 18:42-45

42 So Ahab went up to eat and drink. But Elijah went up to the top of Carmel; and he crouched down on the earth and put his face between his knees.

43 He said to his servant, "Go up now, look toward the sea." So he went up and looked and said, "There is nothing." And he said, "Go back" seven times.

44 It came about at the seventh time, that he said, "Behold, a cloud as small as a man's hand is coming up from the sea." And he said, "Go up, say to Ahab, 'Prepare your chariot and go down, so that the heavy shower does not stop you.'"

45 In a little while the sky grew black with clouds and wind, and there was a heavy shower. And Ahab rode and went to Jezreel. (NASB)

Elijah, in faith, earnestly prayed even when there was not a cloud to be seen in the sky. And he persisted in that prayer. James, in James Chapter 5 verses 13 to 18, writes about the prayer of faith and the earnest prayers of Elijah:

James 5:13-18

13 Is anyone among you suffering? Then he must pray. Is anyone cheerful? He is to sing praises.

14 Is anyone among you sick? Then he must call for the elders of the church and they are to pray over him, anointing him with oil in the name of the Lord;

15 and the prayer offered in faith will restore the one who is sick, and the Lord will raise him up, and if he has committed sins, they will be forgiven him.

16 Therefore, confess your sins to one another, and pray for one another so that you may be healed. The effective *(fervent)* prayer of a righteous man can accomplish much.

17 Elijah was a man with a nature like ours, and he prayed earnestly that it would not rain, and it did not rain on the earth for three years and six months.

18 Then he prayed again, and the sky poured rain and the earth produced its fruit. (NASB) *{Emphasis and additional Greek meaning in parenthesis added}*

The wonderful part about this Scripture is that it tells us that Elijah was a man with a nature like ours. And notice the three elements in this section of James that come together for effective prayer. First, as we previously examined, we must confess our sins and seek God's forgiveness and righteousness, that we can stand justified before Him. Second, we must pray a prayer of faith, not doubt. And third, we must pray earnestly—fervently. Literally, the text reads in verse 17: *he prayed with prayer*—a Greek idiom showing the intensity and zeal of his prayers. Then our prayers can accomplish much or, as some translations put verse 16, they are "powerful and effective"!

In Luke 18:1-8 we have Jesus' parable of the persistent widow:

Luke 18:1-8

1   Then He spoke a parable to them, that men always ought to pray and not lose heart,

2   saying: "There was in a certain city a judge who did not fear God nor regard man.

3   "Now there was a widow in that city; and she came to him, saying, 'Get justice for me from my adversary.'

4   "And he would not for a while; but afterward he said within himself, 'Though I do not fear God nor regard man,

5   'yet because this widow troubles me I will avenge her, lest by her continual coming she weary me.'"

6   Then the Lord said, "Hear what the unjust judge said.

7   "And shall God not avenge His own elect who cry out day and night to Him, though He bears long with them?

8   "I tell you that He will avenge them speedily. Nevertheless, when the Son of Man comes, will He really find faith on the earth?" (NKJV)

The reason Jesus tells them this parable is given in verse 1:

Luke 18:1

1   Then He spoke a parable to them, <u>that men always ought to pray and not lose heart,</u> (NKJV) *{Emphasis added}*

And if there is one thing I want you to get out of today's lesson it is this: If we are asking God for good things—the things which are according to His will, the things which He knows we need and which are just and right—we are always to pray and to persist in prayer and we should never, never lose heart! This is the faith the Lord wants from His people. If the wicked and unjust judge will give justice because of the widow's continual coming to him with her requests, **how much more** will our God, the very source of justice and righteousness, bring about justice and the answer to prayers for His own chosen ones who earnestly and persistently petition Him day and night.

LESSON TWENTY-SIX

———————∝———————

Welcome back to our Bible study series on prayer. In our last lesson, we were studying the section in Luke Chapter 11 where one of the disciples asked Jesus to teach them to pray. In response, the Lord again taught them what we call the Lord's Prayer, but He did not stop the lesson there. He goes on to tell them in verse 5:

Luke 11:5-8

5 …"Suppose one of you has a friend, and goes to him at midnight and says to him, 'Friend, lend me three loaves;

6 for a friend of mine has come to me from a journey, and I have nothing to set before him';

7 and from inside he answers and says, 'Do not bother me; the door has already been shut and my children and I are in bed; I cannot get up and give you anything.'

8 "I tell you, even though he will not get up and give him anything because he is his friend, yet because of his persistence he will get up and give him as much as he needs." (NASB)

In the last lesson, we discussed the importance of persistence in our prayers. If this annoyed friend will give in response to the man's persistence, how much more will our heavenly Father who desires to give us that which is good. And I believe that word "good" is a key to understanding the confidence we have before God. If we are asking for what is good and what is right—that which is according to God's Word—we should have no doubt when we go before our Father in prayer, even if there seems from our perspective to be some delay in receiving an answer. We saw last time, in the case of Daniel's prayer, how a spiritual battle in the heavenly realms can sometimes detain the appointed answer to a prayer request. But we are to continue and persist in faith before God.

Now I do not want to read too much into the parable of the friend that comes at midnight, but notice two things. First, the one who is making the request is asking for the bread to have something to set before a friend of his who has come to him on his journey. Second, this man specifically asks for three loaves. And three in the Bible often signifies a holy number, even as the one God is three—Father, Son and Holy Spirit. So the request is a holy request that is concerned for another. In fact, if you think about it, when we are saved and we truly receive the Lord Jesus, our focus and desires change, and our prayers reflect this. From being self-centered and selfish before, we begin to hunger for the Lord's work and for His gospel to go forward. We receive a yearning to see others saved and made whole and healed and to have their lives arranged right with God and blessed. And we start to take our own responsibilities to loved ones and colleagues more seriously. As Jesus lives inside of us, we want to do what is right. We want to do right by our spouses and our children and in our jobs and for our churches. We want to see Satan's power broken. And we want to be whole spirit, soul and body, so that God can use us effectively as servants for His kingdom.

Now given all that I have just said, as we are asking for the good and holy and right things to change this world for Jesus, will not God hear and answer? Even an evil boss would supply the proper tools needed for his employees to accomplish their work. Certainly God, who is all good, will heal us, make whole our lives, and give us the holy desires of our hearts as we serve Him.

Psalm 37 verses 3 to 5 says:

Psalm 37:3-5
> 3   Trust in the LORD, and do good; so shalt thou dwell in the land, and verily thou shalt be fed.
> 4   Delight thyself also in the LORD; and He shall give thee the desires of thine heart.
> 5   Commit thy way unto the LORD; trust also in Him; and He shall bring it to pass. (KJV)

And the implicit promise in Luke 11:8 is that God will give us as many or as much as we need. But we must persist. That is why

Jesus continues on with the teaching in verse 9, which you will recognize from a similar teaching recorded in Matthew 7:7-11 and which we studied back in Lesson Fifteen. The Lord goes on to instruct about prayer in Luke 11:9:

Luke 11:9-13

9   "So I say to you, ask, and it will be given to you; seek, and you will find; knock, and it will be opened to you.

10 "For everyone who asks receives, and he who seeks finds, and to him who knocks it will be opened.

11 "If a son asks for bread from any father among you, will he give him a stone? Or if he asks for a fish, will he give him a serpent instead of a fish?

12 "Or if he asks for an egg, will he offer him a scorpion?

13 "If you then, being evil, know how to give good gifts to your children, how much more will your heavenly Father give the Holy Spirit to those who ask Him!" (NKJV)

How important it is to prayer that we ask and seek and knock, "For everyone who asks receives." The Scriptures are rich in accounts of people who, in much faith, persisted in their search before God. There was the Canaanite woman who continued in her request of Jesus for the healing of her daughter, even after His initial answers would have discouraged others. And Jesus rewarded the woman's persistence. He answers her in Matthew 15:28:

Matthew 15:28

28 ..."Woman, you have great faith! Your request is granted." And her daughter was healed at that moment. (NIV)

There was Zacchaeus, who would not give up on seeing Jesus but ran ahead and climbed a sycamore tree, and the Lord responded by saying:

Luke 19:5

5 ..."Zaccheus, hurry and come down, for today I must stay at your house." (NASB)

Likewise, there was the woman who for twelve years had a flow of blood but who said:

Mark 5:28

> 28 ..."If I just touch His clothes, I will be healed." (NIV)
> *{Capitalization for deity added}*

And she received her healing as Jesus declared to her:

Mark 5:34

> 34 ..."Daughter, your faith has made you well; go in peace and be healed of your affliction." (NASB)

There was blind Bartimeaus who would not stop, when warned by those around him to keep quiet, but called out all the more to Jesus to have mercy on him. Again Jesus answered his request and said:

Mark 10:52

> 52 ..."Go thy way; thy faith hath made thee whole." And immediately he received his sight, and followed Jesus in the way. (KJV)

And there are so many others who in faith persisted in their belief in the goodness of God and displayed it by both their petitions and actions. This too would be a topic for a whole other study. But the point here is that our prayers should reflect the same faith and spunk and resolve.

Furthermore, in this teaching on prayer in Luke 11:11, Jesus again uses the example of a father who gives gifts of food in response to requests from his child. How much more will our heavenly Father, who is all good, give to us. And when we originally studied this concept in Matthew Chapter 7, the Lord concluded **that** teaching by saying:

Matthew 7:11

> 11 "If you then, being evil, know how to give good gifts to your children, how much more will your Father who is in heaven give <u>what is good</u> to those who ask Him!" (NASB)
> *{Emphasis added}*

But notice here, at the summit of His teaching on prayer, what Jesus says is the gift that the Father will give to those who ask:

Luke 11:13

13 "If you then, being evil, know how to give good gifts to your children, how much more will your heavenly Father give <u>the Holy Spirit</u> to those who ask Him!" (NKJV) *{Emphasis added}*

Jesus ends this lesson on prayer by telling them that they are to ask and seek the Father for the gift of the Holy Spirit. He, the Holy Spirit, is what is needed most by those who are saved by the blood of Jesus. And a prime objective of our prayers should be to receive the baptism of the Holy Spirit and the fullness of the gifts which the Holy Spirit has for us. It is by this great gift, made possible by the cross, that we are filled with the power from on high.

As we have discussed, once we are in the Spirit, prayer itself becomes a more real communication. We experience more power and authority in the prayers we lift up, and we are better able to hear God's response through the various and precious gifts which the Holy Spirit now gives us. We are not orphaned, but have true fellowship with our God. So a constant <u>prayer request</u> for all of us should be to ask the Father to give us the completeness and the abundance of the Holy Spirit. Then, as we receive and are in the Spirit, we will in turn have a more potent and effective prayer life as our connection to the Lord is enhanced.

Now, there is much debate in the Christian community as to just when the Holy Spirit is received. And while part of the debate centers on doctrinal differences, part may really be just the result of semantics. Let me quickly layout what I believe the Bible teaches. First of all, we must recognize that the Holy Spirit is involved with the individual throughout life. In Genesis it says that God breathed the breath of life into Adam and he became a living being. And we know the Holy Spirit is the wind or breath of God. So the Holy Spirit exercises the power of the Father in the actual creating of our individual spirits. And all through our lives the Holy Spirit is contending and striving with us to bring us back to God. On our own we could not even see that Jesus is the Christ, the Son of the living God, but at the right time the Holy Spirit softens us and starts to take away the veil from our eyes that we may say yes to God's salvation. And we are in serious danger if we should harden our hearts again and say no.

Then, when we receive Jesus as our Savior, the Holy Spirit comes and works inside of us in a very special way. We are reborn and begin to truly see the kingdom of God. On the evening of

The Nature and Power of Prayer

Resurrection Sunday, the fearful disciples were behind closed doors; Jesus came to them. And we read in John 20:21-22:

John 20:21-22

21 So Jesus said to them again, "Peace be with you; as the Father has sent Me, I also send you."

22 And when He had said this, He breathed on them and said to them, "Receive the Holy Spirit." (NASB)

I believe those words and the breath of the risen Savior upon them signified two things. First, the Holy Spirit from that point on would be doing a work inside of renewal in a gentle way, even as the gentle breath of the Lord came upon them. We read in Acts Chapter 1 verse 2 that, during this time of the Lord's appearances after the resurrection, He gave commandments to the apostles *"through the Holy Spirit."* And Luke also tells us in Luke 24:45 that:

Luke 24:45

45 ...He opened their minds to understand the Scriptures, (NASB)

Second, I believe Jesus was commanding them to and sealing them for a special event that was still to come, when they would indeed receive the Holy Spirit, but this time the Lord's breath would be as a mighty wind. Jesus had told the disciples at the Last Supper in John 16:7:

John 16:7

7 "But I tell you the truth, it is to your advantage that I go away; for if I do not go away, the Helper will not come to you; but if I go, I will send Him to you." (NASB)

And right before His ascension we read in Acts Chapter 1 starting at verse 4:

Acts 1:4-5

4 And being assembled together with them, He commanded them not to depart from Jerusalem, but to wait for the Promise of the Father, "which," He said, "you have heard from Me;

212

5   "for John truly baptized with water, but you shall be baptized with the Holy Spirit not many days from now." (NKJV) *{Emphasis added}*

Wait for the Promise—wait for the Gift—of the Father. They were going to be baptized—immersed, saturated—with the Holy Spirit. Jesus goes on to tell them in verse 8:

Acts 1:8-9
8   "But you will receive power when the Holy Spirit comes on you; and you will be My witnesses in Jerusalem, and in all Judea and Samaria, and to the ends of the earth."
9   After He said this, He was taken up before their very eyes, and a cloud hid Him from their sight. (NIV) *{Capitalization for deity added}*

They were to wait in Jerusalem until they were "clothed with power from on high," as it says in Luke 24:49. And only then were they to go out and be His witnesses:

Luke 24:49
49   "And behold, I am sending forth the promise of My Father upon you; but you are to stay in the city until you are clothed with power from on high." (NASB)

This is so important in understanding the request of the loaves for a friend. We first have to ask for and receive the baptism of the Holy Spirit if we are going to be able to do the work the Lord has for us in reaching and helping others. We have to ask and seek and knock and believe God for this gift. It should be of the highest priority in our prayer requests.

In Acts Chapter 2, after the Lord's ascension to the Father, we read about an historic event. It occurred on the day of the celebration of Pentecost, also known in the Old Testament as the Feast of Weeks—a sacred Jewish festival marking the wheat harvest and thanking God for His provision.[2] It was celebrated with much joy by the Jews and distinguished by the offering or waving of two loaves

---

[2] This annual feast was one of the three national festivals ordained by God, and it occurred 50 days or seven full weeks after the Passover week's observance of Firstfruits.

of bread made from the finest wheat flour. On this special Pentecost, God would show Himself faithful, fulfilling His promise and providing that which was truly needed:

Acts 2:1-4

1   When the Day of Pentecost had fully come, they were all with one accord in one place.
2   And suddenly there came a sound from heaven, as of a rushing mighty wind, and it filled the whole house where they were sitting.
3   Then there appeared to them divided tongues, as of fire, and one sat upon each of them.
4   And they were all filled with the Holy Spirit and began to speak with other tongues, as the Spirit gave them utterance. (NKJV)

Now, the transformation of the disciples was accelerated in a mighty way. Peter, a new man within and without by this baptism with the Holy Spirit, raised his voice and preached the gospel to thousands in courage and in strength.

LESSON TWENTY-SEVEN

————————◇————————

I continue our study of Jesus' teaching on prayer, as given in Luke Chapter 11 verses 1 to 13, by reminding you of the last verse in that section where the Lord says:

Luke 11:13
13 "If you then, being evil, know how to give good gifts to your children, how much more will your heavenly Father give the Holy Spirit <u>to those who ask Him</u>!" (NKJV) *{Emphasis added}*

We said last time that our highest priority in prayer should be to request the gift of the Holy Spirit. We must ask and seek and knock and persist in seeking God's baptism and outpouring of His Spirit to the fullest. And someone might ask, "Is this a subsequent event to receiving Jesus as our Savior?" As I said previously, we do not want to get too caught up in semantics, but some things **are** evident from the Scriptures. In the last lesson we saw that, on His resurrection, Jesus breathed on the disciples and said, "Receive the Holy Spirit." He then proceeded to open their understanding to the Scriptures and give them commandments through the Holy Spirit. It is my belief that, as they believed on the risen Lord, the Holy Spirit was performing the work of regeneration in their hearts and they began to truly <u>see</u> the kingdom of heaven. But we also read how this work exploded in magnitude, after the Lord's ascension, as the gentle breath of Jesus became a mighty wind. On the day of Pentecost, the disciples <u>entered into</u> the power of the kingdom of heaven as they received the gift of the baptism—the immersion—in the Holy Spirit. They were saturated in the Spirit, and He renewed and changed them dramatically within, and anointed them for service without.

Furthermore, Jesus is the baptizer in the Holy Spirit. John the Baptist said, as recorded in Matthew 3:11:

Matthew 3:11

11 "I indeed baptize you with water unto repentance, but He who is coming after me is mightier than I, whose sandals I am not worthy to carry. He will baptize you with the Holy Spirit and fire." (NKJV)

We can accept the Lord Jesus as our Savior and be baptized by another human in water, but only Jesus can reach down and baptize us in the Holy Spirit. And it was important that the disciples wait and pray in Jerusalem until Jesus sent the Spirit upon them in this way. That is why He tells them in Luke 24:49:

Luke 24:49

49 "And behold, I am sending forth the promise of My Father upon you; but you are to stay in the city until you are clothed with power from on high." (NASB)

Likewise in Acts Chapter 1 verses 4 and 5, just before His ascension, we read:

Acts 1:4-5

4 And being assembled together with them, He commanded them not to depart from Jerusalem, but to wait for the Promise of the Father, "which," He said, "you have heard from Me;
5 "for John truly baptized with water, but you shall be baptized with the Holy Spirit not many days from now." (NKJV)

And they were obedient. We read in Acts 1:12 how they returned to Jerusalem, and they went up into the upper room where they were staying. Acts 1:14 says:

Acts 1:14

14 These all continued with one accord <u>in prayer and supplication</u>, with the women and Mary the mother of Jesus, and with His brothers. (NKJV) *{Emphasis added}*

In Acts Chapter 2, Luke tells us that they were gathered in the same way when the Day of Pentecost had fully come. So again we see how important it is to seek God's gift of the Holy Spirit in prayer. That is why Jesus said:

Luke 11:13b

13 "...how much more will your heavenly Father give the Holy Spirit <u>to those who ask Him</u>!" (NKJV) *{Emphasis added}*

In our last workshop, we read about the dramatic outpouring on the day of Pentecost as a sound came from heaven as of a rushing, mighty wind and how the disciples were filled with the Holy Spirit and began to speak in other tongues—other languages—as the Spirit enabled them. This was a real experience for them. They knew something was happening. The Spirit's presence was manifested and there was no doubt about this tangible baptism. Some who heard and saw them made fun of them and thought they were drunk, but the disciples knew they had come under the power of the Holy Spirit. And Peter saw this as a fulfillment of the Old Testament prophecy. He says to the gathered crowd in Acts 2:16:

Acts 2:16-18

16 "But this is that which was spoken by the prophet Joel;

17 'And it shall come to pass in the last days, saith God, I will pour out of My Spirit upon all flesh: and your sons and your daughters shall prophesy, and your young men shall see visions, and your old men shall dream dreams:

18 And on My servants and on My handmaidens I will pour out in those days of My Spirit; and they shall prophesy:'" (KJV)

Down in verse 33, speaking of Jesus, Peter says:

Acts 2:33

33 "Therefore having been exalted to the right hand of God, and having received from the Father the promise of the Holy Spirit, He has poured forth this which you both see and hear." (NASB)

After Peter completes this powerful sermon, the Bible says that those in the crowd were cut to the heart, and so they ask Peter and the rest of the apostles what they should do. In Acts 2:38 and 39 we have Peter's wonderful response to the people, declaring that God's great salvation in Jesus and His gift of the Holy Spirit were available to them, and not only to them but to others in other generations and from other parts of the world:

Acts 2:38-39

38 Then Peter said to them, "Repent, and be baptized every one of you in the name of Jesus Christ, for the remission of sins, and ye shall receive the gift of the Holy Spirit.

39 "For the promise is to you, and to your children, and to all that are afar off, even as many as the Lord our God shall call." (Webster)

Even as he had said before:

Acts 2:17a

17 "'And it shall come to pass in the last days, saith God, I will pour out of My Spirit upon <u>all flesh</u>: ...'" (KJV) *{Emphasis added}*

While all current born-again believers accept that salvation in Jesus is available today to any person who repents and receives the Lord, some unfortunately have difficulty seeing that the manifest power and anointing in God's Holy Spirit is also available to us today. And this real encounter with God through the outpouring of His Spirit should be even more significant and evident for the true believer as we approach the last days.

Sometimes the reason is understandable why some are hesitant to believe that the gifts and anointing of the Holy Spirit are for today. Too often there have been abuses and sin by those who profess to having received this dynamic baptism. But Paul clearly instructs us in 1st Thessalonians 5:19-22:

1Thessalonians 5:19-22

19 Do not quench the Spirit.

20 Do not despise prophecies.

21 Test all things; hold fast what is good.

22 Abstain from every form of evil. (NKJV)

OK. To more fully answer our original question, let us look at three instances that occurred after the day of Pentecost. The first is in Acts Chapter 8 starting at verse 5:

Acts 8:5-8

5   Then Philip went down to the city of Samaria, and preached Christ to them.

6   And the people with one accord gave heed to those things which Philip spoke, hearing and seeing the miracles which he performed.

7   For unclean spirits, crying with loud voice, came out of many that were possessed: and many taken with palsies *(paralytics)*, and that were lame, were healed.

8   And there was great joy in that city. (Webster) *{Clarification in parenthesis added}*

Then in verse 12 we read:

Acts 8:12

12   But when they believed Philip as he proclaimed the good news of the kingdom of God and the name of Jesus Christ, they were baptized, both men and women. (NIV)

Notice that the people in this city believed the gospel of Jesus and were baptized in water. These were born-again believers and obviously the Holy Spirit had to be working on their hearts in a special way. Yet we read something interesting starting down in verse 14:

Acts 8:14-17

14   Now when the apostles who were at Jerusalem heard that Samaria had received the word of God, they sent Peter and John to them,

15   who, when they had come down, prayed for them that they might receive the Holy Spirit.

16   For as yet He had fallen upon none of them. They had only been baptized in the name of the Lord Jesus.

17   Then they laid hands on them, and they received the Holy Spirit. (NKJV)

So even though we are told that the Samaritans received the word of God, they had not yet received the Holy Spirit in the way the first believers had on the Day of Pentecost. "They had only been baptized in the name of the Lord Jesus," implying that they had not been baptized in the Holy Spirit. But after this, Peter and John went down and prayed for them, and once again we see the important role of prayer to receiving this baptism. They laid hands on them and we are told that these people of Samaria then also received the Holy Spirit. And the receiving of the Spirit was a tangible event—they knew it and experienced it. He "fell upon them." The occurrence was even obvious to an observer named Simon, a corrupt man who had previously practiced sorcery:

Acts 8:18-21
    18 Now when Simon saw that the Spirit was bestowed through the laying on of the apostles' hands, he offered them money,
    19 saying, "Give this authority to me as well, so that everyone on whom I lay my hands may receive the Holy Spirit."
    20 But Peter said to him, "May your silver perish with you, because you thought you could obtain the gift of God with money!
    21 "You have no part or portion in this matter, for your heart is not right before God." (NASB)

Therefore, I strongly believe that the baptism in the Holy Spirit is a subsequent event to the acceptance of the Lord Jesus as Savior. And it makes sense then that Jesus tells us in Luke Chapter 11 to pray and ask for the Holy Spirit. Now we should not be rigid in our teaching here, because that subsequent event could be a significant time later, as it was in the above example, or it could be almost instantaneous, as we will see in the next reading.

In Acts Chapter 10 we read about a centurion called Cornelius:

Acts 10:1-2
    1 There was a certain man in Caesarea called Cornelius, a centurion of what was called the Italian Regiment,
    2 a devout man and one who feared God with all his household, who gave alms generously to the people, and prayed to God always. (NKJV)

Peter, who is in Joppa praying on the housetop, is directed by the Holy Spirit to go to Cornelius in verses 19 and 20, and we see here just one of the many times the Spirit gives guidance in the book of Acts. Obediently, Peter goes to Caesarea and preaches to Cornelius and all his relatives and close friends who had assembled. Then we read in verse 44:

Acts 10:44-48a

44 While Peter was still speaking these words, the Holy Spirit fell upon all those who were listening to the message.

45 All the circumcised believers who came with Peter were amazed, because the gift of the Holy Spirit had been poured out on the Gentiles also.

46 For they were hearing them speaking with tongues and exalting God. Then Peter answered,

47 "Surely no one can refuse the water for these to be baptized who have received the Holy Spirit just as we did, can he?"

48 And he ordered them to be baptized in the name of Jesus Christ. ... (NASB)

These people were so opened to the Lord and the gospel that they were able to accept everything God had for them. Before Peter could even finish his message, they had accepted Jesus and were baptized in the Holy Spirit. Again the baptism was evident: they knew it and experienced it as the Spirit came upon them. And it was evident to Peter and the Jewish believers with him as well.

Much later on, in Acts Chapter 19, Paul comes across some believers in Ephesus who had only been baptized into John the Baptist's water baptism of repentance. Paul must have noticed something different about these men, because he asks them if they received the Holy Spirit when they believed in Messiah. They answer him that they had not so much as heard whether there is a Holy Spirit. Paul preaches to them that they should believe on Christ Jesus—a deeper belief than they understood. You see, it is not enough to "believe" in the sense of knowing and accepting that Jesus is Lord. We have to actively put our trust in Him as the source of everything for our salvation and follow that belief by submitting ourselves to Him and making Him the Lord of our lives. Moreover, we have to truly desire to receive His life, the only hope for change, inside our hearts. Paul then re-baptizes these believers in water, but this time not just into repentance. Rather, he submerges them fully into Christ Jesus:

Acts 19:5-6
> 5 On hearing this, they were baptized in the name of the Lord Jesus.
> 6 When Paul placed his hands on them, the Holy Spirit came on them, and they spoke in tongues and prophesied. (NIV)

And notice the fulfillment of the water baptism. They are then baptized in the Holy Spirit in power and with signs. As Paul says in Galatians 3:27:

Galatians 3:27
> 27 For as many of you as have been baptized into Christ have put on Christ. (KJV)

And again in 2nd Corinthians 3:17-18:

2 Corinthians 3:17-18
> 17 Now the Lord is the Spirit, and where the Spirit of the Lord is, there is liberty.
> 18 But we all, with unveiled face, beholding as in a mirror the glory of the Lord, are being transformed into the same image from glory to glory, just as from the Lord, the Spirit. (NASB)

I remember back when I was first saved. I was a young skeptic and a quasi-agnostic who was not interested in religion or the Bible. I was working at a company that had moved us up to Connecticut. Out of the blue, questions started to arise in my heart, which I now know was the Holy Spirit working on me. And He had placed Christians around me who could provide answers to some of those questions. One person was a man named Jim who worked with me at the company. He had a chemistry background just as I had, and we would talk about science and Christianity. The short time he worked at the company was hard for him because he came up against an office and warehouse that would constantly ridicule his faith. At this same time, an event happened in my life that caused me to get down on my knees and ask God to show me if He was real and if Jesus was indeed His Son. And God gave a miraculous answer to my prayer.

I can still remember the shocked look on my wife's face that evening when I said that I had to go to the store to buy a Bible. I purchased a New Testament and I do not know if I had even finished the gospels before I believed on Jesus and accepted Him. But a test came very quickly. One day in the office, Jim was on a call and the office workers and some fellows from the warehouse were sitting around joking and disparaging him. As I was about to leave for the day, the main instigator turned to me expecting a sympathetic response from a fellow skeptic and said, "Do you believe how that Jim thinks Jesus is God?" With all the eyes of the room fixed on me, I answered, "If you had asked me last week I would have said Jesus was just a man, but now I say He's God." The room was silent. I can remember the feeling as I walked out the door and into the car. I was shaken. How could I ever do that again? It was embarrassing and it just was not my nature. Being denominationally illiterate—not knowing a Baptist from a Pentecostal—I prayed with all my heart, "Lord, I believe in You, but I can't do this on my own. Send me Your Holy Spirit. I need Your Holy Spirit. Please, Lord Jesus, give me Your Holy Spirit!" And as I prayed, the Holy Spirit was poured out all over me. I was showered with the presence of God. I had never before felt the glory of heaven, and I praised Jesus with a new found anointing. I have proclaimed my faith in Jesus ever since.

LESSON TWENTY-EIGHT

———————⟨×⟩———————

I n our last few lessons, we have been speaking about the importance of persisting in prayer to the Father, especially in asking
for the baptism and outpouring of His Holy Spirit upon us. As Jesus
taught in Luke Chapter 11 verses 9 to 13, we are to ask and seek
and knock and persist in prayer to the Father for that which we need
the most—the Holy Spirit. For if we then, being evil, know how to
give good gifts to our children, how much more will our heavenly
Father give the Holy Spirit to those who ask Him!

But someone might say, "I've received the Holy Spirit already. I
have been baptized with the Spirit. How does this teaching apply to
me?" It is a good question. And I would direct them to Acts Chapter
4, to the prayer of the assembled believers which we studied in the
first lesson of this workshop on prayer. Now the disciples had already
received the baptism in the Holy Spirit on the day of Pentecost in
Acts Chapter 2, and the church in Jerusalem was growing. By the
time we get to this prayer in Chapter 4, Peter and John had been
used by God to heal the man who was lame from birth and to preach
to the amazed people at the temple. The two apostles, as a conse-
quence, had been arrested and brought before the Council. And the
Sanhedrin had severely threatened them to no longer speak or teach
in the name of Jesus. On their release, they and their companions
lifted their voices in the prayer we have recorded in Acts Chapter 4
verses 24 to 30. We will read the end of that prayer from verse 29
and into verse 31:

Acts 4:29-31

29 "And now, Lord, take note of their threats, and grant that Your
bond-servants may speak Your word with all confidence,

30 while You extend Your hand to heal, and signs and wonders take place through the name of Your holy servant Jesus."

31 And when they had prayed, the place where they had gathered together was shaken, and they were all filled with the Holy Spirit and began to speak the word of God with boldness. (NASB)

Understanding the difficulties that were ahead, these Holy Spirit baptized believers recognized that they needed to pray for courage and for the miraculous manifestations of the Spirit. Notice what happened. We read that they were again mightily *filled with the Holy Spirit* and they spoke the word of God in boldness.

Likewise, if we are to face the challenges before us as Christians, we should always and constantly seek all the Lord has for us in the Holy Spirit. We should desire the changes He will make in our hearts and personalities. We should desire and pray for the fruit He will bear in our lives. We should ask the Lord for an abundance of the anointing and outpouring of His Spirit to make our faith alive and to know the joy of His presence—as Jesus instructed His disciples, to be clothed with power from on high. And we should earnestly seek the gifts that Jesus will give us through the Holy Spirit. These requests should be made to the Father in prayer throughout our Christian walk in this world. We should ask and seek and knock; it should not be simply a one-time experience.

Now concerning these gifts which we can receive through the Holy Spirit: We already read how Jesus, having ascended to the right hand of the Father, received the promise of the Holy Spirit which He then poured out on His followers. Paul, speaking of this ascension in Ephesians Chapter 4 verses 7 to 8, tells us:

Ephesians 4:7-8

7 But to each one of us grace was given according to the measure of Christ's gift.

8 Therefore He says:

"When He ascended on high,
He led captivity captive,
And gave gifts to men." (NKJV)

Throughout the book of Acts and the epistles, we see these various gifts of the Holy Spirit which believers received. In 1st Corinthians Chapter 12 we get a sampling:

1 Corinthians 12:7-11

7 But the manifestation of the Spirit is given to each one for the profit of all:
8 for to one is given the word of wisdom through the Spirit, to another the word of knowledge through the same Spirit,
9 to another faith by the same Spirit, to another gifts of healings by the same Spirit,
10 to another the working of miracles, to another prophecy, to another discerning of spirits, to another different kinds of tongues, to another the interpretation of tongues.
11 But one and the same Spirit works all these things, distributing to each one individually as He wills. (NKJV)

One of these gifts which I would like to take a moment and discuss is the gift of tongues or other languages, which we also came across when we read about the Day of Pentecost, the conversion of Cornelius's household, and Paul's baptizing of the believers at Ephesus. And without getting into all the controversy that surrounds this gift, I would like to emphasize to you that the gift of tongues can be a tremendous aid to your private prayer life. For by it the Spirit helps us when we do not know how to pray. In Romans 8 verses 26 to 27 we read:

Romans 8:26-27

26 Likewise the Spirit also helps in our weaknesses. For we do not know what we should pray for as we ought, but the Spirit Himself makes intercession for us with groanings which cannot be uttered.
27 Now He who searches the hearts knows what the mind of the Spirit is, because He makes intercession for the saints according to the will of God. (NKJV)

The *New American Standard Bible* translates verse 26 this way:

Romans 8:26

26 In the same way the Spirit also helps our weakness; for we do not know how to pray as we should, but the Spirit Himself intercedes for us with groanings too deep for words; (NASB)

Other translations render it, "groans that words cannot express," "groanings that cannot be expressed in words" or "that cannot be put into words" or "words cannot explain." In the Spirit we can pray God's will even if we do not grasp it with our understanding—even though we are not using normal familiar words. And I think everyone realizes that there are times when we just do not know how to pray. Even after everything we said about knowing the will of God, there will still be situations where we will be at a loss, having little or no idea of the correct way to petition God. And there will be times when we do not even seem to have the mental strength to formulate the words of a prayer with our understanding. That is why the gift of tongues is so precious. We can feel the Holy Spirit praying through us to the Father. He might be using the different language of other humans past or present, or a language of angels. We do not comprehend the meaning of the words with our minds—with our understanding—but miraculously our spirits are built up and taught and receive God's power and peace. In 1st Corinthians 14:2, Paul teaches:

1 Corinthians 14:2

2 For he who speaks in a tongue does not speak to men but to God, for no one understands him; however, in the spirit he speaks mysteries. (NKJV)

And down in verse 4 he writes:

1 Corinthians 14:4a

4 One who speaks in a tongue edifies himself; ... (NASB)

In the gift of tongues, there is both the aspect of submission of self to God and the exalting of God in praise. As we are in the presence of the Holy Spirit and as we receive heavenly insight into the greatness of our God, the Holy Spirit gives us this gift to express those things that are literally too magnificent and dynamic for our normal speech. Our spirits may express in a moment what it would take volumes to express with our minds. That is why the gift is so powerful for private prayer and worship (though Paul places wise regulations on its use in public assembly in 1st Corinthians Chapter 14). When we pray in other tongues, in our spirits we can almost perceive things happening in the heavenly realms. And as we ask for discernment and the interpretation of the tongues, our minds can receive understanding as well. Also, sometimes when we receive the gift of tongues, it is akin to a new baby learning a language from his parents. We may only get a few words at first. But as we are faithful to speak those words, the Spirit adds and teaches us more.

My study partners should know that I am not saying any of this to belittle in any way the necessity of praying with our reason and under-standing in regular, plain words. And if you have been studying along in this series you do know this, since we have spent the previous 27 lessons discussing how we should pray with our understanding. But even when we pray with words which our minds understand and which are according to the reason and logic of God's Scriptures, we should still always seek to be, as we say, "in the Spirit" when we pray, asking the Holy Spirit's help and following His guidance and direction in those prayers. And sometimes that guidance can be very gentle and subtle, and sometimes it can be highly evident. As we quietly come before our Father in prayer, we should be open to the visions the Spirit might bring across our minds or the words of Scripture He may highlight in our memories, or even the blessed words of prophecy He may bestow on us. And even as Elijah heard the still small voice (1st Kings 19:12), we may hear in our hearts the voice of the Lord Jesus. Obviously, we should check everything we receive against the canon—the Scriptures—so that we are not deceived by our own imaginations or the enemy. But we should never be discouraged in seeking all the Father has for us in the Promise of His Holy Spirit.

In the last lesson, we spoke about being under the outpouring of God's Spirit, and one of the most beautiful ways the Holy Spirit com-municates with us is through His presence. Romans 8:16 tells us that:

Romans 8:16

16 The Spirit Himself bears witness with our spirit that we are children of God, (NKJV)

The Holy Spirit is the Spirit of truth, and one of the ways He guides us into truth is through the confirmation of His presence—the witness of His Spirit to our spirits. And there is a manifestation in our bodies that this Wind from heaven brings with Him to let us know when something is holy and righteous and true. Those who have experienced this anointing in the Spirit know exactly what I am speaking about. That is why it is important for believers in the Lord Jesus to ask and seek and knock for the fullness of God's Holy Spirit.

And this might be a good point in our study to remind you that prayer is not just a communication with God that occurs at a specific time. In 1st Thessalonians 5:16-18 Paul writes:

1 Thessalonians 5:16-18

16 Rejoice always;
17 pray without ceasing;
18 in everything give thanks; for this is God's will for you in Christ Jesus. (NASB)

Pray without ceasing or pray continually. We have seen how we can pray with others and in the assembly of believers. And we have spoken about how we should dedicate that special time each day to be in the secret place with our Father and spend time devoted to prayer. And yet our walk with God in prayer is more than this. For if we are a believer who loves God, we will find ourselves speaking to God constantly all during the day, no matter the situation, no matter what is transpiring. We are at all times asking for His help and guidance. We can be at our various works and duties, we can be deeply focused at some task, and still have a part of our heart resting in and worshipping Him. Prayer is our lifeline to God, and our spirits should always be attuned to Him and listening for Him.

As we are in Christ and His Spirit is in us, the continuous nature of prayer as part of this personal communion is only to be expected. We should always and in all circumstances be talking to our heavenly Father. In Ephesians Chapter 6, in the section where Paul instructs us how to win the conflict against the spiritual forces of evil, Paul says in verse 18:

Ephesians 6:18a

18 And pray <u>in the Spirit</u> on all occasions with all kinds of prayers and requests. … (NIV) *{Emphasis added}*

Even as he tells them in Colossians 4:2:

Colossians 4:2

2   Continue <u>earnestly</u> in prayer, being vigilant in it with thanks-giving; (NKJV) *{Emphasis added}*

Please also notice how important it is for us to pray with *thanks-giving*. Just as we read before in 1st Thessalonians 5:17-18:

1 Thessalonians 5:17-18

17   pray without ceasing;

18   in everything give thanks; for this is God's will for you in Christ Jesus. (NASB)

It is a terrible thing when we forget to thank the Lord after we receive that for which we have prayed. Instead our prayers should be filled with thanksgiving for what God has done. We should not be like the Israelites at the time of Moses who saw only what was not yet manifested rather than thanking God for the numerous miracles He had already done for them. And consider the New Testament account of the lepers. In Luke Chapter 17, we read how Jesus heeded the request of ten lepers for healing. But once healed, only one, a Samaritan, came back to give Him thanks. And Jesus said,

Luke 17:17-18

17   …"Were there not ten cleansed? But the nine — where are they?

18   "Was no one found who returned to give glory to God, except this foreigner?" (NASB)

Too often we are like those other nine. We do not take time to thank God for the answers to our prayers, but immediately focus on some new problem that has come along. Romans 1:21 cautions us that thanklessness is a sign of ungodliness. But power is added to our prayers when we give God thanksgiving. Our faith and joy are built up in the Holy Spirit. And not only should we express gratitude for what He has done, but we should thank Him for what He will do and has promised to do. Philippians 4:6 reads:

Philippians 4:6-7

6   Be anxious for nothing; but in every thing by prayer and supplication with thanksgiving let your requests be made known to God.

7   And the peace of God, which passeth all understanding, will keep your hearts and minds through Christ Jesus. (Webster)

LESSON TWENTY-NINE

———————∝———————

In this lesson, as we continue our study on prayer, we want to focus on praying in the name of Jesus. There is power in the name of the Lord, and there is probably no better or more proper way to close our prayers and petitions to God than to say, "Father, I ask you these things in the name of Your Son Jesus. Amen." The name of the Lord Jesus is the great identifying mark of His believers. We have studied what Jesus taught His disciples in Matthew 18:19-20 where He says:

Matthew 18:19-20

19 "Again I say to you that if two of you agree on earth concerning anything that they ask, it will be done for them by My Father in heaven.

20 "For where two or three are gathered together in My name, I am there in the midst of them." (NKJV) *{Emphasis added}*

And, in our last lesson, we looked at the prayer offered up by the disciples in Acts Chapter 4 which concluded with a request that miracles be done through the name of Jesus. Starting at verse 29 we read:

Acts 4:29-30

29 "And now, Lord, take note of their threats, and grant that Your bond-servants may speak Your word with all confidence,

30 while You extend Your hand to heal, and signs and wonders take place through the name of Your holy servant Jesus." (NASB) *{Emphasis added}*

Through the name of Jesus we identify to all the earth and to all the heavenly realms the foundation for what we do and why it is that we have any reason to expect to receive anything. It is because of Jesus. There is no one else. We are His. When we gather together, we gather together in His name as His people. When God works through us, He works through us to bring glory to His name—the name of Jesus—and to no one else. And when we come before the Father in prayer, it is as His children wrapped or clothed in the precious name of His Son—the name which is above every name—Jesus the Christ.

Actually, Paul tells us in Colossians 3:17:

Colossians 3:17

17 And <u>whatever you do</u>, whether in word or deed, do it all in the name of the Lord Jesus, giving thanks to God the Father through Him. (NIV) *{Emphasis and capitalization for deity added}*

That "whatever" includes prayer. Our prayers should be lifted up to God in the name of Jesus, and the Lord Himself gives us promises for when we do this. We will use for the text of our study the account of the Last Supper in the gospel of John. Let us read from Chapter 14 verses 12 to 14. Jesus says here:

John 14:12-14

12 "Truly, truly, I say to you, he who believes in Me, the works that I do, he will do also; and greater works than these he will do; because I go to the Father.

13 "Whatever you ask in My name, that will I do, so that the Father may be glorified in the Son.

14 "If you ask Me anything in My name, I will do it." (NASB)

The Lord repeats here for emphasis that if we ask anything in His name, He will do it. That is a powerful promise.

But does this promise mean that some can simply, by using the words "in the name of Jesus" in their requests, guarantee success? Not at all! Not if they are using His name deceitfully or in emptiness. Asking in His name is not some magical charm that opens the door for just anyone off the street who wants to give it a try. That would be taking the holy name of the Lord in vain. Let us take a moment to consider something that happened at the time of the early church which is recorded in the book of Acts. In Chapter 19, beginning at verse 11 we read:

Acts 19:11-19

11 Now God worked unusual miracles by the hands of Paul,

12 so that even handkerchiefs or aprons were brought from his body to the sick, and the diseases left them and the evil spirits went out of them.

13 Then some of the itinerant Jewish exorcists took it upon themselves to call the name of the Lord Jesus over those who had evil spirits, saying, "We exorcise you by the Jesus whom Paul preaches."

14 Also there were seven sons of Sceva, a Jewish chief priest, who did so.

15 And the evil spirit answered and said, "Jesus I know, and Paul I know; but who are you?"

16 Then the man in whom the evil spirit was leaped on them, overpowered them, and prevailed against them, so that they fled out of that house naked and wounded.

17 This became known both to all Jews and Greeks dwelling in Ephesus; and fear fell on them all, and the name of the Lord Jesus was magnified.

18 And many who had believed came confessing and telling their deeds.

19 Also, many of those who had practiced magic brought their books together and burned them in the sight of all. And they counted up the value of them, and it totaled fifty thousand pieces of silver. (NKJV)

"The name of the Lord Jesus was magnified." I like that verse. In this account, we see that the name of the Lord is not some blessed rune disconnected from its owner, the way in which the seven sons of Sceva and perhaps many of those who practiced magic arts had considered it. To them the name of Jesus was looked upon as simply some seal to get what they wanted, or so they thought. It did them no good and, in the case of Sceva's sons, misuse of the name actually led to their harm. They did not really belong to the Lord, so they did not have His authority.

That word *authority* is an important one. When we say someone is praying or doing anything in the name of Jesus, we are saying that they are doing it under the authority given them from Jesus as His disciples. They are doing it under His auspices and as His agent, even as Paul was His agent: Paul came in the name of Jesus. This is a critical concept and maybe a modern example will help us to grasp it.

Consider someone that works for a company. Years ago I worked for a large corporation. I had a business card that had my name and title down the bottom, but which, in much larger and prominent text, displayed the name of the company I was representing. And as a representative, an agent of that company, I was able to call on other sizeable companies which were our clients and enter into negotiations. Had I just walked off the street and tried to have access based on my name, I would have been turned away. But I came in the name of my company—as a legitimate representative of that company—and I was received. Someone else could try falsely saying they were also from my company but it would not do them any good. Once their credentials were checked, they would be shown up even as the seven sons of Sceva were discredited. You can not come in the name of a company unless you are truly part of the company and have been given the authority to represent it.

And notice the trust required: that you are a faithful representative concerned with the owners' business and duly exercising your agency in a responsible manner. If an employee given such an important responsibility abuses the position or negotiates in a way opposite from the good of the company or outside the parameters set, they are not long for that company. In the same way (and as we have studied in previous lessons), if we are acting as members of the kingdom of darkness rather than the kingdom of light, we should not think our prayers will be heard no matter how large the name Jesus may be emblazoned on our vehicles. We have taken the name of the Lord in vain. But if we are a good and faithful representative, the enemy may say to us, "Who are you? You are nobody and you can do nothing," but then he looks again and sees a spiritual name card from heaven placed on our lapel. The pin says, "This one comes in the Name of Jesus," and the enemy must flee, not because of us, but because we belong to the company of Him who is! Praise the Lord!

When Jesus makes this great promise of asking Him in His name, He is speaking to His close disciples and He is speaking to those who truly believe in Him, as He says:

John 14:12-15

12 "Truly, truly, I say to you, he who believes in Me, the works that I do, he will do also; and greater works than these he will do; because I go to the Father.

13 "Whatever you ask in My name, that will I do, so that the Father may be glorified in the Son.

14 "If you ask Me anything in My name, I will do it.

15 "If you love Me, you will keep My commandments." (NASB)

He goes on to say that He will give them the Helper, the Spirit of truth. This passage speaks of agency: "greater works than these he will do; because I go to My Father." This is the agency He is giving to those who truly believe in Him. As His agents in this world we love Him and trust in Him and desire to keep His commands. And so when we ask for something as His agents, Jesus promises **He will do it**. This is what it means to ask in the name of Jesus. We are truly His and He promises to help us. Furthermore, He will equip us for the task through the Holy Spirit, by whom also He comes and lives inside of us. And notice in verse 13 what happens when Jesus does whatever is asked in His name by His believers: the Father is glorified in the Son. Therefore God is glorified by the answered prayers of His people. Amen.

So that it is clear that this is not an isolated Scripture, let us continue on in the gospel of John, at the Last Supper, to Chapter 15 verses 14 to 16. Jesus tells His disciples:

John 15:14-16

14 "You are My friends if you do what I command you.

15 "No longer do I call you slaves *(or servants)*, for the slave does not know what his master is doing; but I have called you friends, for all things that I have heard from My Father I have made known to you.

16 "You did not choose Me but I chose you, and appointed you that you would go and bear fruit, and that your fruit would remain, so that <u>whatever you ask of the Father in My name</u>

He may give to you." (NASB) *{Emphasis and clarification in parenthesis added}*

We see, first, that the disciples were chosen and appointed to bear lasting fruit. Second, they knew their Master's business: He made known to them all the things He heard from the Father. And third, even as they so knew, if they did the things He commanded them, they were His friends and could act as His agents asking the Father in His name. Once again we have a great promise that "whatever you ask of the Father in My name He may give to you."

In the very next verse, verse 17, we have the commandment of the Lord clarified:

John 15:17

17 "These things I command you, that ye love one another." (KJV)

As chosen vessels with knowledge of the kingdom, as they walked according to the love of that kingdom they could ask in the name of Jesus and receive "whatever they ask" in His name. They were chosen for this relationship, and Peter, in the first letter of Peter, calls all true believers the elect or chosen of God. In Chapter 2 verse 9 he says:

1 Peter 2:9

9 But you are a chosen generation, a royal priesthood, a holy nation, His own special people, that you may proclaim the praises of Him who called you out of darkness into His marvelous light; (NKJV)

Therefore, as we know His business and walk according to His ways, we too are His friends and may ask in His name as His representatives in this world. And if the corporations of this world will give their representatives whatever they need to do their businesses, will not our Father give to us whatever we ask that we may bear fruit? Jesus promises that He will.

As we continue reading down in John to Chapter 16, Jesus speaks of their time of sorrow, referring to the crucifixion and His death, and then of their joy when they will see Him again. But He says something interesting in verse 23 about how it will be after His resurrection. Up to this point the disciples have had a lot of questions and they have needed Jesus right there with them for answers. Really they have needed Him there for everything. But Jesus has told them in verse 16:

John 16:16

16 "A little while, and ye shall not see Me: and again, a little while, and ye shall see Me, because I go to the Father." (KJV)

He speaks of His death and resurrection and ultimate ascension, after which He would not be right there with them in the flesh, though He would be with them always, even to the end of the age. He would come to them and all His disciples through the Holy Spirit and tell them plainly about the Father. But they were no longer to be onlookers from the side watching Him in His relationship with the Father, somewhat befuddled and constantly questioning Him to explain. Rather He tells them in verse 23:

John 16:23-24

23 "And in that day you will ask *(or question)* Me nothing. Most assuredly, I say to you, whatever you ask the Father in My name He will give you.

24 "Until now you have asked nothing in My name. Ask, and you will receive, that your joy may be full." (NKJV) *{Emphasis and clarification in parenthesis added}*[3]

---

[3] Note: the Greek word translated "ask" in the first part of John 16:23, "And in that day you will ask Me nothing," is *erotao* {er-ō-tah'-ō}. This is different from the word translated as "ask" in the second part of that verse, "whatever you ask the Father," which is *aiteo* (ahee-teh'-ō). *Aiteo* is also the word used above in John 14:13, 14:14, 15:16, and 16:24 and suggests the petition or request of one who is lesser in position than he to whom the petition is made. It is the humble entreaty to a superior—a man asking something from God or a subject asking something from a king. *Erotao* instead suggests familiarity between the parties and also has as its original meaning "to question." Hence John 16:23 is better rendered, "And in that day you will ask Me no question." This is confirmed up above in John 16:19 where the disciples desired to ask *(erotao)* Him a question. See Vine's Expository Dictionary of Biblical Words, © 1985, Thomas Nelson Publishers: "If the Holy Spirit had been given, the time for 'asking' questions from the Lord would have ceased." In John 14:14, where, not a question, but a request is to be made by the disciples to the ascended and glorified Lord, *aiteo*, is used.

Now the believers in Jesus were to stand in the place of the Lord, as His body on earth, and pray in the power of His name with the certainty that whatever they asked the Father in His name, the Father would give them. This is why we pray in the name of Jesus. Jesus said, "Until now you have asked nothing in My name. Ask, and you will receive, that your joy may be full."

LESSON THIRTY

———————∝———————

W ith this lesson, we come to the close of our study series on *The Nature and Power of Prayer*. I hope that you have been encouraged by the series and that you will have a more effective prayer life with the Lord. I have tried in these workshops not just to speak about prayer but to look at the many questions and Biblical topics that impact just how we perceive the things that go on around us and which ultimately will affect the way we pray. Really, when we look back at the study, it has not only been a teaching on prayer but also on knowing the will of God, the coming of the kingdom of God, the spiritual battles in the heavenly realms, salvation, receiving the Holy Spirit, forgiveness, trials and temptations, and so many other important Biblical matters.

Today I would like to address a question that has come up from time to time. In our last lesson we looked at the importance of praying in the name of Jesus. The question we want to answer today is, "Is it proper to pray to Jesus?" In our study of the Lord's Prayer, we saw that this model prayer was addressed to God the Father. And there are some very strong feelings on this issue. Quite honestly, I believe that much of the dispute that often arises is really rather silly. You see it typified by some of the groups that will come to your door which claim to follow the Bible but which have some very twisted theology. If you ever get into a discussion with them, you find out that they will ridicule born again Christians for worshipping and praying to Jesus. I think you know the groups I am referring to. I have debated their members many times.

Sometimes they will say something like, "We will pray in the name of Jesus, but we never pray to Jesus. That's not allowed. We only pray to the Father." And unfortunately there are some Christians that border on saying the same. One common thread you can note in these other groups though, which is not surprising: they deny salvation by a personal relationship with Jesus Christ. Well, I guess if you cannot pray to Him you cannot ask Him to come into your heart and save you.

And that right there should be a clear answer to any Christian that has a question about the appropriateness of praying to the Lord Jesus. While frequently our prayers **are** directed to the Father, it is natural in the Spirit to also pray to the Lord Jesus. Actually, one of the first prayers we make as a Christian is directed to Jesus, asking Him to come into our lives and hearts and to be our Savior. John Chapter 1 verse 12, speaking of Jesus, reads:

John 1:12

> 12 But as many as <u>received Him</u>, to them He gave the right to become children of God, even to those who believe in His name, (NASB) *{Emphasis added}*

In the gospel invitation, we are to believe in the Lord Jesus and receive His life and Lordship into our lives. Paul, in Colossians 1:27, calls this the hope of glory: Christ in you. And this communication with the Lord Jesus does not end with salvation. Rather Paul tells us in 1st Corinthians 1:9:

1 Corinthians 1:9

> 9 God is faithful, who has called you into <u>fellowship</u> with His Son, Jesus Christ our Lord. (NIV) *{Emphasis and capitalization for deity added}*

And John, in 1st John 1:3, says that:

1 John 1:3b

> 3 …truly our fellowship is with the Father, and with His Son Jesus Christ. (KJV)

The word translated fellowship there means a fellowship recognized and enjoyed, a communion—to participate together in, to communicate. And prayer is obviously part of that fellowship and communication. We are called to be in fellowship with <u>both</u> the Father and His Son Jesus Christ. Therefore, it is not only proper to direct prayers to Jesus, but it is expected of believers who should always be talking to the Lord whom they know.

It is interesting to watch what happens when those groups we were speaking about earlier (who come to the door with their Bibles as well as their church's publications and tracts) are confronted with a question about Stephen the martyr. The question which I ask usually leaves them dumbfounded. After bringing up Stephen, I lead into the question by simply stating, "Then you feel that Stephen sinned when he was stoned and was dying?" As they look perplexed or answer, "When did we say that?" I will open the Bible to Acts Chapter 7 verse 59 and I'll say to them, "You said it was wrong to pray to the Lord Jesus, but let's see what Stephen prayed at the end of his life in this world:"

Acts 7:59

59 They went on stoning Stephen as he called on the Lord and said, "Lord Jesus, receive my spirit!" (NASB)

"Now, Stephen asked the Lord Jesus to receive his spirit. That is a prayer—a very important prayer. Did Stephen sin when he did this?" That is the point at which they usually say they do not know and then they make a quick exit, because they have been confronted with the error of their reasoning. It is clear from the book of Acts that Stephen is being presented as an example of what a believer should be. Obviously he did not sin, obviously his prayer to the Lord Jesus was a righteous one, and obviously it is proper and right for us to do likewise. John 5:23 says that:

John 5:23b

23 ...He who does not honor the Son does not honor the Father who sent Him. (NASB)

And, in 1st John 2:23, John writes:

1 John 2:23

23 Whoever denies the Son does not have the Father; the one who confesses the Son has the Father also. (NASB)

Some of these pseudo-churches unfortunately go to great lengths to take the salvation in Jesus and the real fellowship we are called to have with the Lord out of the gospel. And their gospel then is no gospel at all. Consider one last Scripture on this point. Look at Revelation Chapter 22 verse 20. It is the next to last verse in the Bible.

Revelation 22:20

> 20 He who testifies to these things says, "Surely I am coming quickly." Amen. Even so, come, Lord Jesus! (NKJV)

John's response to the Lord's message that He is coming quickly is the prayer, "Amen. Yes, come Lord Jesus!" And we should pray likewise to the Lord looking forward to His return. Thus our prayers can be directed to the Father <u>and</u> to the Son, as the Holy Spirit leads us.

Moving on, I would like to end this series on prayer with a note about the importance of intercessory prayer for others. Intercession is the act of going before God and petitioning Him on behalf of another individual or group. Paul told the church at Ephesus, in Ephesians Chapter 1 verses 15 to 18, that having heard of their faith in the Lord and their love for all the saints, he did not cease to give thanks for them, making mention of them in his prayers. His petition was that the God of our Lord Jesus Christ, the Father of glory, may give them the spirit of wisdom and revelation in the knowledge of Him, and that the eyes of their understanding would be enlightened. Down in Chapter 3 and verse 14 we read more about his prayers for these believers:

Ephesians 3:14-21

> 14 For this reason I bow my knees to the Father of our Lord Jesus Christ,
> 15 from whom the whole family in heaven and earth is named,
> 16 that He would grant you, according to the riches of His glory, to be strengthened with might through His Spirit in the inner man,
> 17 that Christ may dwell in your hearts through faith; that you, being rooted and grounded in love,
> 18 may be able to comprehend with all the saints what is the width and length and depth and height —
> 19 to know the love of Christ which passes knowledge; that you may be filled with all the fullness of God.

20 Now to Him who is able to do exceedingly abundantly
above all that we ask or think, according to the power that
works in us,

21 to Him be glory in the church by Christ Jesus to all generations, forever and ever. Amen. (NKJV)

God is able to do **exceedingly abundantly** above all that we
ask Him. It is easy to be moved by the way the apostle Paul cared
and prayed for these believers—these saints. And all those who
truly believe in Jesus are called saints in the Bible. If you belong to
the Lord, He has set you apart, sanctified you, and you are indeed
a "saint in Christ Jesus" (Philippians 1:1; Ephesians 1:1; Romans
1:7). And these prayers of intercession for the saints were central to
Paul's understanding of winning the victory meant for us in Jesus.
Remember how we studied the end of the letter to the Ephesians,
in Chapter 6 verses 10 to 12, where Paul tells them to be strong in
the spiritual battle against principalities, against powers, against the
rulers of the darkness of this age and the spiritual host of wickedness
in the heavenly places? He goes on to describe the spiritual armor
they must wear, and as part of the preparation he directs them in
verse 18 to be:

Ephesians 6:18-20

18 praying always with all prayer and supplication in the Spirit,
being watchful to this end with all perseverance and supplication for all the saints —

19 and for me, that utterance may be given to me, that I may open
my mouth boldly to make known the mystery of the gospel,

20 for which I am an ambassador in chains; that in it I may speak
boldly, as I ought to speak. (NKJV)

To win this battle it was important for them to pray in the Holy
Spirit with all kinds of prayers and requests always, and to pray for
each other—for all the saints. In addition, they needed to pray for
him as well. Paul himself sought their prayers, that he would say the
things he should say and preach the gospel with courage. Paul knew,
as we all should know, that no man can stand on his own and we
each need others to go before the throne of God, interceding for us
in prayer. How especially true that is for those who publicly preach
and teach the gospel of Jesus Christ as Paul did. The demonic battle

against them and their families is fierce. Your pastor and all the ministers of the Lord need your earnest prayers.

It is important that we also intercede in prayer for our families and loved ones whom the Lord has placed in our lives almost as a trust. We think of Abraham who interceded before the Lord for the righteous persons that might be in Sodom, because of his concern for his nephew Lot who lived there. Some of us may have loved ones who are not living where they should, in the spiritual sense. But Abraham's persistence in intercession probably resulted in the angelic rescue of Lot and his daughters when that city was destroyed. And our persistence in prayer before God for our loved ones may be to their salvation as well.

Furthermore, our prayers of intercession should extend beyond the church and even our immediate familiar circle. Paul tells us in 1st Timothy Chapter 2 and verses 1 to 4:

1 Timothy 2:1-4
1   I urge, then, first of all, that petitions, prayers, intercession and thanksgiving be made for all people —
2   for kings and all those in authority, that we may live peaceful and quiet lives in all godliness and holiness.
3   This is good, and pleases God our Savior,
4   who wants all people to be saved and to come to a knowledge of the truth. (NIV)

Amen. I will close these lessons with a beautiful illustration of prayer given to us in the Scriptures. In the Old Testament, Moses was told to make a tabernacle which was actually a copy or shadow of heavenly things. The tabernacle would be a place where God would come down and dwell, His presence being over the mercy seat of the ark of the testimony which was behind a veil in the Most Holy Place. Just outside that veil, in the Holy Place, was an altar of incense overlaid with pure gold upon which every morning and every evening the priests, who were descendants of Aaron, offered or burned specially compounded, sweet incense before the Lord. Every morning and every evening its beautiful smell would fill the tabernacle and, later on, the temple in Jerusalem.

In Psalm 141 verse 2, David sings:

Psalm 141:2a

2   Let my prayer be set forth before Thee as incense... (KJV)

And in the book of Revelation we have a vision of the true throne room of heaven. In Chapter 5 verse 8 we read:

Revelation 5:8

8   Now when He had taken the scroll, the four living creatures and the twenty-four elders fell down before the Lamb, each having a harp, and golden bowls full of incense, <u>which are the prayers of the saints</u>. (NKJV) *{Emphasis added}*

So our prayers are as the incense that goes up before the Lord God in heaven. These prayers of His saints are a sweet and pleasing aroma to Him. Down in Chapter 8 of Revelation, in verses 3 to 4 we read:

Revelation 8:3-4

3   Then another angel, having a golden censer, came and stood at the altar. He was given much incense, that he should offer it with the prayers of all the saints upon the golden altar which was before the throne.

4   And the smoke of the incense, with the prayers of the saints, ascended before God from the angel's hand. (NKJV)

It is ultimately these prayers, heard and answered by God, which will usher in the end of the age and the return of Jesus Christ. As it says in verses 5 and 6:

Revelation 8:5-6

5   Then the angel took the censer and filled it with the fire of the altar, and threw it to the earth; and there followed peals of thunder and sounds and flashes of lightning and an earthquake.

6   And the seven angels who had the seven trumpets prepared themselves to sound them. (NASB)

As you pray to God morning and evening, offering your time and desiring fellowship with Him, as you lift up your petitions according to His will, consider how pleased He is that your prayers and the prayers of all the saints fill that throne room with the wonderful fragrance of a church victorious. Amen. Come Lord Jesus.

"Cast your burden on the LORD,
And He shall sustain you;
He shall never permit the righteous to be moved."
Psalm 55:22 (NKJV)

ABOUT THE AUTHOR

Gregory J. Scalzo is the Pastor and founding director of Shear-Jashub Christian Tabernacle and the featured speaker on the weekly *Shear-Jashub* radio program. His Bible teaching ministry combines a scholarly knowledge of God's Word with Holy Spirit anointed wisdom and insight.

Greg Scalzo was born and raised in Queens, New York. He received his undergraduate degree in chemistry, graduating with honors from New York University. Starting out as a physical chemist for a scientific equipment manufacturer, Greg transitioned into technical sales and interacted with PhD's from major corporations. This led to a position with McKesson Chemical, the largest chemical distributor in the United States, where he was quickly promoted to Territory Manager of their Connecticut branch. After several years, he was successfully recruited away by Lonza, a global specialty chemical manufacturer. At night, Greg also completed his Master's degree in Business Administration from the University of Connecticut, where he graduated at the very top of his class.

In the spring of 1981, while Greg was still working at McKesson Chemical and attending UCONN, he and his wife Patty accepted the Lord Jesus Christ and were saved. Freed from agnosticism and the evolutionary teaching of his education, Greg then poured himself into a study of God's Word. And as he grew in his Christian faith, the Holy Spirit made clear to Greg that God was calling him to a special work of ministry. At the leading of the Lord, he finally left the corporate business world to prepare to build a ministry and church in the dry ground of New England. In 1984, he and Patty founded Shear-Jashub Christian Tabernacle, a non-denominational Christian church in Madison, Connecticut. The church is a true Bible church, upholding the inspiration and inerrancy of the Scriptures, preaching the born again relationship with the Lord Jesus Christ, and testifying to the reality of the gifts of the Holy Spirit for today. Found in Isaiah 7:3, *Shear-Jashub* means "A Remnant Shall Return" and there is a strong emphasis in the church's teaching on the Jewish roots of the faith.

Pastor Greg's sermons have been featured on the *Shear-Jashub* radio broadcast since 1997. They are heard weekly in Connecticut and parts of New York on WFIF 1500AM and around the globe daily on the *Shear-Jashub* website at www.shear-jashub.org.

In 1985, in order to support themselves in the ministry, Pastor Greg and Patty started a small business which drew on their mutual hobbies of art and woodworking, Patty's background in decorating, and Greg's knowledge of the technical aspects of wood chemistry and finishes. In the Greg & Patty Scalzo furniture shop, they still to this day create artistic reproductions and restore fine furniture and antiques. In 2016, Pastor Greg and Patty celebrated their 40th wedding anniversary. They have three children: Greg III, who is a software engineer for a defense contractor and married to Michelle; Patricia Deborah Orris, MBA, who is an audit analyst and married to Billy; and Francis-David, who is an undergraduate student at Regent University majoring in Biblical and Theological studies and who is a classical violinist.

CPSIA information can be obtained
at www.ICGtesting.com
Printed in the USA
BVOW06s0014211216
471420BV00005B/6/P